Education, Work and Social Capital

Education, Work and Social Capital is a major study of the nature, aims and context of vocational education at the beginning of the twenty-first century. It provides a comprehensive, integrated treatment of the relationship between the aims of economic activity and those of education. Approaching the subject from a philosophical perspective the author engages with debates about

- the work-related aims of education
- the moral and spiritual significance of work
- the conceptualisation of political economy
- high-skill economies and vocational education
- the 'end-of-work' thesis
- the relationship between education and training in vocational education
- future work patterns
- the educational consequences of the economic theories of influential economists such as Smith, Mill, List, Marx, Marshall and Keynes

This is an essential and ground-breaking study for academics and students of business studies, economics, political economy, and the sociology of work. It will equally be of interest to policy-makers concerned with the future development of vocational education and training.

Christopher Winch is Professor of Philosophy of Education at University College Northampton. His recent publications include *The Philosophy of Human Learning*, and coauthoring *Key Concepts in the Philosophy of Education*, both published by Routledge.

Routledge International Studies in the Philosophy of Education

Education, Work and Social Capital

Towards a new conception of vocational education

Christopher Winch

London and New York

First published 2000
by Routledge
11 New Fetter Lane, London EC4P 4EE

Simultaneously published in the USA and Canada
by Routledge
29 West 35th Street, New York, NY 10001

Routledge is an imprint of the Taylor & Francis Group

Typeset in Baskerville by Steven Gardiner Ltd, Cambridge
Printed and bound in Great Britain by St Edmundsbury Press, Bury St Edmunds, Suffolk

British Library Cataloguing in Publication Data
A catalogue record for this book is available from the British Library

Library of Congress Cataloging in Publication Data
Winch, Christopher
Education, work, and social capital: towards a new conception of vocational training /
Christopher Winch.
    p.   cm. – (Routledge international studies in the philosophy of education; 11)
Includes bibliographical references and index.
1. Vocational education – Philosophy. 2. Vocational education – Economic aspects.
3. Infrastructure (Economics). I. Title. II. Series.
LC1042.5.W56   2000
370.11'3'01 – dc21   00–035311

ISBN 0-415-20434-8

This book is dedicated to Cathy, Alison and Paul

Contents

Preface

Vocational education is a relatively neglected topic in philosophy of education in the English-speaking world. A few pioneers have raised issues in the subject but have been little heeded. Yet there can be few subjects of greater importance to the well-being of modern societies than the way in which they prepare young people for work. A subject of equal importance is the quality of the work that a society offers its citizens and the broader aims of economic activity beyond the necessary achievement of economic viability and competitiveness. I quickly discovered that it is not possible to do justice to the subject of vocational education without at the same time dealing with the issues of the quality of working lives and the broader aims of economic policy. Thus the philosophy of vocational education becomes a subject that is inextricably connected with broader ethical and political questions about the nature of human well-being and how it can best be achieved. So far then, from being a peripheral part of philosophy of education, we should see the study of vocational education as one of its central preoccupations, one which, moreover, binds the discipline to the study of the presuppositions of economic activity.

Given the cultural predisposition against taking vocational education seriously, one must feel cautious about the impact that a book of this nature is likely to have. I would consider it to be a success if it provokes debate among both philosophers and economists and leads to a reappraisal of the importance of vocational education to philosophy of education.

The male pronoun is used generally to denote both males and females unless otherwise stated.

Acknowledgements

I have benefited greatly from discussions over the years with John Gingell, whose views and mine concerning the importance of vocational education are very close. I am also indebted to Linda Merriman, Linda Clarke, Lorraine Foreman-Peck and John White for discussions of some of the topics treated in this book. Comments from anonymous reviewers of the *Oxford Review of Education*, *New Political Economy* and *Studies in Philosophy and Education* have also proved invaluable.

I also owe a particular debt to some of those who have written on these topics before me. These include: David Finegold, Sig Prais, Harold Entwistle, Richard Pring, Terry Hyland, Madawc Williams, Kevin Williams and Theodore Lewis. The use that I make of their ideas is entirely my own responsibility.

I would like to acknowledge the following publishers and journals for permission to reproduce material previously published.

Kluwer Academic Publishers
PO Box 17
3300 AA Dordrecht Holland
for permission to use material in:
'Vocational Education: a liberal interpretation', 1995,
Studies in Philosophy and Education, 14, 4, pp. 401–415.

Taylor and Francis Ltd
PO Box 25, Abingdon, Oxfordshire OX14 3UE
for permission to use material in:
'Listian Political Economy: Social Capitalism Conceptualised?', 1998, *New Political Economy*, 3, 2, 1998, pp. 301–316.
and
'Two Rival Conceptions of Vocational Education: Adam Smith and Friedrich List', 1998, *Oxford Review of Education*, 24, 3, pp. 365–378.

1 Introduction

THE MAIN ARGUMENT

There are relatively few books about the philosophy of vocational education, published in English. This is due, in large part, to a persistent cultural bias, particularly in the UK, against contaminating educational concerns with such gross matters as work and the economy. Anyone interested in promoting vocational education is thought to be a philistine, concerned only with material gain rather than with higher forms of human achievement. The main aim of this book is to show that this view is a travesty, that our deepest concerns with moral and spiritual well-being are bound up with work, and that any education directed towards the well-being of the vast majority who are not going to live the life of the country gentry of yesteryear needs to concern itself with preparation for work in the broadest sense. The richness and complexity, as well as the importance, of vocational education will then become apparent, and the subject may at last be taken with the seriousness it deserves by philosophers of education. That it should at last be taken seriously is the ambitious aim of this book.

The main theme is the relationship between politics, economic well-being and education. It is not a treatise in economics or politics, but in philosophy of education. However, in developing a philosophical view about education in general and vocational education in particular, it is unavoidable that certain theses about politics, economics and their respective relationships with education are advanced. These theses are, on the one hand meta-political, meta-economic and meta-educational, and, on the other, substantive normative theses about the conduct of politics, economics and education in developed and developing societies.

Put briefly, the 'meta' theses can be stated as follows. The view of politics presented here owes much to Aristotle. Any political society consists of different groups with different particular views of the good to be pursued in human life which are integrated in some way into a view of the common good for the society as a whole.[1] Day-to-day politics concerns the working out of particular group and individual conceptions of the good within the framework of the society's view of the common good. Such a common view of the good is necessarily complex and reflects both the diversity of the society and the relative strengths of the various groups whose contesting conceptions of the good happen to predominate. There are many different political structures, both democratic and non-democratic, in which political questions can be contested and resolved, but the normative side of the discussion in this book will be particularly concerned with democratic, although not necessarily liberal in any metaphysical sense, forms of polity. The liberalism argued for will be the contingent and non-foundational kind described by Gray as 'agonistic' or contested.[2]

The view of economics presented here is much broader than that usually presented by professional economists. Keynes wrote that 'Consumption—to repeat the obvious—is the end and object of all economic activity.'[3] This definition follows the classical tradition of conceiving economic activity in terms of maximising the production and circulation of consumable commodities, a conception derived from Adam Smith in particular. A little reflection shows, however, that although the academic study of economics may largely be concerned with the mechanics of the production, circulation and consumption of goods, a political conception of the subject (a political economy) will necessarily be concerned with a broader conception, which will encompass the scope of the discipline hinted at in Keynes' definition of the aims of economic activity. This broader definition would have it that the aim of economic activity is the maintenance and reproduction of the society. Consumption will be a large part of that aim, since without consumption humans could not survive, let alone prosper. It is another matter to maintain, however, that consumption is the *sole* goal of economic activity or that the maximisation of consumption is the only goal of the study of economics and of economic policy.

For it is obvious, in the first place, that certain forms and certain degrees of consumption may actually be harmful to a society, either to individuals, to the environment they inhabit or to the interests of those yet to come, on whose well-being the future of the society depends. In this sense, political economy is concerned with the good of the society as a whole, not just with the maximisation of consumption. For such reasons did Mill advocate the redistribution of inheritances, List the development of national strength and even Keynes, the elimination of unemployment and the civilisation of the acquisitive instinct that underlies capitalism.[4] Given this approach, the aims of economic activity will be complex, reflecting the various points of view and interests of different groups with competing conceptions of the good, together with the current balance of forces between them. The normative thesis of this book is very much concerned to give consumption its due place within broader concerns for the physical and social environment and the preservation and further development of society. The maintenance of intrinsically worthwhile activities, institutions and ways of life is to be accorded as much importance as the maximisation of consumption and more when they come into conflict.

Finally, the concept of education advanced here is also political in the broad, Aristotelian sense set out earlier. Education as a concept is concerned with preparation for life in its broadest sense, primarily, but not exclusively, with the preparation that takes place in childhood and youth. However, since there are different points of view as to what are appropriate forms of preparation for life, there are also different conceptions of education. These are subject to the contingent play of the relative strengths of different points of view as to what these form of life should be, and are inextricably bound up with different conceptions of what the ends of economic and political life should be.[5] In this sense, one cannot disentangle a particular conception of education from particular conceptions of economic and political life. The importance and nature of vocational conceptions of education in any particular society is bound up with these contesting conceptions of economic life and the contesting conceptions of the good that animate politics. One of the main aims of this book is to explore the consequences for vocational education of taking genuine account of the different political conceptions of economic activity that are alive within developed and developing societies and, normatively, to link a preferred conception of vocational education with preferred conceptions of normative politics and political economy.

Two *caveats* concerning these contesting conceptions should be entered. First, a contest in this sense is not necessarily a zero-sum game where a gain for one conception is pure loss for an opposing one. Different conceptions of the good may only be incompatible to a degree, for example, if they contain common elements but differ in the respective emphases that they put on some of them. Very often contests about these competing conceptions amount to the *degree of priority* that should be accorded to one element rather than another, rather than about whether some elements should be totally eliminated from national life. For example, it is unlikely that anyone would wish to see the aim of consumption banished from conceptions of the economic good, but there may well be contesting conceptions concerned with the relative balance between present and future consumption, with the *allocation* of consumables, with the relative importance of private and public goods or with the balance between consumption and investment. Likewise in education, few would dispute that in some sense education is concerned with the growth of individual independence. However, the proponents of different conceptions may well dispute concerning the *degree* of independence desirable, the *stages* in life at which it should occur and the *contexts* in which it should be exercised.

It would also be wrong, in painting this picture of societies in which conceptions of the good compete with each other, to ignore the fact that rigidities within a society may cramp or even ossify that society's ability to maintain such competition. In some ways this is good and necessary. There are times at which particularly bitter disputes must be settled and left behind. But it can also be unfortunate. As Hume pointed out, men are creatures of habit to a large extent and the *status quo* can easily be seen as having eternal validity. It frequently happens that if a prevailing conception takes hold at a crucial transition point in a society's history then it comes to have an almost permanent status and surrounds itself with such prestige that it is only with great difficulty that it can be dislodged by conventional political means. Such was the case with the conception of economics as the maximisation of the production of commodities in the early stages of the industrial revolution, due largely to Adam Smith. Such was also the case with the conception of education as personal realisation that was adopted in the state system of education in the UK in the latter part of the nineteenth century, under the impact of the prestige of the education of the gentry, the influence of the churches and the prevailing *laissez-faire* view of economic activity.[6]

Briefly, the normative theses that will be argued for against the background of these respective conceptions of politics, economics and education are as follows. In relation to politics a non-foundational, contingent liberalism with a strong emphasis on collectivist, rather than individualist, solutions to political and social issues will be argued for. In relation to economics, it will be argued that economic policy in the kind of normative political context described above, needs to adopt as aims consumption and competitiveness, but also the opportunity for people to enjoy a certain degree of self-fulfilment in their lives predominantly, although not exclusively, through the production and consumption of high-skill, high-value goods and services. In relation to education, there needs to be a mix of liberal, vocational and civic-related aims of education, which take account of the need for social diversity, economic specialisation and social cohesion.

SOCIAL CAPITAL

In recent years it has become fashionable to use the term 'capital' in a much wider sense than that of labour power, raw materials, buildings and machinery. These can be *physical* or *financial* (the latter the power to command physical capital).[7] It will be helpful to call this 'economic capital'. We now speak about 'human capital', 'cultural capital' and 'social capital'. To avoid confusion, it will be helpful to distinguish the senses in which these terms are used and to outline the way that they are going to be used in this book. Human capital is what Smith called 'productive powers', conceived of as the potential for labour of individuals.[8] Nowadays it has been increasingly recognised that the skill and knowledge that an individual brings to work is an important part of that potential. Cultural capital refers to the moral and cognitive assets laid down by someone's culture which they can draw upon as individuals; for example, a certain ability to use language. In Bernstein's theory of codes, the ability to use an elaborated, as well as a restricted code in order to communicate in an impersonal, context-free manner would be an example of the ability an individual has in virtue of the capital on which he can draw through his membership of a community with a common culture, under-stood here as the rules, social relationships, customs, institutions and norms of a particular social group.[9]

The term 'social capital' has a longer history, but a more varied etymology. In the work of Mill and Marshall it refers to economic capital that is socially owned.[10] In recent years, it has acquired meanings more akin to those of human and cultural capital. 'Social capital' can take an individualistic interpretation, referring to the sum total of human capitals or it can refer to the cultural assets on which individuals can draw in their individual economic activity. On the individual-istic interpretation it has no reality beyond that of each quantity of human capital, that is the skill and knowledge that each individual in the society possesses.

As such, it reflects a widespread interpretation of *methodological individualism*, that social assets have no further reality than the collections of individuals that associate together numerically, constituting a social collectivity.

'Cultural capital' on the other hand, points to a more collectivist interpretation of these social assets. Although ontologically, proponents of the notion of cultural capital may concede that there is no society without the individuals who compose it, they also hold that a society's human assets consist of more than individual knowledge and skill. These cannot be understood independently of the social milieu in which they are created and in which they exist. One, Wittgensteinian, way of putting this point is to admit the ontological priority of human creatures for any society, but to argue that in terms of understanding human society it is necessary to appreciate the norms, customs and institutions that constitute that society. The individual human *qua* social being can only be understood as a member of a particular society and has his cognitive, moral and social life constituted in terms of the society in which he lives.[11]

The modern use of the term 'social capital' trades, at least implicitly, on this insight. For writers such as Coleman, social capital is constituted through the social relationships that people have with each other, through the collective knowledge of a group, and the moral, cognitive and social supervision that the group exercises over its members.[12] On this view, one cannot understand individual human capital independently of understanding the social relationships within which it arises and which nurture and perpetuate it. Social capital in this sense has a strongly moral dimension. For example, it is often described in terms of norms of trust prevalent within a society.[13]

Something important is missing from these accounts of cultural and social capital. Without an understanding of the *cognitive* as well as the cultural and moral aspects of human association, the relevance of society for economic life cannot be properly appreciated. It could immediately be replied that one cannot understand the cognitive, moral and cultural aspects of life independently of each other. This is happily conceded. It is maintained, nevertheless, that there are important distinctions that need to be drawn between the three and that in focusing on two of them largely to the exclusion of the third, something important is lost.

It may be helpful to consider the question in relation to a particular example. A country such as France has a strong tradition of cuisine which is deeply rooted in the national life and diffused throughout all strata of society. It plays a central part in the social and economic life of the society. The tradition of cuisine can be looked at in various ways in terms of capital. As economic capital it can be seen as the agricultural and manufacturing assets for food production, together with the distributive system and gastronomic industry that are linked to it. A large work-force, skilled to varying degrees, is employed to make this raw material and fixed capital productive (variable capital). In addition, there is a human capital element to this variable capital, which consists in the agricultural, selling, service and culinary skills that are employed within all aspects of cuisine. This, in turn, is supported by a vocational and educational system, both formal and informal, which develops future generations of human capital.

This human capital is, however, embedded in social networks and norms that shape and regulate the institutions and customs associated with gastronomy in all its forms. These include familial practices of shopping, farming and caring about food, as well as norms relating to the social and sexual division of labour and to the preparation of meals. Such relationships exist in the agricultural industry that serves families and in the gastronomic industry that serves the dining public. In this way, the moral dispositions that underlie the continuation and control of gastronomy are maintained.

However, cuisine also involves much knowledge and skill. This is conveyed from generation to generation in both formal and informal ways, through educational and workplace institutions and in both private and commercial contexts. This knowledge and skill, it could be maintained, is the property of individuals, but it is, on the argument above, more than that. Any individual can only learn, practice and develop his knowledge and skill within the institutions through which the gastronomic practices have their existence. It is only within families, kitchens and restaurants, for example, that cuisine has a medium of existence. The knowledge and skill are social assets in the sense that their parts are not held individually, but only in their totality within a collective. Much of this collective knowledge is informal and unwritten and often embodied only in practices, where the sole discursive element is the display of skill. Sometimes it is available socially, for example in gatherings of agriculturalists or chefs who may exchange or divulge elements of practice as part of social life. Furthermore, the individual has to exercise his knowledge and skill in association with other people, and part of this skill consists in his ability to work with, manage and respond to other people. Social capital, then, is an amalgam of moral, cultural and cognitive elements all dependent on one another. Indeed, it might be better to say that the cultural, moral and cognitive aspects are all sides of of one complex phenomenon, that of social capital.

The distinction between social capital on the one hand, and physical and financial capital on the other, allow us to see how investment in certain forms of physical capital can destroy existing forms of social capital. Let us suppose that the traditional Parisian bistro which is essentially a family concern embodying the lore and skills of generations of restaurateurs, together with the *collective* knowledge and skills of their trade, is threatened by the successful development of fast-food outlets which rely on mass-produced food, centrally sourced and distributed throughout the city, which are able to undercut the bistros in price. If we suppose that the bistros start to disappear, then it is natural that the social capital embodied in them will also disappear, since the economic conditions for its future existence will no longer obtain. That in turn represents a loss of social capital for the whole of France. Whether this kind of change matters for a society and whether or not it should attempt to do anything about it is one of the major themes of the later chapters of this book.

The concept of social capital, then, comprises what is meant by human, cultural and social capital by other authors, together with an emphasis on two points. First, that social capital has cognitive, as well as moral aspects. Second, that it is not an aggregation of individual human capitals, but is also the medium of expression of human capital (since human labour is usually deployed in a social context), and also the medium for its renewal and creation (since it is through social relationships that human capital is realised and developed).

Productive powers

Social capital in this sense constitutes an important aspect of the economic life of any society, however that economic life is conceptualised. But social capital only constitutes a part, albeit an important part, of the economic potential of any society. The nineteenth-century German economist Friedrich List used the term 'productive powers' of a society to express this notion of general economic potential. For List, the productive powers of a society include social capital in the sense that it has been described here. It also includes, however, the physical and financial capital of the society, together with its physical resources and its overall organisational capacity. 'Physical capital' in this sense includes 'social capital' in the sense in which Mill and Marshall used the term, that is, socially owned physical and financial capital. But it also includes public and semi-public goods including natural resources (e.g. water, air), socially or state-produced goods (e.g. lighthouses, roads, canals, bridges, railways), associations in civil society (e.g. churches and charities), functions of the state (e.g. education, health and legal systems), and, finally individual attributes (abilities, skills, virtues).

On this account, *social capital* constitutes an important part of *productive powers*. It consists of social assets, one of the functions of which is to promote production for consumption and for the maintenance of productive powers for the future. There is a very important point to make about these social assets. Many of them exist for no particular purpose. For example, spontaneous and customary habits of sociability and trust which extend beyond the family are often considered by people to have a value in themselves, they are part of what makes life worth living and do not have any overt ulterior purpose.[14] On the other hand, such associational habits have other consequences. To use again the example of cuisine in France, one can easily point to its economic significance in oiling the wheels of commerce, in promoting the morale of citizens and in helping to develop the tourist industry. Churches exist for the purpose of worshipping God and helping to sustain religious belief within a community of believers. This is the main function which is *assigned* to them when they are built and is primarily what they are built *for*.[15] On the other hand, they serve other purposes, such as providing opportunities for socialising and match-making, and the religious beliefs and teachings which they sustain in their turn allow for spiritual renewal and promote habits and virtues of diligence, perfectionism and trustworthiness that are important for economic activity.[16] Once such functions are ascribed to social institutions they may become valued for them and promoted and defended both by the state and by society, without it being suggested that these are now functions assigned to them.

On the other hand, some institutions have functions assigned to them that directly promote economic activity. These include the legal system, education, housing and infrastructural works. They, too, may well come to have ascribed functions which tend to promote economic activity, for example, consider the role of a state education system in promoting the building and publishing industries. Carrying out an audit of the productive powers of a society would be a difficult undertaking, particularly as the effects of certain institutions may be, in their nature, hard to gauge. By taking productive powers seriously one approaches the conceptualisation of economic life from a completely different direction from that of both Marxism and classical economics in its neo-liberal form. For Marxists and neo-liberals the economy is conceived of as a set of relationships that are largely independent of the rest of society, but which in turn effect these other institutions. These non-economic institutions are also *supervenient* upon the economy. Legal, moral and religious institutions exist because of economic exigencies. Were these exigencies to change, then the supervening institutions would change as well. The primary explanatory principle underlying non-economic societal change is, then, economic change.

The idea of productive powers conceived in the way that Friedrich List did, sees society as a whole, of which the economy is an aspect, whose parts interact with each other in ways that can only be revealed by detailed study. One of the major themes of this book is the development of the idea of social capital as a component of the productive powers of a society with a particular examination of the role that education plays in the formation, maintenance and development of social capital.

ARGUMENT OF THE BOOK

Three overlapping themes concerning economics, politics and education are developed throughout the book. Inevitably, themes are introduced in one chapter only to be taken up again in another, later one. However, the general structure is pretty clear.

Chapter 2 attempts to disentangle the relationships between work, leisure, effort and necessity as a preliminary to getting clear about key distinctions between pleasurable and non-pleasurable, difficult and easy, productive and non-productive activity. The general concept of activity is then related to the work–leisure distinction and paid employment is distinguished from other sorts of activity. These distinctions allow the later account of vocational education and economic activity to be developed.

Chapter 3 is concerned with the concept of education and different conceptions of it, which include liberal, vocational and civic education. These are distinguished and their relationships with each other described.

Chapter 4 introduces the dominant conception of economics in terms of consumption, inherited from Adam Smith, but also to be found in the work of Marx. Chapter 5 outlines the key ideas of List, which lie behind an alternative conceptualisation of economic activity in terms of the development of social capital and productive powers.

Chapter 6 returns to the theme of work, concentrating on paid employment and the continuing of education, particularly moral education through the social demands and relationships that arise in the workplace. It is argued that the workplace is an important site of moral formation and a potential source of intrinsic satisfaction and self-fulfilment for the worker, in some respects as important as the domestic and leisure spheres of life.

Chapter 7 is a critical examination of the common misconception of vocational education as training. Training and conditioning are distinguished and the role of training in vocational education is outlined. The historical reasons for the identification of vocational education with training are outlined and their current legacy in the form of competence-based vocational education is examined. This chapter includes reflections on the importance of assessment in vocational education that are taken up again in Chapter 15.

Chapter 8 is an examination of learning in and around the workplace. The complexity of education and training for complex and responsible forms of work is described, together with associated forms of assessment. Chapter 9 develops the idea of vocational education as a process of *formation* rather than training and develops its affinities with liberal conceptions of education. Different kinds of paid employment are distinguished, together with their implications for vocational education.

Chapter 10 marks a return to the more overtly economic themes of the book with an account of the relationship between vocational education and the labour market, paying attention to the moral implications of preparing individuals for seeking employment. Chapter 11 draws on contemporary economic discussions of the conditions for a high-skill economy and argues for the important non-material benefits that result from running one. The relationship between a high-skill economy and vocational education is briefly discussed.

Chapter 12 examines dominant contemporary ideas about the moral role that employment plays in our lives and criticises some of these ideas because of the lack of balance that they threaten to introduce into our conceptions of a worthwhile life. Chapter 13 looks at the issue of the role of employment in our lives through another angle, namely the 'end-of-work' thesis and illustrates its empirical and philosophical defects. The continuing central role of employment in the lives of many is argued for, taking account of the arguments of the previous chapter.

Chapter 14 takes up the topics of social capital and productive labour in a high-skill context and considers the implications for vocational education of taking the development of social capital seriously. The related and fashionable topic of 'life-long learning' is subject to critical examination in this context. The book closes at Chapter 15 with a discussion of the relationship between school-based education and work-based vocational education and the conceptual and institutional relationships between the two. The state of policy concerning vocational education in the UK at the end of the century is appraised in the light of the arguments of the book as a whole.

Notes

1 This can vary enormously, from a 'thin' view of the common good, which is nothing more than a disjunction of permissible possibilities to a 'thicker' structured hierarchy whereby higher order values held by different groups nevertheless result in a set of lower order values held in common. Superimposed on such a structure is also the outcome of decisions about the *extent* to which different values are implemented within the public sphere and the *relative weighting* given to values held in common but allotted different degrees of importance between different groups. For more on these issues, see John Gray (1995) *Enlightenment's Wake*, London, Routledge; John O'Neill (1998), *The Market: Ethics, Knowledge and Politics*, London, Routledge, Chapters 2 and 3; and Christopher Winch (1996) *Quality and Education*, Oxford, Blackwell, Chapters 3 and 4.
2 Gray, op. cit.
3 J. M. Keynes (1973) *The General Theory of Employment, Money and Interest*, second edition, London, Macmillan, p. 104.
4 For a contemporary introduction to social economics, see Mark Lutz (1999) *Economics for the Common Good*, London, Routledge.
5 Cf. Andy Green (1990) *Education and State Formation*, London, Macmillan.
6 See, for example, D. Ashton and F. Green (1996) *Education, Training and the Global Economy*, Cheltenham, Edward Elgar, Chapter 5; Green, op. cit.
7 For a useful discussion see A. Marshall (1890) *Principles of Economics*, eighth edition, London, Macmillan, Book I, Chapter IV.
8 A. Smith (1981) *The Wealth of Nations*, Indianapolis, IN, Liberty Fund, Volume I, p. 10.
9 Cf. B. Bernstein (1973) *Class Codes and Control*, Volume I, London, Paladin.
10 Cf. Marshall, op. cit. p. 66; J. S. Mill (1994) *Principles of Political Economy*, edited with an introduction by Jonathan Riley, Oxford, Oxford University Press, p. 321. First published 1848.
11 See D. Bloor (1997) *Wittgenstein, Rules and Institutions*, London, Routledge.
12 See, for example, J. Coleman (1988) 'Social Capital in the Creation of Human Capital', *American Journal of Sociology*, 94, Supplement S, 95–120.
13 For a representative example, see F. Fukuyama (1995) *Trust*, London, Penguin, Chapter 3.
14 Fukuyama, op. cit.
15 On the distinction between *ascribed* and *assigned* functions of institutions see J. Searle (1995) *The Construction of Social Reality*, London, Penguin, Chapter 3.
16 See F. List (1991) *The National System of Political Economy*, New Jersey, Augustus Kelley, pp. 143–144. First published 1841. See also Longfellow's poem, 'The Builders':

> In the elder days of Art,
> Builders wrought with greatest care
>   Each minute and unseen part;
> For the Gods see everywhere.

> H. W. Longfellow (1919) *The Poetical Works of Henry Wadsworth Longfellow*,
> London, Humphrey Milford, p. 186

2 Necessity, work, effort and leisure

INTRODUCTION: THE DEFINITION OF WORK

In this chapter I will argue that the search for watertight definitions of the concepts of *work* and *leisure* is philosophically futile. Instead, it will be argued that the relationships between these concepts are, nevertheless, worthy of careful philosophical exploration. Such an exploration will be illuminating because it will make clear when these distinctions have a point in our lives, which is, after all, why we make them. When we have understood the roles that these two concepts play, we can begin to understand the meaning of 'vocational education' and thus move on to a study of its potential and actual importance.

There have been several recent attempts to define work. White offers a critique of various arguments that attempt to show that work is, in some sense, a human need.[1] I have a great deal of sympathy with that critique, as I hope to show in the course of this chapter. However, White also defines work as activity that aims at an end-product.[2] This position, to some extent following an analysis of *play* offered earlier by Dearden, is not, however, sustainable.[3] Dearden argues that play is by its nature *non-serious* in that it is devoid of real ethical and cultural value; that it is *self-contained*, being set apart from the 'duties, deliberations and developing projects which make up the serious web of purposes of ordinary life' and that it is *immediate in its attractiveness*.[4]

Gingell has shown that none of Dearden's criteria for distinguishing play from non-play activities (which one may take to be largely work activities) will do, since counter-examples can always be found.[5] It is clear, for example, that many play activities are taken very seriously indeed. Bill Shankly's famous remark that football is not a matter of life and death, it is much more serious than that, makes the point well, if somewhat ironically. The self-contained nature of play is not universal either, as Wellington's saying about the battle of Waterloo being won on the playing-fields of Eton makes clear. Many a reluctant child urged by its parents to 'go away, stop bothering me and play' will testify to its frequent lack of immediate attractiveness. White's own definition of work in terms of an end-product is similar to Dearden's criterion of non-self-containedness for play activities, but fares no better. Many leisure activities have an end-product, both as their aim and their outcome: building a model railway in one's attic, for example.

Likewise, many work activities have no easily identifiable end-product. Indeed, the contemporary malaise in the British workplace identified as 'presenteeism' is precisely the carrying out of work activities with no tangible benefit, simply to impress one's employer with one's presence in the workplace, by carrying out ritualistic activities.

These examples do not show that there are no meaningful distinctions between work and non-work activities, but rather that the conceptual relationships between them are much more complex than the search for simple definitions would suggest. Two points are apparent when one looks into the matter. The first is that the concepts of *work*, *leisure* and *play* seem to have the characteristics of what Wittgenstein called 'family resemblance concepts'; indeed his own example, that of games, is closely related to the concepts under discussion. Wittgenstein's account of these concepts suggests that they have the following features. First, there is no central core of use such that one aspect of the concept is more important than the others. Thus, we cannot say, for example, either that games are always competitive or that it is a central mark of the concept *game* that games are competitive. Second, the marks of the concept form a complex and overlapping pattern. Some games are self-contained and non-serious, others self-contained and serious, others again, immediate in their attractiveness but not self-contained, and so on. The important point is not that one could not, if one tried hard enough, offer a definition that would cover all the cases, but that such definitions play no role in our grasp of these concepts.[6] One very important reason for this arises from another of Wittgenstein's remarks, namely that one draws boundaries for particular purposes.[7] In this context, the boundaries between work and leisure, or work and play are drawn in order to make a point, for example to distinguish between the time when you 'clock on' and 'clock off' at your place of employment and when you use your own time. One might want distinguish between the time that one's employer has paid for and the time that he has not. Or again, it may be used to distinguish between the serious and non-serious parts of the day when you are employed earning a wage. This might be an important aspect of job evaluation, for example. One may even distinguish between work and non-work aspects of leisure activity, for example, playing a game of bridge and repairing a child's toy, when one is concerned to contrast those leisure activities that have a tangible end-product and those that do not.

The reason for making a distinction one way rather than another often depends on the context in which the distinction is being made.[8] Thus one might, in the context of paid employment, make the distinction between work and leisure in one way (teaching children is work and talking to one's colleagues is leisure) and, in the context of home life, make it in another way (where putting up shelves is work and watching the television is leisure). Not only then is the distinction between work and leisure, or between work and play, unlikely to be captured satisfactorily in a definition, it is also likely that any attempt to do so will be seriously misleading concerning the use and therefore the meaning of these concepts. I conclude, therefore, that any attempt to neatly separate work from leisure or play activities is most unlikely to succeed. This, however, is not to say that these distinctions do not have some force, but that they need to be handled carefully and case by case. First, however, it is necessary to look at two concepts that are highly relevant to attempts to characterise work, but that have been relatively neglected in the literature. The discussion that immediately follows should make the philosophical discussion of the nature and importance of work and its relationship to vocational education much more illuminating.

EFFORT AND NECESSITY

The experiences of trying to make, and of making, an effort are an important and unavoidable feature of human life and must be recognised by any education worthy of the name. *Effort* is concerned with the overcoming of obstacles to our own purposes and those of others, and thus with the recognition of necessity in our lives. *Necessity* involves the recognition and overcoming of barriers to our plans, but it also involves the demands that both nature and other people make upon us. We need, for example, to seek food and shelter and to maintain the sources of these if we are to pursue any of our own plans. The fact that our lives are bound up with others, not only in our family and immediate circle, but also in the wider society, obliges us to respond in various ways to the demands of other people.

The encounter with obstacles and demands of both a personal and an impersonal nature is fundamental to our existence as beings whose powers are limited, but who, nevertheless, wish to bring our projects to fruition, engage in projects with others and who have to submit to the exigencies of nature. The experience of the world as resistant to our wills begins in earliest childhood. Our helplessness leads us to seek assistance from others in order that our most basic needs are attended to. Soon we learn to enlist the help of others in a more imperious way, which is not always successful. Rousseau observes that our first cries are prayers and counsels us to beware that they do not become commands.[9] Even if one does not accept the likelihood of gross psychological damage that Rousseau believed would result from the satisfying of an arbitrary infant will, there are, nevertheless, grounds for thinking that the realisation of the limited nature of its powers of persuasion are important at this stage in a child's life. This realisation constitutes the beginnings of recognition of the need to enlist the co-operation of others in the fulfilment of its needs and, later, of its more long-term projects.

At the same time, young children learn that their actions produce *reactions*. Sometimes these are of comfort and pity, when a child is distressed. Sometimes they are reactions of encouragement and pleasure when the child makes an effort to do something that it has not done before, such as learning to talk and to walk. Sometimes the reactions are of resentment and displeasure when the child does something to hurt or upset another.[10] These encounters, which occur as part of the child's growing mastery of language, constitute the beginnings of a moral realisation of the child's own finitude, its dependence on others, its need for co-operation to solve life's problems and the requirement to pay due regard to the feelings and needs of others. It is no exaggeration to say that these are lessons that a human being never stops learning if they are well taught at the outset, but which are never learned adequately if they are not. In this sense, moral education is a part of general education and a key lesson learned, if it is effective, is that the approval and co-operation of others is vital to our success in most of what we do. In this sense too, the approval of others is a need, but it is not strictly based on a biological drive,[11] but exists as a condition of flourishing for beings whose fate is unavoidably social.

These early episodes of learning are not automatic, as it has become fashionable to think. It is observed, correctly, that much of early learned behaviour, such as communicating and walking, has an instinctual, animal basis. From this it does not follow that they are instinctive *behaviours*. The point is that learning to communicate, to move, to feed in ways that are appropriate to the society that one is growing up in, involve a recognition of, and adaptation to, norms which are those of that society. An essential part of learning to do these things involves a recognition of and adaptation to the requirements of others.

Learning to communicate, for example, involves not merely mastering a vocabulary and syntax, but developing an ability to get the willing attention of others and to make oneself understood, and to understand and respond to the responses of others. The picture that Chomsky and others present of neural linguistic circuitry being 'switched on' as a result of minimal exposure to the mother tongue, is a travesty of the truth.[12] It does not follow from the fact that a child need not make *self-conscious* efforts to be understood that it does not make efforts. Neither does it follow from the fact that early action has an instinctive basis, that it is *effortless* instinctive behaviour. The experience of a world that is not wholly subject to our will is fundamental to our learning anything and to our making efforts in order to do so. In so far as successful learning is necessary for us to act effectively, effort is necessary to acting effectively in many parts of our lives. The expenditure of effort is an unavoidable and pervasive feature of learning and acting.[13]

As children grow older, society's demands of what they need to learn become more complex and the actions they accomplish and the projects they undertake also become more complex, more dependent on the co-operation of others and more long-term in their ambition. This is not to say that there may be children who find themselves in a position, such is their social power, that they have to make very little effort to secure what they want. Children in such a position may be in moral hazard if the micro-environment of their upbringing is seriously misleading as to the demands that a larger stage will bring to bear on their abilities to act and to respond to the expectations of others. Even if it is not, there are dangers attached to a child's failure to notice the complex interdependence of human life and the need to pay due regard to the expectations, needs and desires of others in the pursuit of its own life. Rousseau was, no doubt, correct in seeing that the upbringing of the young can go well or badly (although this was hardly an original insight) but wrong to think that its going well could only occur in the absence of a socially-based normative structure.[14] On the argument above, such a structure is necessary for any reasonable form of education. More fundamentally, it is inconceivable that one could learn to communicate outside such a structure, so that there is an important sense in which the encounter with the normative nature of human life is unavoidable.[15]

A fundamental condition of human well-being is satisfaction of the wish to be approved of and accepted by others, not only as a member of one's society but as someone recognised as an *active* member of society, who can both pursue their own ends and contribute to the fulfilment of social ones. This is meant in a minimal sense; it is not a universal condition of life that people seek to impress or overawe others by displays of power and wealth, merely that they seek to be accepted as individuals with a proper place in society in their own right.[16] In order to do this, people need to grow morally as well as intellectually and physically. Thus the development of enduring traits of character (often called the virtues), which contribute to the flourishing of both individual and society, are a vital part of education. Since moral education is preparation for living well with other people, it is a central part of any education. It must be developed in particular social contexts, initially the family and the school, but later in other, less explicitly educational, contexts. The virtues practised in any particular society constitute, to a large extent, what counts as the good in that society. A society whose sense of its worth is partly constituted by the practice of other-regarding virtues, such as trust, charity and sociability, will practice, and educate children to practise those virtues for their own sakes. The same point applies to the more self-regarding of the virtues, such as perfectionism, persistence and industriousness.[17] Moral education is thus, to a large extent, concerned with the satisfaction of intrinsic social goods which only manifest themselves in social situations: domestic, economic, public and political.

There is no one set of virtues that fit every society's ideas of what constitutes the good life, although it is arguable that a minimal core are required in any.[18] Not only may the particular virtues vary, but the balance between social and other-regarding virtues may vary from society to society and may also vary diachronically, within societies. Thus to characterise morality in a meta-ethical sense as concerned with the cultivation of virtue is not to say very much about the *particular* virtues that will be cultivated in any one society. This is important to the debate about the place of work in human life since it is often maintained that *autonomy* or the ability to carry out one's own projects is a central human need. On the view being developed here, the degree of autonomy regarded as a suitable framework for the practice of virtues will vary from society to society and, to the extent that it is a universal human need, will only be so in the minimal sense that some form of self-directedness is a necessary condition of happiness.

The capacity for voluntary action is necessary for us to carry out projects. If the arguments above are correct, that capacity has to be exercised through the application of effort. No philosopher has argued that the capacity to act is not a fundamental feature of human life, they have, however, disagreed about the importance of *work*. Voluntary activity involving effort, in pursuance of a self-determined project, in co-operation with others or at the behest of someone else, is a commonly accepted necessary condition of an activity's counting as work. We have already noticed the difficulties involved in offering definitions of this kind. My own view is that definitions, even of this minimal kind, are not helpful because the employment of terms such as 'effort', 'work' and 'leisure' is too complex and context-dependent to be susceptible to watertight definitions. The problems that arise in attempting to define it as White does in terms of end-product arise with this new attempt at a definition. For example, some work is involuntary (e.g. slave labour). In some contexts 'effort' means 'conscious physical exertion' (running up a hill while out of condition), while in others it means 'trying a bit harder than usual' (e.g. in making conversation with one's distant relations). Again, the most we can do is make a series of contrasts, bearing in mind that they may not always apply in particular contexts. There are two general points worth making, though, and they are that work involves *activity* of some kind and that effort involves *overcoming some kind of barrier* (even if it is just the inclination to read the newspaper rather than make conversation with a distant cousin). But these general points are enough to develop the case that I wish to make.

We can say that purposive activity which involves some degree of effort is a pervasive and central feature of human experience, and that consequently, any education worthy of the name would prepare children for that experience in ways appropriate to the values and way of life of the society in which they are growing up. In our society, some fairly general but useful points can also be made about this. First, there is a *moral* dimension to our activity in so far as it affects the well-being of ourselves and others. Second, activity in societies like ours falls into one or other of the categories of domestic labour, voluntary work, leisure or paid employment. Third, a relatively high value is placed on *autonomy* in one or more of these spheres of activity. That is, to some extent, the means and the ends of the activity are at least partly determined by the individual who is to carry it out. The more autonomous one is in one's activity the greater is the latitude to choose means and ends. It follows readily that greater autonomy has an impact on the autonomy of others and leads to the necessity of systems of rules to regulate cases where one person's exercise of autonomy comes into conflict or potential conflict with that of another.

DIFFERENT ASPECTS OF WORK

Some time has been spent drawing attention to the fact that it is difficult to provide a definition of 'work'. However, there are important distinctions that will broaden our understanding of the concept.

Making and doing

Work always involves some degree of activity, even if it neither leads to an end-product nor requires a great deal of effort. However, there are many reasons why we might wish to distinguish between activity that does lead to an end-product and activity that does not. A lot of work, particularly in the manufacturing and agricultural sections of the economy, involves the production of artefacts that are quite tangible, like cars, clothing, tools or food. Service industries, on the other hand, also involve the creation of end-products, but these are invariably of a less tangible kind. For instance, a bank will manage a customer's account and offer services such as loans. Both these examples share in common the fact that they are commodities, that is, they can be traded. A bank sells its services for profit just as much as the manufacturer or farmer. But this, as we shall see, is not a necessary condition of activities that involve 'making'. On the other hand, there are activities that do not involve making anything, either tangible or intangible. Riding a horse or swimming with no further end in mind other than entertainment are examples. Such activities are not usually tradeable, although one may buy the opportunities to carry them out and then they are a service that is traded. Both 'making' and 'doing' activities can be carried out without any pecuniary reward.

Paid and unpaid work

This has quite a few complications. We are most familiar with it in terms of the distinction between those activities for which we receive a wage or salary and those for which we do not. One's employment is an example of the first and domestic labour is an example of the other. However, 'paid work' is a little more complicated. One may be self-employed, for example, and here, although one works in order to sustain a certain standard of living, one's work is to a large extent self-directed and one's income comes from the proceeds of the business that one runs.[19] More important, perhaps, is the distinction that Marx drew between the work which is necessary for self- and familial reproduction and that which is imposed on a person for the sustenance of someone else through the prevailing social arrangements. This is clear in the case of modes of production like slavery (where work is imposed and the necessities of life are provided for) and serfdom (where a portion of the working year is spent in self-employment and another portion in obligatory unpaid service to a social superior). It is much less clear in the case of capitalism, as Marx pointed out, because there is no point in the working day where one can say definitely that a worker is sustaining himself and where he is contributing surplus value (through the contribution of labour additional to what he needs to sustain himself) to the employer.

The situation is further complicated under capitalism, as Marx argued, by the contest between the worker and his employer. There are three possible arenas for such a contest. The first is over what constitutes the resources necessary for reproduction of workers and their families. The second is over the amount of time at the disposal of the employer over and above that necessary for reproduction, that the employer may require for paying for a worker's reproduction. The third concerns the intensity of work that is required from the employee, which affects both the time required for reproduction and the amount of surplus value that can be extracted from an employee. The three crucial variables which affect the solution of these questions through some kind of conflict of interest between worker and employer consist in: (a) the productivity of an employee's work (the main factor here is the capital employed in the work process) and (b) the intensity with which they have to work (the main factor here is the individual effort that the employee has to expend) and the length of the working day. The formal conditions of being a waged or salaried employee in capitalist conditions may mask vastly different working practices and conditions, but also the size of the reward that one receives from 'paid employment'.[20]

Remuneration need only be one aspect of the stake that one has in paid employment. The 'wage slave' of Marxist political economy may correspond to reality in many cases, but there are other ways in which an employee may be involved in the affairs of an enterprise, including its reward system, other than through the payment of a wage. The employee may, for example, be part of a profit-sharing or share-ownership scheme. More radically, the enterprise may have decision-making procedures that involve the employees to a considerable extent so that they have a role in making decisions that have an impact on their remuneration. The German system of *Mitbestimmung* or 'codetermination' is an example of one such system.[21] Even slavery sometimes included a form of 'incentive scheme' which encouraged slaves to use their own initiative and, eventually, to gain their freedom.[22] These variations on the institution of paid employment are important because they alter the moral as well as the material relationship between worker and owner and thus have a larger impact on the institution of paid work itself and the role that it plays in people's lives. This is a point that will be returned to in Chapters 3–5.

'Productive' and 'non-productive' work

This is perhaps, one of the distinctions that causes most confusion to laypeople and economists alike. It is drawn very clearly and in a very particular way in Adam Smith's *The Wealth of Nations*, and this account has largely been accepted ever since, although, since the work of Friedrich List, with some dispute.[23] Smith meant by 'productive' labour, activity the outcome of which is capable of being sold as a commodity on the market. Thus work that contributes to the making of pins or watches for sale is productive in this sense, as is work which contributes to the creation of marketable services such as meals in a restaurant or a perfomance in a cabaret.[24] All other kinds of work are, however, deemed 'unproductive'.

> There is one sort of labour which adds to the value of the subject upon which it is bestowed. There is another which has no such effect. The former, as it produces a value, may be called productive; the latter, unproductive labour. Thus the labour of a manufacturer adds, generally, to the value of the materials which he works upon, that of his own maintenance and his master's profit. The labour of a menial servant, on the contrary, adds to the value of nothing.[25]

Smith here makes a distinction that has almost passed into society's conventional wisdom, as has the corollary that productive work is something good and

unproductive work something bad, despite Smith's protestations about the useful-
ness and necessity of some functions of the state. In doing so, however, he ignored
a key distinction which, once it has been drawn attention to, undermines the
basis of the way in which he makes the distinction between unproductive and
productive work (or labour—the terms are synonymous in this context). The
'menial servant' referred to in the quotation may well be the agent of a nobleman
engaged in conspicuous consumption who contributes in no way, however
indirect, to the production of goods and services, whether saleable or not. The
same cannot be said for the judge or the soldier, who ensures that internal and
external peace is kept, thereby allowing for productive activity, in the sense of work
that leads to the creation of tradeable goods and services, to be produced. It by no
means follows that the work of such individuals is 'unproductive' in the way in
which the work of the menial servant might be.[26] If Smith had said that the work
of soldiers and judges was unnecessary, he would not have been taken seriously; by
using the term 'unproductive' to cover two kinds of very different case, he covers
up an absurdity.[27] Much the same point that has been made about soldiers and
judges can be made about doctors, teachers and many other workers who make an
indirect contribution to productive work through the non-trading sector of the
economy.

Marx may have contributed to this misunderstanding of the importance of
'non-productive' work through his modified form of the labour theory of value,
which was originally developed by Locke, Smith and others. If value is only
embodied in tradeable goods and the only identifiable input to that value is the
quantifiable labour that has gone into their production, then it is very difficult,
although not impossible, to take seriously the contributions from inputs that
cannot be readily quantified through some direct measure of the paid labour that
has gone into their production.[28] Smith's distinction between productive and non-
productive work is therefore tendentious and conceptually dubious. In Chapter 3
and beyond, that distinction, in the form that it has traditionally been made, will
be questioned in greater detail.

Voluntary and non-voluntary work

This distinction is, to a considerable degree, context-dependent. For example,
work which one is forced to do is considered to be non-voluntary, an instance of
this would be if the courts order one to do community service tidying up a park.
Again, one might, in another context, consider work that is necessitated, either
by one's conscience or for economic reasons, to be non-voluntary. Yet again, in
the context of any of these three cases one may, in some circumstances, have a
measure of choice over what one is doing and in others not.

Voluntary work is unlikely to be paid (although it is common for expenses to be
paid for this kind of activity, for example, sitting as a member of a local council),
it may or may not involve effort for some or all of its duration. It makes perfect
sense to say, in an appropriate context: 'now that he has more leisure he works
very hard in the voluntary sector, for a charity'. It may or may not involve an

end-product and it may or may not be productive in either of the senses described above.

Domestic and non-domestic work

This distinction is very important and is often neglected in the literature on vocational education. Marxist and, latterly, feminist thinking within economics has argued for the recognition of domestic labour as an important aspect of economic life. Its importance arises in three ways: first, the fact that it is a vital component of the reproduction of the society, including the labour power of employees (and, as unpaid labour, is non-productive in Smith's sense). Second, in the era of artisanal and guild-dominated production much of the labour that was traded (and was thus productive in Smith's sense) was carried out in the domestic environment and thus fell within the organisation of the household. Indeed, it can be argued that this type of workplace is again becoming significant through small-scale artisanal activities, the rise of consultancy and so-called 'teleworking' using new tech-nologies for communication. Third, the division of labour within the household, and the recognition of the contribution it makes to the more conventional forms of economic activity, have become the subject of debate, notably with arguments put forward concerning the formalisation of the role of domestic labour in the first sense through, for example, the introduction of a wage system. The decline of a sexual division of labour outside the household has led to increased questioning of the current status of the sexual division of labour within it as well.

It is possible to see domestic work sometimes motivated by necessity and sometimes not. It has both voluntary and involuntary and productive and non-productive aspects. Some domestic work may be accounted leisure activity and some 'proper' work. Sometimes it may involve effort and sometimes not.

Pleasurable and non-pleasurable activities

It is perhaps tempting to think that the distinction between *work* and *leisure* could be drawn in terms of activities that are pleasurable and those that are not. A moment's reflection shows that this will not do, since it is very easy to find examples of conventional work experiences that are, at least in part, pleasurable and leisure experiences that are not. But perhaps this is too hasty; surely the important distinction is between activities that are carried out *for the sake of pleasure* and those that are not. One might say that leisure activities are those that are carried out for the sake of pleasure, this need not make them, however, in every instance pleasurable.

Now it is true that classifying activities in this way will yield a crude distinction between leisure and non-leisure activities, but equally it will obscure important distinctions. One perfectly legitimate use of the term 'leisure' refers to non-remunerated activity. Much non-remunerated activity is undertaken out of necessity and is not necessarily pleasurable. Conversely, many people undertake paid employment, not because they need the money, but because they wish to work for the pleasure that it gives them. This only seems odd if one identifies the pleasure that is obtained from an activity as arising from its completion.[29] One might, for example, identify the pleasure of drinking with the feeling of satisfaction of thirst being slaked. This is to be distinguished from the case where someone receives pleasure from indulging in the activity itself, rather than satisfying, say, the desire engendered by thirst. This can also be intentionally pursued.[30] In a more active sense, pleasure in an activity may be obtained through the release of one's active powers through intentional physical activity.

Not all pleasure is to be associated with sensual activities. Humans are capable of desiring states of affairs or objects because of their perceived value in an emotional, moral or aesthetic sense. We may desire a loved person for the emotional value that we attach to being in their company. Now it seems clear enough that we can obtain pleasure through the attainment of something to which we attach value; it is not, perhaps, as clear that the carrying out of activities which are intended to bring about such ends could themselves be pleasurable. One might think this is impossible if one believes that pleasure related only to the achievement of the ends that one had selected and not to the means. This might be true of certain cases, but not be universally so. The means themselves might be chosen because of their own value or desirability (clearly not just any means will be acceptable in the pursuit of a valued goal).

But even if this is not so, it may come about that an individual comes to experience pleasure through the carrying out of activities that lead to the valued goal. Thus, a couple might wish to decorate their house (a valued end) and find that the experience of doing so is pleasurable through the feeling of spiritual closeness that the activities involved engender. One may, then, experience pleasure in carrying out activities that lead to a goal invested with emotional, aesthetic or moral significance. This may well impact on the means employed to reach such a goal; the couple prefer to decorate themselves rather than to hire a professional decorator, for example.

This has an implication for those activities called 'work', particularly those that seem to be carried out because of necessity in a person's life. In these cases, it is perhaps obvious that the goal (a wage or a vital job accomplished) will bring pleasure or a means to pleasure, but it is also intelligible that the means to such an end be also pleasurable, and that the pleasure may come about through the release of one's active powers or through being in a certain social situation in the course of doing that work. And, to pursue this thought further, it becomes intelligible that the means of achieving a work-related end may be chosen for the pleasure that the work-process itself engenders, giving rise, perhaps, to an enhanced fulfilment of the original end. These are not merely fanciful speculations. Marx, for example, in his study of different work processes, draws attention to the 'animal spirits' engendered among the workers in a workshop not characterised by the strict division of labour and draws attention to the fact that work may be carried out with excessive intensity when one is overly bent on exercising one's active powers.[31] Smith, too, draws attention to the degradation of active powers and consequent human degradation under conditions where little latitude is given to human judgement in the workplace.[32] German, unlike English, has a word for precisely this phenomenon of pleasure or zest *in* rather than as a result of work, *Arbeitsfreude*. *Arbeitsfreude* is a complex phenomenon which is, it will be argued, of considerable importance for vocational education. At one level, it involves the sensual pleasure that one gains from a work process; at another, the pleasure in the release of active powers of either strength or skill. At another, it involves the social pleasures of association in a work process. Finally, it may involve a heightened spiritual awareness of the significance of the activity, the way in which it is being done and its wider consequences. These issues will be returned to in greater depth in Chapter 5.

An important tradition of thinking about the differences between work and leisure can be found in the work of Aristotle.[33] In this tradition, leisure consists largely in the cultivation of friendships. This vision of leisure in turn reflects the way of life of a well-off citizen in a largely self-sufficient *polis*. While it is true in modern societies that the cultivation of friendship is an important aspect of our activities outside work, it is also an oversimplification. In the first instance, friendships are very often formed in the workplace. These may or may not be confined to the work situation. The enjoyment of friendship then becomes an important aspect of people's working lives. The cultivation of these friendships may tend to take place in the more 'leisurely' periods of working life but this is by no means necessarily the case. They may often be forged in the realm of necessity, where intense mutual reliance between partners in the workplace generate a sense of mutual trust and liking and may even involve the sense of heightened spiritual awareness that working with others at the limits of one's skill and endurance may engender.

CONCLUSION

It has been the aim of this chapter to indicate something of the complexity of the relationships between the concepts: *work*, *leisure*, *effort* and *activity* and, in addition, to indicate the role that necessity plays in life. Furthermore, the chapter has attempted to show the complex relationships that exist between different kinds of work, how their classification is context- and purpose-dependent and how these aspects link with the other, related, concepts that we have examined.

Two things should be evident from this discussion. The first is that it is unhelpful to attempt definitions of these concepts which will include all relevant cases and exclude all irrelevant.[34] The second is that, however we classify work in different contexts and for different purposes, there are a whole range of legitimate uses of 'work' which are not directly related to economic activity in the sense of directly remunerated employment. However, paid work plays an important role in most people's lives. Any discussion of vocational education has got to take preparation for a life of remunerated employment very seriously, without falling into the trap of supposing that it is the only, or even the most important, activity that they undertake as adults.

Notes

1 J. White (1997) *Education and the End of Work* (1997), London, Kogan Page.
2 White, op. cit. p. 4.
3 R. Dearden (1968) *The Philosophy of Primary Education*, London, Routledge.
4 Dearden, op. cit. p. 100.
5 C. Winch, J. Gingell (1999) *Key Concepts in the Philosophy of Education*, London, Routledge, pp. 173–174.
6 L. Wittgenstein (1953) *Philosophical Investigations*, Oxford, Blackwell, paras 65–67.
7 Wittgenstein, op. cit. para 76.
8 R. Beardsmore (1992) 'The Theory of Family Resemblances', *Philosophical Investigations*, 15, 2, pp. 111–130.
9 J.-J. Rousseau (1966) (1762) *Emile ou l'Education*, Paris, Editions Flammarion, Book 1, p. 76, see also p. 80.
10 P. F. Strawson (1974) 'Freedom and Resentment' in *Freedom and Resentment and other Essays*, London, Methuen.
11 For such an account, see R. Sheaff (1996) *The Need for Health Care*, London, Routledge.
12 For example, N. Chomsky (1988) *Language and Problems of Knowledge*, Cambridge MA, MIT Press, pp. 62–63.
13 White unfortunately seems to have been tempted by the Chomskyan account of learning with minimal effort, see White, op. cit. pp. 97–101.
14 Rousseau, op. cit.
15 Cf. N. Malcolm (1982) 'Language and the Instinctive Basis of Human Behaviour', Swansea, University College of Swansea.
16 As Adam Smith recognised, one of the morally less attractive features of money-based societies is precisely that not only do they allow people to impress others through the display of accumulated wealth, but they positively encourage it as well; *The Wealth of Nations*, Indianapolis, IN, Liberty Fund (1776) (1981), Bk. I, x, b, p. 125; Bk. V, I, b, p. 712; (1759) (1984), *The Theory of Moral Sentiments*, Indianapolis, IN, Liberty Fund, Ch. II. Aristotle (1988), *The Politics*, edited by Stephen Everson, Cambridge, Cambridge University Press, Bk. I, 9, pp. 12–14.
17 F. List (1991) *The National System of Political Economy*, NJ, Augustus Kelley.
18 J. Gray (1995) *Enlightenment's Wake*, London, Routledge.
19 There are circumstances in which the distinction between employment and self-employment is largely formal, for example, when the self-employee is completely dependent on one or two large contractors who closely supervise his work.
20 K. Marx (1887) (1970), *Capital*, London, Lawrence and Wishart, Chapters X, XV.
21 W. Streeck (1992) *Social Institutions and Economic Performance*, London, Sage, Ch. 5.
22 Cf. Montesquieu (1973) *The Persian Letters*, London, Penguin, Letter 115, p. 208.
23 Smith, op. cit.; List, op. cit.
24 Smith himself did not, although his followers have, included tradeable services as well as goods, as possible results of productive labour.
25 Smith, op. cit. Bk. II, Chapter III, p. 330.
26 As Keynes showed, however, the work of the 'unproductive' menial servant can also have 'productive' consequences' if it leads to increased demand.
27 Gwydion M. Williams (2000) *Wealth Without Nations*, London, Athol Books, Part 3.
28 Marx recognises that training and education are inputs that have an effect on the market value of labour, because they represent labour embodied in further labour, but does not develop this insight further to consider the social conditions of production. For him, the economy comes first and the rest of society is built on it. He does not recognise sufficiently the complex social relationships on which an economic system is built.
29 This discussion owes a great deal to N. Dent (1984) *The Moral Psychology of the Virtues*, Cambridge, Cambridge University Press, especially Chapters 2 and 3.
30 Dent, op. cit. p. 49.

31 Marx (1970) op. cit. for the first, Ch. XIV, p. 341; for the second, Ch. XXV, p. 694, on agricultural labour in England.
32 Smith (1981) op. cit. Bk. V, i, f, p. 782.
33 Aristotle (1925) *Nichomachean Ethics*, London, Dent.
34 Not all concepts are like this, of course. *Education*, for example, as will be seen in the next chapter, does not lend itself so easily to classification as a family resemblance concept.

3 The economic and work-related aims of education

INTRODUCTION: CONCEPTS AND CONCEPTIONS OF EDUCATION

Education is neither a clearly defined nor a family resemblance concept. One cannot satisfactorily define 'education' to exclude all uses of the term that do not fall within the definition.[1] On the other hand, neither is it a series of overlapping usages without an identifiable central core, the relationships between which vary according to context and purpose.[2] It is, however, susceptible of a loose definition that will serve for most purposes. It can be defined as 'preparation for life'. This could be characterised as a 'second-order' definition since it contains minimal normative content and commitment to particular values.[3] 'First-order' conceptions need follow no such restraint. Such a definition implies that learning is an important component of education, since preparation for life involves learning. Learning *per se*, however, is not education, because some of it is too trivial or too misdirected to qualify. It is therefore misleading to define 'education' merely in terms of learning.

The loose definition has the advantage of neutrality between different kinds of learning: propositional, practical, tacit and social. It is also broad enough to capture such phenomena as post-compulsory and adult learning, not to mention vocational education. Preparation for life does not end with childhood, and even when one is an adult who has been adequately prepared it remains true that there will remain *aspects* of life for which one may not have been prepared. A further advantage is that it incorporates the value-laden and normative elements of education. A preparation for life is a preparation for the pursuit of some conception of the good, expressed within the beliefs, institutions and customs of societies. The *concept* of education is neutral between these. However, it has been customary among philosophers of education since Plato to incorporate into their philosophical theory of education a first-order normative account of some aspects of the good. This approach has been followed by, among others, Aristotle, Rousseau, Dewey and Peters.[4]

There is nothing wrong with first-order normative accounts of education. Whatever the first-order commitments that a philosopher has, however, he also has the prior duty of clarifying the concept of education, and that task does not *necessarily* involve the articulation and defence of a particular first-order account.

CONCEPTIONS OF VOCATIONAL EDUCATION

I have already distinguished between first- and second-order accounts of education and claimed that the second-order account involves minimal normative content. No such restraint applies to first-order accounts, which invariably define education in terms of some particular view of the good. Different conceptions of education vary both between and within societies. It is not difficult to see how different societies may have different conceptions of the good; it is, perhaps, more difficult to see how those conceptions could co-exist *within* them. Aristotle's description of the *polis* allows for the pursuit of competing conceptions of the good by individuals and associations.[5] Although Aristotle does not express this view, it is also compatible with his meta-theory of politics that different *cultural* conceptions of the good can also be accommodated within the *polis*, understanding 'polis' in a more modern sense as a form of political association of which the nation state is a primary example.[6]

Within a political society, different conceptions of the good have different relationships with each other. This also holds for different conceptions of education, since these involve preparation for different forms of the good. Thus, some conceptions will be compatible with, and even require each other, since they relate to different phases of education. For example, education in the basic sense of 'grounding', that is learning to read and to count, are prerequisites of preparation for a vocation or for acquaintance with one's culture.[7] Some have a more limited compatibility; it may be possible for one person to become both acquainted with their culture and to pursue a vocation. Given the alternatives available and the finitude of human ability and lifespan, however, such permutations will be limited.

More difficult to reconcile are conceptions that are mutually exclusive. I may think that traditional liberal education is desirable for A and that preparation for life as a carpenter is desirable for B. What is desirable for A is not likely to be desirable for B and vice-versa, on this view. It does not follow, of course, that just because a liberal education is desirable for A and not for B, that it is undesirable *per se*, or even undesirable for a whole section of society. The situation becomes more problematic, however in the following circumstances. First, I may hold that some conceptions of education are desirable for some groups in society and not for others and this view of education may be disputed by those others. For example, I may hold liberal education is only a good for the gentry. For the peasantry, I may think a preparation for agricultural labour is the only desirable good. The peasantry, however, might believe that they too should have some form of liberal education. In this situation one has a very common form of political conflict of interest. One group rejects the conception of the good that another is trying to impose on it and there are consequent conflicts about political power and the distribution of resources.

It is normal and politically healthy for a society to have a plurality of conceptions of education, provided that there are ways of arriving at commonly agreed sets of educational arrangements. It is now necessary to look at these conceptions, how they are arrived at and, tentatively, at how they might be reconciled. In the previous section it was suggested that different conceptions of education were associated with different conceptions of the good. One should not assume that all sections of society or all individuals will have the same conceptions. The imaginary example of the peasantry and the gentry suggested that one group may wish to pursue a conception of the good which another regards as its exclusive possession. Other possibilities exist: that one group may regard its conception as universal and seek to impose it on the whole society or that different groups may adopt largely exclusive and differing conceptions of the good.

Given that a political society will contain within itself groups holding different conceptions of the good, how can one identify who these are? One answer, derived from Vico and Marx, is that society consists of different economic interest groups. The gentry/peasantry example fits this pattern. But this is far too simple, for three connected reasons. First, there is more than one way of classifying interests. Sexual, ethnic and religious divisions may be just as important as economic ones.[8] Second, one's individual point of view concerning the good may not coincide with the majority view of the sectional group to which one belongs—a peasant may think it perfectly appropriate that the gentry have exclusive political power. As Marxists used to put it, one's subjective perception of one's interests might fail to coincide with what, 'objectively', is in one's interests. Third, individuals may belong to different sectional groups depending on context. A worker may adopt the position of a *rentier* when considering his private pension fund; an entrepreneur the viewpoint of a trade unionist when his daughter is given the sack; a teacher the view of a parent when his son is doing badly at school. A child may adopt a short-term view of his well-being; the same individual may later adopt a long-term view as an adult both of his own well-being and that of his children.

The diversity and shifting nature of sectional groups, particularly in diverse and complex societies, makes it dangerous to attempt to classify differences about conceptions of education as if they corresponded neatly with one way of classifying interest groups. A more helpful approach is to suggest that different individuals' *points of view* are not only related to their personal preferences, but also to the complex of positions that they have in society. Those points of view may shift according to circumstance and context. Although this makes the task of tracing and forming patterns of conceptions of educational good highly complex, it helps to illustrate how important it is to accommodate different conceptions to establish areas held in common as well as areas of conflict. As suggested above, *political dialogue* which explores the implications of different value positions has great value for doing this.[9] One way of encapsulating these points is to say that people have an interest in the political and educational system of the society from the point of view of *stakeholders*. They may adopt more than one stakeholder position, and positions may vary from time to time in a person's life and from context to context. In what follows, the three main first-order conceptions of education and their relationships with each other are described. A preferred first-order conception of vocational education will be developed in this context.

DIFFERENT CONCEPTIONS OF EDUCATION

All education is vocational in a *thin* sense: preparation for life is preparation for following a particular conception of the good, that is, a calling to a particular way of life. However, it is generally, and rightly, understood that the difference between a vocational and a liberal education involves, at the very least, a difference in emphasis.[10] In what follows I will try to describe the different conceptions of education that exist in modern complex societies and their relationships with each other.

These will be described in terms of their *aims*, since these underpin their other principal features: curriculum, institutional context, pedagogy and assessment.[11] Conceptions of education can be conveniently divided into three main categories: liberal, vocational and civic. It will be shown that these classifications, although convenient, in fact display certain significant overlaps.

Liberal educators

Liberal educators generally emphasise the goal of personal development and self-fulfilment as the overriding good. Within this broad tradition, it is possible to discriminate between three distinct tendencies, distinguished in most cases, as much by emphasis as anything else (this is not so true, however, of the third category, the radical liberal). First, *conservative liberalism* in education has tended to place most emphasis on the development of cultured individuals, usually understood in terms of acquaintance with the dominant culture of the society, which is considered to be, in the words of Arnold, 'the best that has been thought and said'.[12] There are numerous philosophers and educators who have written in this tradition in recent years: Bantock, Peters and Cooper to name but three.[13] The key characteristic of this tradition is the emphasis on the acquisition of propositional knowledge of key elements of the dominant traditional culture as the means to personal development and cultivation. Not only is such an education a preparation for the leisured classes, but, for the professional, it is a useful preliminary for a subsequent vocational calling.[14] Traditional liberal education as it developed in the nineteenth century also placed great emphasis on *character development*, particularly as a preparation for a calling as a military or imperial servant of the state. Acquaintance with classical culture was one element of this, as was the inculcation of qualities of stoicism and physical endurance associated with physical games and uncomfortable living conditions.

Modern liberalism in education has tended to downplay the significance of knowledge and cultural acquaintance in favour of the development of *autonomy* or the ability to lead an independent life. Writers such as J. P. White and R. F. Dearden belong to this tradition. The pursuit of autonomy requires acquisition of appropriate cultural knowledge, but does so because it is a means to the end of developing the autonomous person, to be understood as someone who can choose the ends as well as the means of life and who is properly equipped to determine what ends he will pursue.[15]

Radical liberalism shares with other tendencies in liberal education a concern with personal development, but, unlike the other two tendencies, emphasises the need to change society through the process of education in order to achieve the goal of a fully developed and self-realising human being. The effective founder of this tradition is Rousseau in *Emile*, but the other great contributor is John Dewey.[16] Like modern liberals, radical liberals emphasise autonomy as a key aim of education. Unlike the conservatives, they have limited or even no time for inculcation into traditional culture.[17] Unlike modern liberals, they place a great deal of emphasis on the ability of autonomous individuals to choose from among ends which are not necessarily approved of by society. They are strong autonomists about ends. Those who are resolutely non-cognitivist about values also tend to downplay the possibility of a rational choice of ends, regarding this as essentially a subjective matter. Radical liberals have tended to adopt a strong strain of vocationalism within their general outlook. For Rousseau, the acquisition of useful skills was an important condition of acquiring a healthy self-respect of *amour propre*. For Dewey, the position is less clear; he seems to oscillate between a belief in vocational education as an instrument of personal growth and a belief that education should aim to promote the growth of society.[18]

Civic educators

Civic educators may be subdivided into conservatives, liberals and radicals—although with some surprising results. Conservative civic educators tend to stress the aim of preserving a contented and reasonably quiescent citizenry who will not make revolutionary demands or upset the *status quo*. Bantock, for example, stresses the importance of a specific form of cultural initiation for non-academic pupils to fit them for a world in which they will not be among the leaders.[19] Smith, however, through his concern with the degenerating effect that the division of labour would have on working people, and through his concern that large corporate bodies would start to dominate the political life of a society thus characterised, advocates elementary education as a condition of engendering at least a minimal degree of scepticism and independence among the common populace.[20] There are, then, potentially conflicting strands within the conservative civic education tradition.

Liberal civic educators stress the importance of common and equal citizenship and the inculcation of civic virtues commensurate with that ideal. They tend to discount the inculcation of traits such as obedience and quiescence which conservative citizenship educators tend to find desirable for at least certain sections of the population.[21] For the liberal civic educator, the general priority is the development of an autonomous individual, but one also endowed with civic virtues, namely those that promote an active and sceptical citizenry capable of playing a full part in all aspects of the life of a democratic society, including in the public and domestic spheres.

Radical civic educators stress, as one might expect, the role of education in developing a citizen who will initiate radical change in his society. It might seem obvious that this would be achieved by *prefigurative* education, that is, by radicalising the child in order to develop a radical adult. Surprisingly, one of the most thoughtful radical civic educators of the twentieth century took a somewhat different view. Gramsci held the opinion that prevocational education had two bad effects on children from less exalted backgrounds. First, it led them into habits of docility and submissiveness, second it deprived them of the epistemic means of developing a critique of their society. Gramsci believed that traditional habits of study developed the self-discipline, determination and independence that would be necessary for social emancipation. He also believed that a traditional classical curriculum, as opposed to a vocational one, would enable the citizen to understand the history and politics of his society the better to transform them.[22]

Vocational educators

Vocational educators can be classified according to the different emphases that they place on the aims of education, although it must be stressed that these classifications do not preclude overlap in aims in certain respects.

First of all, there are the *instrumental vocationalists*, who, following Adam Smith, see the vocational element of training purely in terms of preparation for specific occupations. Generally speaking, instrumental vocationalists are hostile to institutionalised forms of vocational education, seeing them as having the effect of bidding up prices in the labour market.[23] Smith also believed that, due to the increasing use of the division of labour, prolonged skill formation periods would become unnecessary.[24] There is, however, also a *civic* element to Smith's account of education. Inevitably, employers tend to take a more instrumental view of vocational education, particularly for lower-status workers.

Liberal vocationalists have become increasingly influential in recent years.[25] They stress the continuity in aims between liberal and vocational education, generally holding that some of the most important liberal aims, such as those of autonomy and self-realisation, can best be achieved, at least for many people, through vocationally oriented curricula, partially at the latter stage of the compulsory curriculum, but especially after the compulsory stage. They differ from conservative and modern liberal educators in their curriculum choices, particularly at the upper end of the compulsory years of schooling. They may, however, also differ from radical liberals in advocating a more liberal form of curriculum during the earlier years of compulsory schooling.[26] Liberal vocationalism has come to attract increasing interest at the level of government and some sections of the business interest in the UK. In addition, it has become more popular with parents, some of whom have come to consider that it confers future employment advantages on their children. Liberal vocationalism is important for the development of the argument in this book.

Finally, there are *radical vocationalists*, who see vocational education as offering a transformational role for the individual in his future interactions with society. Rousseau's aim of producing an individual self-reliant through his ability to pursue a craft or trade, and thus to move society towards a community of independent citizens, is an example of radical vocationalism. Rousseau-influenced twentieth century radicals like Illich also fall into this category.[27]

JUSTIFICATION OF THE VOCATIONAL CONCEPTION OF EDUCATION

It is now time to consider the preferred conception of vocational education that this the main concern of this book: liberal vocationalism. It is advocated as an important strand in the educational philosophy of developed industrial countries for a number of reasons. First, because vocationalism corresponds to the interests, both perceived and real, of large numbers of young people, of government and sections of business.[28] Second, because it is a more effective way than modern liberalism of meeting liberal aims for some people. Third, because it can be pursued alongside modern liberal and liberal civic education to give a balanced range of opportunities which reflect the diversity of ability and interest that exist in any modern pluralist society. Finally, subscribing to it entails economic changes that are not only appropriate to an advanced society concerned with material prosperity, but offer new possibilities to a large majority of those who see their aims in life largely defined in terms of work.

Liberal vocationalism rejects the instrumentalist conception of training, which sees vocational education largely as an immediate preparation for comparatively low-skill work. It emphasises the importance of individual development and the ability to choose a satisfying occupation. The liberal vocationalist, like the modern liberal, lays stress on the importance of choosing one's ends in life, although the emphasis on occupational choice situates the liberal vocationalist as a weak autonomist, rather than a strong autonomist in the post-Millian liberal tradition. That is, the liberal vocationalist encourages young people to make occupational choices from amongst those that society considers worthwhile or, in the idiom of the previous chapter that are 'productive' rather than 'unproductive'.

The main contrast between the liberal vocationalist and the modern liberal at the compulsory stage of education is that the former is much more prepared than the latter to spell out what the choices involved in making plans for a future life are and what the means to attaining them are, while the modern liberal is more inclined to think of ends in an unconstrained way, as if the future adult will be an isolated person of leisure. In the language of the previous chapter, the liberal vocationalist seeks to develop autonomy, but within the inevitable constraints of the necessity of earning a living that shape the life-choices of the great majority of the population. The necessity involved, however, is not just that of the occupational *status quo*. It is one that, although it recognises the necessity of working, is also concerned to make work a worthwhile experience.

Likewise, in his more radical mode, the liberal vocationalist emphasises the importance of preparing future workers for a role in the governance of their enterprises, through institutional forms of industrial democracy (see Chapter 13). In this guise, he offers an extension to liberal civic education with radical implications. Liberal vocationalism has, then, close affinities with, and is largely compatible with aspects of, both modern liberal and liberal civic conceptions of education.

In order to delineate the scope and limits of liberal vocationalism, it is of the first importance to distinguish the common phase of education, prevocational education and postcompulsory education (which is the main focus of this book). At the common phase is the requirement of grounding and cultural literacy (which are sub-aims that liberal, civic and vocational conceptions hold in common). Grounding can be defined as that part of education that provides the prerequisites for *independence* (the ability to choose means, which is a prerequisite of autonomy), and consists mainly of literacy and numeracy.[29] Cultural literacy is the common set of knowledge and assumptions that society shares, which provides the basis for mutual understanding and reasoning in both everyday contexts and established subjects. The primary and early secondary curriculum is concerned with grounding and cultural literacy, which are prerequisites for liberal, civic and vocational education.[30] The questions that concern us should be: 'How flexible is the core curriculum? What options does it allow? And at what stage does it allow them?' Liberal vocationalism suggests the need for flexibility in answering these questions.

Prevocational education, occurring in the middle secondary years (14–16) is concerned with two sub-aims. First, the preparation of young people for the understanding of work and the economy (in this sense it is an extension of cultural literacy) and second, through the provision of generic vocational programmes, which give the opportunity to make more informed choices about work for those contemplating entering an occupation or going into an apprenticeship or further education at the end of the compulsory phase. It is important to provide credible qualifications (e.g. at GCSE level in the UK context) in order to both keep options open and to give a good foundation for postcompulsory vocational education.

Liberal vocationalism builds on the recognition, which has steadily gained ground since the discrediting of theories of unitary ability, that ability is activity specific and that abilities vary widely and are related to interests. It recognises and celebrates the diversity of human life and aspirations. It also fulfils many of the main criteria of a liberal education: it initiates young people into worthwhile activities, building on cognitive breadth it seeks to provide cognitive depth in certain areas and it emphasises choice and forms of learning that are ethically acceptable.[31] It parts company with traditional liberalism in putting limits on the depth to which 'forms of knowledge' are pursued and substitutes in their place more practical modes of knowledge.

The prerequisites for effective *postcompulsory* liberal vocational education are, first, that there is a good system of postcompulsory vocational education to move into and, second, an economy organised in such a way that skills are valued and used. The implications of liberal vocationalism, far from being conservative, are radical, both in the educational and the political sense.[32] Liberal vocationalism is a call to arms to those who wish to cater for a wider range of interests and aspirations amongst stakeholders than are currently catered for. It not only implies changes in secondary education (see below) but, much more fundamentally, implies changes in the way in which young people are inducted into work and, in many cases, the way in which work is organised and tasks are configured into occupations. When taken to its natural conclusion in a society accustomed to instrumental vocationalism and an economy organised to match, such as ours largely is, it is, to all intents and purposes, a radical form of vocationalism.

LIBERAL UNIVERSALISM

Given the liberal vocationalist's emphasis on autonomy and on the pursuit of activities of intrinsic value, together with his acceptance of the necessity of a common core curriculum, one may well ask whether the difference between him and the modern liberal is significant. What is at issue?' Is it more than a mustard seed? There is a significant difference despite the large areas of agreement.

Liberal vocationalism takes into account and even extends liberal civic education by suggesting the possibility of extending citizenship into the workplace. Unlike modern liberalism, it maintains that interests and abilities are too diverse to be contained in a common curriculum up to the age of 16, and that equity in a plural society suggests that the interests and wishes of the vocationally inclined be accorded the same respect as those of the liberally inclined. Here it parts company with those liberal educators who see vocational education as a poor substitute for a full-blooded liberal education, by acknowledging that the academic route is not the only means by which most people exercise their abilities. This is not 'tokenism'; to accord an alternative approach equal status to the liberal one is to take seriously its material, human and structural requirements, and that requires heavy invest-ment in both human and material resources. Liberal vocationalism implies a reordering of financial priorities in education towards those whose needs have been long neglected.

Despite its affinities with modern liberalism, modern liberals might still be inclined to reject it, however, on arguments based on the need to preserve liberal democracy. This is a mistaken strategy. Even political liberal universalism, which seeks to justify liberal democracy through fundamental principles like rights or a hypothetical contract, does not require liberal universalism in education. It requires what we have seen that liberal vocationalism can already provide for those sections of the population who choose a vocational route: grounding, cultural literacy and a programme of liberal, if not radical, civic education. However, it remains true to say that, logically speaking, liberal universalism is passive towards vocationalism and tends to emphasise the standard themes of liberal education.[33] The rejection of system-based political liberalism suggests a more positive orientation towards different routes to education. Educational pluralism can be justified on the grounds of *agonistic liberalism*, as a reflection of the diversity of currents within a society and of the need to provide for them. Once one recognises the existence of different points of view and is prepared to accept contingent political arrangements for accommodating them, the emphasis shifts from procedural requirements for democracy to substantive issues of defining and making room for these diverse interests.[34] Given the pervasiveness of contingent rather than *a priori* political arrangements, agonistic liberalism has a great deal to recommend it as a framework for defining and accommodating diverse educational interests. Rejection of liberal political universalism undermines one of the main justifications for ignoring vocationalism as a serious option.

GOOD AND BAD EDUCATION

We can now see how it might be possible to characterise education as *in general* a good and *in particular circumstances* a bad thing. To say that education is a preparation for life is to imply, uncontroversially, that it is a good. It is difficult to deny that some preparation is necessary for anyone who wishes to lead a satisfying life, or for any society that wishes to prosper. It does not follow that for any person, that a particular conception of education is necessarily a good for *them*. Traditional thinking in the conservative liberal traditions has tended too readily to make this assumption as concept and conception are confounded and an account of one conception is taken as the definition of the concept of education.[35]

It follows that there are senses in which, although in general education is good, it can, under certain circumstances, be bad. First, and most generally, an inappropriate conception of education may be adopted for someone, for a group or for a society. Second, an inappropriate conception may be adopted for a particular phase of education. Third, there may be deficiencies in the execution of a particular conception, so that, for example, aims are poorly formulated, curricula poorly designed, assessment misconceived or pedagogy bungled. In the terms of the foregoing argument, many people in our society may be receiving a bad education.

First, in terms of point 3, their grounding and development of cultural literacy may have been mishandled. Second, many children have been given limited or inappropriate choices which do not conform to their developing ideas of the way in which they would like their lives to go. Although the earlier part of education may be largely appropriate, they are receiving a bad education, in the sense of point 2, for a particular phase. Any form of education can turn out to be bad under certain circumstances. It is the argument of this book that liberal education has no monopoly of the title of educational good. But it also follows that neither do the other conceptions. Given a certain conception of the good, it will follow that a certain kind of education is preferable. However, there is still room for argument concerning the extent to which any particular programme does in fact constitute an adequate preparation. Then there are questions concerning how well that programme is executed. These latter two groups of question cannot receive an *a priori* answer; they must be settled by empirical investigation.

TRADITIONAL LIBERAL EDUCATION

The vocational education of the eighteenth-century English gentry

It was claimed earlier that all education is, in some sense, vocational. What can we say of the model of liberal education that has long been dominant in the UK?[36] To whose needs did it answer when it was originally constructed? To whose needs does it answer now? In order to answer these questions, it is necessary to look to the model of education that was incorporated into the state system towards the end of the nineteenth century. There are two aspects to this issue. First, the elementary civic education that Smith advocated had already reached a proportion of the population. This became the backbone of the elementary school system which served the great majority.

Secondary education was, however, the preserve of a few and was confined to the grammar and independent schools. The general aim of such an education was, together with personal cultivation, preparation for university and the liberal professions. Later, it came to include preparation for the science-based professions and the newer science and technology courses that increasingly came to be offered in the universities. However, the underlying model remained personal cultivation and preparation for an adult life which was not primarily concerned with paid employment. Such was the kind of education offered to the gentry, both major and minor, of seventeenth- and eighteenth-century England.

England, from the time of the Civil War until the Reform Act of 1832, was, to a considerable degree, governed by a large oligarchy of country gentlemen and aristocrats whose power base was the House of Commons. The particular conception of the good that this large oligarchy adhered to was that of a leisured person who, in addition to pursuing country pursuits, was expected to show some engagement with intellectual life and to participate in the governance of his society and his community. A curriculum based on the historical and cultural experience of the ancient world, together with an acquaintance with the history and main cultural achievements of the contemporary world was thought to be the the appropriate preparation for such a life.[37]

The English conception of liberal education by its nature blurred the vocational/liberal distinction. The vocation *was* enjoyment of life and a cultivation of the mind on the one hand, and, on the other, a leisured participation in local governance and the affairs of state.[38] There would be no apparent absurdity in describing such a conception of the good life as non-vocational in character, if by that one were to mean that it was not concerned with *work* in the sense of paid employment. It was clearly vocational in the sense in which it prepared people for *a particular kind of life* which had the characteristics of an engagement with society at quite a demanding level, at least for those who entertained ambitions to be active members of the ruling class.

The transfer of this particular conception of education to the preparation of different classes of citizens for a different kind of life was bound to lead to difficulties. These were to a large extent obscured by two factors. The first was that the growing professions required the kind of background acquaintance with the nature of the society and its cultural heritage that the education of the gentry provided. The second is that the curriculum underwent evolutionary change over the years, with a slow, but increasing attention being paid to science. A third important factor was the broadening of the franchise, particularly after 1832, which enabled sections of the middle class to play an active part in the political life of the society. All these factors continued to make a gradually shifting version of the traditional education of the gentry relevant to the preparation of some children of middle-class background. The rest of the society were catered for through conservative civic and instrumental vocational education (where the latter was thought to be necessary). In the hands of some modern philosophers of education, as well as in practice, and especially through the introduction of comprehensive education, traditional English liberal education has been transformed into a timeless ideal, suitable for all citizens. This chapter shows its historically and politically contingent nature.

It does not follow that such an education is, in itself, a suitable preparation for all future citizens, particularly those who do not wish to seek an occupation in the professions. The construction of any alternative does, however, need to take account of the need for an appropriate form of civic education for the citizens of a democracy, as well as for the personal cultivation of the individuals, if it is to be attractive. Contemporary British education still bears the marks of the gentry conception with its emphasis on preparation for life as if it is to be a leisured life, when patently, for most people, it is not.

CONCLUSION

Although this book is primarily concerned with post-compulsory vocational education, it is based on an assumption that a prime aim of vocational education is personal development and fulfilment through work for all citizens if they so wish it. Economically active adults, who are also citizens of a democracy, therefore need a range of common understanding and knowledge that allow them to take an active part in the affairs of their society and to have the opportunity of enjoying leisure and domestic life. All citizens, therefore, need a common liberal and liberal civic education on which to build worthwhile vocational education. Vocational education can exist in embryonic form, as part of moral and civic education at the primary stage, additionally as an element in the study of the main subjects at the lower secondary level and, for those who choose it, as a more explicitly pre-vocational strand at 14+ years of age. Vocational education is not a distinct strand in education separate from the rest, it is one branch that grows out of a common trunk which encompasses liberal and civic, as well as vocational aims.[39]

Notes

1 Contrast the essentialist definition that O'Neill gives to 'market'. John O'Neill (1998) *The Market: Ethics, Knowledge and Politics*, London, Routledge.

2 See L. Wittgenstein (1953) *Philosophical Investigations*, Oxford, Blackwell; R. Beardsmore (1992) 'The Theory of Family Resemblances', *Philosophical Investigations*, 15, 2, pp. 111–130.

3 These commitments would normally involve a concern that one's society should continue in the future in a form that has recognisable continuity with the past. Beyond this it is difficult to be more explicit without invoking a first-order account.

4 Plato (1950) *The Republic*, London, Macmillan; Aristotle (1925) *Nichomachean Ethics*, London, Dent; J.-J. Rousseau (1966) *Emile ou l'Education*, Paris, Editions Flammarion; John Dewey (1916) *Democracy and Education'*, New York, Macmillan; R. S. Peters (1966) *Ethics and Education*, London, Allen and Unwin.

5 See, for example, Aristotle (1988) *The Politics*, Cambridge, Cambridge University Press, Bk. 2. The following discussion owes much to O'Neill (1998), op. cit. Chapter Two and to J. Gray (1995) *Enlightenment's Wake*, London, Routledge, Chapter 6.

6 For a defence of the modern view of nationality as it is typically embodied in modern nation states, see David Miller (1993) 'In Defence of Nationality', *Journal of Applied Philosophy*, 10, 1, 3–16.

7 See Oliver Letwin (1988) *Education: The Importance of Grounding*, London, Centre for Policy Studies.

8 Hobbes, for example, in Part Three of *Leviathan* (1967) London, Penguin, is greatly concerned with the management of religious differences within a plural society.

9 Market solutions, with their adoption of a non-cognitivist view of value and reliance on *exit*, rather than *voice* for resolving conflicts about goods, seem to be in a rather poor position to do this, to the detriment of the general political health of a society. For a market account of education, see James Tooley (1995) *Disestablishing the School*, Aldershot, Avebury, and for a critique of markets O'Neill, op. cit.

10 This seems to be the view of for example, Richard Pring (1995) *Closing the Gap: Liberal Education and Vocational Preparation*, London, Hodder and Stoughton.

11 This point is developed in more detail in C. Winch (1996) *Quality and Education*, Oxford, Blackwell.

12 Cf. M. Arnold (1932) *Culture and Anarchy*, edited by John Dover Wilson, Cambridge, Cambridge University Press.

13 Cf. G. H. Bantock (1963) *Education in an Industrial Society*, London, Faber; Peters, op. cit.; David Cooper (1980) *Illusions of Equality*, London, Routledge; Paul Hirst (1974) *Knowledge and the Curriculum*, London, Routledge; Anthony O'Hear (1981) *Education, Society and Human Nature*, London, Routledge.

14 J. S. Mill (1867) 'Inaugural Lecture at the University of St. Andrews' in F. A. Cavanagh (ed.) (1931) *James and John Stuart Mill on Education*, Cambridge, Cambridge University Press.

15 Cf. J. P. White, (1982) *The Aims of Education Restated*, London, Routledge; R. F. Dearden, (ed.) (1984) *Theory and Practice in Education*, London, Routledge, see chapter entitled 'Theory and Practice in Education'.

16 Rousseau, op. cit.; J. Dewey, op. cit.

17 Cf. Rousseau, op. cit. writing of the education of a child on the brink of adolescence: 'Des Livres! Quel triste ameublement pour son age!' p. 204.

18 On Rousseau as vocationalist, John Darling (1993) 'Rousseau as Progressive Instrumentalist', *Journal of Philosophy of Education*, 27, 1, 27–38. On the uncertainties of

Dewey's position, see H. O. Mounce (1996) *The Two Pragmatisms*, London, Routledge, Chapter 8.

19 Bantock, op. cit.

20 Cf. A. Smith (1981), *The Wealth of Nations*, Indianapolis, IN, Liberty Fund, Bk. V, Chapter 1, section f.

21 In the UK this approach has been strongly associated with the work of J. P. White (1982) op. cit.; (1990) *Education and the Good Life*, London, Kogan Page; (1997) *Education and the End of Work*, London, Kogan Page. See also J. White, P. Gordon (1979) *Philosophers as Educational Reformers*, London, Routledge for a historical account. The epistemological dimensions of liberal citizenship education are explored by E. D. Hirsch (1987) *Cultural Literacy: What Every American Should Know*, Boston, MA, Houghton Mifflin, from a more conservative perspective to that of White.

22 Antonio Gramsci (1971) *Selections from the Prison Notebooks*, London, Lawrence and Wishart.

23 Smith, op. cit., Bk. I, Chapter X, c, p. 139.

24 Ibid. pp. 139–140.

25 Pring, op. cit.; H. Entwistle (1970) *Education, Work and Leisure*, London, Routledge; C. Winch (1995) 'Vocational Education: A Liberal Interpretation', *Studies in Philosophy and Education*, 14, 4, 401–415; Kevin Williams (1994) 'Vocationalism and Liberal Education: Exploring the Tensions', *Journal of Philosophy of Education*, 28, 1, pp. 89–100, are all examples.

26 See Winch, op. cit., and Pring, op. cit.

27 I. Illich (1971) *Deschooling Society*, London, Penguin.

28 For UK evidence concerning young people, see, for example, National Commission on Education (1993) *Learning to Succeed*, London, Heinemann, p. 151, 'The vast majority [*sc.* of children] believed that schools should help them to do as well as possible in their exams and teach them things that would be useful when they entered jobs'.

29 See Letwin, op. cit.

30 The concept of cultural literacy is controversial partly because it has conservative and liberal interpretations and E. D. Hirsch, the originator of the idea of cultural literacy, was a conservative interpreter of the concept. It is unfortunate that, in the furore over the political interpretation, Hirsch's epistemic point about common understanding has tended to be ignored. For a defence see C. Winch (1998) *The Philosophy of Human Learning*, London, Routledge, Chapter 12; for cultural literacy see Hirsch, op. cit.

31 R. S. Peters recognises that vocational education (he uses the expression 'vocational training') can be done in a liberal way in his discussion of the criteria of education (Peters, op. cit. pp. 44–45).

32 It is important to note the difference in emphasis between the case being made out here and that of liberal educators like Peters and Bantock, who, while sympathetic to some form of liberal vocationalism, nevertheless saw it as a substitute form of liberal education for the less able (see Peters, op. cit. pp. 85–87), rather than something of equal value to liberal education. This is partly to do with Peters' and Bantock's acceptance of some deficit theories of ability.

33 Gutmann, for example, points to the centrality of secular standards of reasoning and Callan to the development of autonomy. For a useful survey of some aspects of this debate, see Kenneth Strike (1998) 'Freedom of Conscience and Illiberal Socialisation: The Congruence Argument', *Journal of Philosophy of Education*, 32, 3, 1998, 345–360. See also Amy Gutmann, *Democratic Education*, Princeton NJ, Princeton University Press, 1987; Eamonn Callan, 'Political Liberalism and Political Education', *Review of Politics*, 58, 1, 1–33 (1996).

34 Gray, op. cit. Chapter 6.

35 Peters, op. cit.; Hamm (1989) *Philosophical Issues in Education*, Brighton, Falmer; R. Barrow (1981) *The Philosophy of Schooling*, Brighton, Harvester, but see White (1982) op. cit. for a much more cautious approach from the modern liberal tradition.

36 This is not to imply that it is exclusive to the UK, but to point to its exceptionally privileged position and the historical roots of that position.
37 Such an outlook had close affinities both with an Aristotelian conception of the good life for a citizen and for the kind of education that was appropriate for such a person.
38 J. Morley (1993) *Edmund Burke*, introduced by Brendan Clifford, Belfast, Athol Books.
39 See C. Winch (1990) *Language, Ability and Educational Achievement*, London, Routledge, for an elaboration of this view.

4　Conceptualising economic life

Part one: the consumptionist tradition

INTRODUCTION: THE AIMS OF ECONOMIC ACTIVITY

Concepts and conceptions

The next two chapters will consider different ways in which economic life can be conceptualised. The issues have similarities with those concerning the aims of education discussed in the previous chapter. Just as one can maintain a distinction between a *concept* of education as a preparation for life and different *conceptions* of what that might be, so it is possible to distinguish between the concept of economic activity and different, often contested, conceptions of what it might be. A useful place to start is Marshall's definition of economics as 'a study of men as they live and move and think in the ordinary business of life'.[1] Economic life can therefore be characterised as 'human activity in the ordinary business of life'. Although very broad, the definition will serve our purpose better than an etymological account based on the Greek term *oikos* or 'household' which is too restrictive, since economic activity in Marshall's sense extends well beyond the activities of a household. Within the 'ordinary business of life' some activities will come more to the attention of economists than others, but the definition has the great virtue of resisting the separation of economic aspects of life from others, which, although it has allowed the technical development of the economics in ways which would otherwise not have been possible, also has the vice of leading people (including economists) to think that economic life is somehow structurally detached from the other aspects of living.

Those aspects of the 'ordinary business of life' that will particularly come to the attention of economists will include: activity which results in the mutual exchange of goods and services to satisfy needs and preferences, and activity which is directed to the physical and social maintenance and renewal of individuals and the societies in which they live. However, within this focus it is possible to discern three broad conceptions of what economic life is *primarily* about. As with the conceptions of education that we examined in the previous chapter, whether or not these conceptions come into conflict and their manner of doing so depends on the relative weighting that is put on each. There is no necessity for any of them to be mutually exclusive.

First, there is a conception which is probably the most vigorous in the contemporary world, which sees economic activity as primarily concerned with consumption.[2] This is closely linked with one that sees economic activity as concerned with the production of 'vendible commodities' or items that can be bought and consumed. This definition of Adam Smith's makes the point that economic activity is primarily carried out through the medium of markets, although, as we shall see, this need not necessarily always be the case.[3]

Second, there is a conception which ties economic activity to the pursuit of the good life. This ancient conception derives from Aristotle and can be found in the *Politics*. Economic life is concerned with the pursuit of the proper ends of a *polis* or political society which is the achievement of well-being (*eudaemonia*) which is itself an intrinsic good. Aristotle does not maintain that *eudaemonia* is maintained in the same way for each person, nor that each part (association or community) of a *polis* contributes in the same way.[4] There are characteristically different kinds of life pursued by different kinds of household, association or community and it is the business of the *polis* to express a set of common ends which, at the same time, embody the more particular ends of households.[5] For Aristotle, activities of production and exchange should be directed towards the pursuit of the good life, not to consumption as such, nor to the production of exchangeable values as such. *Economic* activity, which is directed towards the pursuit of the good life within the context of the household, is contrasted with *chrematistic* activity, which is concerned with exchange on the market, not necessarily with use.[6] 'Economic acquisition, that of the household, considers acquisition only with respect to the object's primary use, as an object that satisfies a need.'[7] Modern Aristotelian conceptions of economics take it for granted that there is a chrematistic element to the pursuit of the good life. There is a question, however, as to the extent to which this should be so. Perhaps the most striking representative of the Aristotelian tradition is Marx, particularly in the historicist scheme of the ultimate evolution of human society into communism. In relation to capitalism, however, he broadly accepts a classically oriented consumption-based teleology.

The third conception sees economic activity as primarily related to the maintenance and strengthening of the polity or nation. This conception is usually associated with *mercantilism*, a system of economic thought that flourished from the early modern period until the end of the eighteenth century. Mercantilism is usually regarded as an outmoded way both of conceptualising and regulating economic activity, but, as Keynes argued, contained a great deal more virtues than its best-known critic, Adam Smith, was prepared to allow it.[8] However, the idea that the end of economic activity is nation-building was, perhaps, most forcibly developed by Friedrich List, a German economist of the early nineteenth century. List, if he is known at all in the contemporary UK, is thought of in connection with the policy of protective tariffs for nascent industries competing on an international market.[9] List, however, is far more sympathetic to free trade than the mercantilists, and his case for limited protection has had an extraordinary influence on the policies of the US and Japan, not to mention the Soviet Union.[10] Both Marshall and Mill acknowledge the strength of his case.[11] List's overall position is, however, more complex than this, and has important connections with the second conception of economics advanced in the previous paragraph. His thinking will be examined more closely in Chapter 5, where it will become apparent that he made significant contributions to the school of thought which identifies the primary aim of economic activity with the promotion of the common good.

ECONOMICS AS THE PROMOTION OF CONSUMPTION

Classical political economy (Smith, Ricardo, Mill, Marx) characterises the capitalist economy as one whose inner purpose is the consumption of 'vendible commodities' (Smith). One should, however, be wary of forcing economists into classifications into which they fit uncomfortably. While Smith and Ricardo fit unambiguously into the 'consumptionist' category, care is needed in assessing the contributions of the others. Mill, in particular, and, following him, Marshall, were careful to argue that the nature of what is consumed will itself alter with the growth of a commodity economy. In particular, wants and needs will change with an increase in the satisfaction of primary needs and education (itself a consequence of growing economic wealth). They both, therefore, envisaged a qualitative change in the nature of consumer society as it developed. Keynes, too, did not see see quantity of consumption as an end in itself. He not only believed that the *quality* of consumption was important, but also that there was another important social goal of economic activity, namely, full employment. Marx accepted the inner purpose of capitalist economic activity as the consumption of commodities within the historical phase of capitalism itself, but held that it would eventually consume itself through the full working out of the internal forces that govern it. Changes in the mode of production will have an effect on people's attitudes such that their needs will become redefined in more humane ways, particularly under communism, when material abundance will be taken for granted. Marx differs from the others just mentioned in believing that this is not possible under capitalism.

Not all these economists took the same attitude to capitalism. Smith and Ricardo took for granted both capitalist forms of ownership and the desirability of allowing market forces to dominate economic activity. Mill, although accepting the theoretical basis of *laissez-faire* economics, was more sceptical about capitalist ownership and the ability of a market economy to distribute wealth appropriately. This led him to advocate both co-operative ownership and a vigorous redistributory policy for inherited fortunes.[12] Marshall placed much more emphasis on the role of the state in promoting and sustaining economic activity than do any of these three.[13] On the other hand, Keynes, while believing in greater state intervention than Marshall, thought, unlike Mill, that it is justifiable and even beneficial for society for there to be greater accumulations of wealth than are necessary for self-sufficiency.[14] Marx was the major classical economist who rejected both capitalist forms of ownership and the use of the market as long-term forms of economic organisation. Nevertheless, in his analysis of what he regarded as the contemporary and temporary mode of production which he describes as capitalism, he used many of the ideas of his predecessors in describing its 'laws of motion'. Even when these important qualifications have been made, it is possible to discern four common key themes in the development of their account of capitalist economic activity, which will be looked at in a more critical way in Chapter 5.

Labour, value and the quantification of labour

Smith, Ricardo, Mill, Marshall and Marx all subscribe to some version of the labour theory of value, whereby the value (or, in some versions, the cost), of labour reflects the costs of its reproduction.[15] Marshall was careful to distinguish between the short- and long-term conditions affecting the cost of labour, arguing that the labour theory of value only held over the long term. He was also careful to distinguish between the costs of bare physical reproduction and those of a socially acceptable level of reproduction that took into account the accepted amenities available at any given level of civilisation. Unlike Marx, he argued that labour is not the only component of cost, apart from profits, and drew attention to interest, earnings of management and a risk premium as well. He also hinted that the quality of workers and their work were of crucial importance in determining costs, but this theme remained relatively undeveloped.

These writers tended to analyse labour primarily in terms of its *duration*, its *organisation* and its *intensity*. The level of *skill* involved is usually factored into the equation in terms of the length of time taken to develop a level of skill in order to produce a commodity; in other words it becomes another element to be taken into account as a cost of reproduction, thus stretching out the duration of labour necessary to reproduce the labourer and his family.[16]

Skill and diligence

In order to take seriously the element of skill in labour, classical economists, as we have seen, tend to reduce it to an aspect of the time taken to produce a commodity. The higher educated worker's product costs more because of the education and training that has to be factored into his labour. However, at least some of this education takes place outside the production process. General education takes place outside the workplace altogether. If one argues that the price of a product embodies the labour used, then part of that labour will have been performed prior to the direct process of production, but is a contributor to it. In this sense, the labour involved in making a piece of jewellery, say, has to include that involved in making the craftsman. This observation undermines the distinction between productive and unproductive labour made in the next section.

As we are much more aware, through the rise of the quality movement in commercial operations, the elimination of error is also an important factor in both keeping down the costs of production, but also in keeping market share and raising position in the market place (going 'up-market' to higher value-added and higher priced commodities). *Diligence* is an important factor in error elimination and quality enhancement and is a product, not only of systems employed in production, but also of the education and training of workers, both on the job and at the prevocational stage. Diligence and the ability to work with others is an aspect of *social capital* that has to be developed and maintained. Most of the classical economists had very little to say about this, but both Marshall and List saw it as a crucial factor in production, both recognising the role of education in developing it and List, in particular, recognising the importance of deep-rooted social and moral attitudes.[17] Once again, the points made about the contribution of education to skill development apply to a certain extent to the development of diligence and other-regarding virtues indispensable for certain kinds of economic activity. However, as we shall see in Chapter 6, the workplace is also an indispensable site of moral formation, so that some aspects of vocational education cannot be counted straightforwardly as on-the-job skill formation either. Marx, no less than those economists more sympathetic to capitalism, neglected the contribution of education and training to successful production, partly because he, too, largely accepts the distinction between productive and unproductive labour (see below) and partly because he, like Smith, tends to downplay the importance of skilled and independent labour in capitalist production.

The effective organisation and use of capital to make labour more efficient is a key feature of the development of capitalism, and Marx also identified the *intensity* of labour, which was a function of the bargain that employees could strike with employers, as another crucial feature in determining the efficiency with which capital could be utilised. Smith, in particular, saw the organisation of production into small, discrete components, each of which individually requiring little skill, as a critical factor in developing the efficiencies that created a growing commodity economy. Without any evidence, he assumed that the development of a process division of labour was an exclusive characteristic of capitalism.[18] Neither did Smith pay much attention to the use of machinery in the production process. It was left to Ricardo to draw full attention to the labour-saving aspects of the use of machinery and this analysis was further developed by Marx.[19] Smith also stressed the way in which the division of labour progressively eliminated the use of virtually any aspect of the human intellect in production. This point was developed by Marx into a further indictment of the inhumanity of capitalist production methods, while at the same time he acknowledged the 'necessity' of the process. Others, however, were more cautious; Marshall, in particular, was anxious to stress the personal attributes, both technical and moral, that accompanied the introduction of machinery. Unlike Smith and Ricardo he actually looked at real examples and his account of watchmaking, for example, not only contradicts that of Smith at various points, but is also based on attention to the way in which the industry actually developed.[20] It is fair to say, however, that all these economists pay relatively little attention to the social organisation of work and human activity generally, and the role that this organisation plays both in determining the value of work.[21] Considerations of its quality and the quality of social relations necessary to obtain it figure strongly in some economic theories which are not so directly in the consumptionist tradition.

Productive and unproductive labour

As mentioned in Chapter 2, one of the most influential contrasts ever made in economic theory is that between productive and unproductive labour. It has entered ordinary habits of thought about the value of work and effort, despite vigorous criticism by, for example, List.

Smith states that the employment of non-productives leads to poverty, while the employment of productives leads to wealth. Furthermore, the category of non-productive labourers includes everyone who does not directly contribute to the production of a vendible commodity 'which lasts for some time at least after that labour is past.'[22] This includes: the sovereign, churchmen, lawyers, physicians, men of letters, players, buffoons, opera singers.[23]

While it is quite legitimate for certain purposes to distinguish between those who produce commodities directly and those who do not, it is quite another to imply that anyone who does not do so does not thereby *contribute* to the production of goods, let alone to economic activity more generally. Even within the confines of commodity exchange Smith's doctrine is very restrictive, since it appears to imply that the provision of services for exchange contributes nothing to wealth creation. Modern economists accept that the service sector has an important part to play. The sticking point for many, however, is that of fully accepting the role of those who contribute *indirectly* to commodity exchange as essential to the working of the economy as a whole. If Smith had not implied that non-productive workers were all like menial servants in their contribution, the idea would not so easily have gained ground that all non-productive work is, in some sense, not strictly necessary. Smith's distinction seems to have been largely accepted by Ricardo, Mill and Marx, although vigorously contested by List (see Chapter 5). Keynes, while not directly tackling it, drew attention to the importance of paid remuneration, which even if not, strictly speaking productive, contributes to the maintenance of demand, to the circulation of commodities and hence to the maintenance of full employment.[24]

Even if one acknowledges that the principal aim of economic activity is consumption, it is difficult to accept that only productive activity in Smith's sense contributes to it. Once, however, one no longer accepts this as a principal aim, the distinction itself loses much of its importance, being superseded by an evaluation of the worth of labour in terms of contribution to the common good or the strength of the nation. There is little doubt that the distinction between productive and unproductive labour, and the tendentious way in which Smith makes it, has contributed to the hostility with which many look at activities carried out by non-commercial organisations and, in particular, by the state. The very generality of Smith's distinction has contributed to its success. Socialists have tended not to like the characterisation of nurses and teachers as unproductive. They have been less unhappy about entrepreneurs, policemen, lawyers and bankers being so categorised.[25]

It could be maintained, in favour of the distinction, that there is an important economic difference between activity which results in the existence of a tradeable commodity and activity which does not and that it is, ultimately, the existence of the tradeable commodity that ensures economic success and wealth creation. One can admit all this, but the general point still remains, even in the terms preferred by classical and neo-classical economics. If costs and hence prices of commodities are, in the long run, determined to a considerable extent by the human effort that has gone into their creation, then the cost of the human effort that is a *precondition* of the direct and immediate effort involved in production cannot be ignored as factors in the overall costs. There may well be difficulties, in an accounting sense, of quantifying the contribution that this effort makes, for it cannot just be the time forgone from earning which is involved in being educated, which would explain the wage premium of the educated worker as a kind of interest,[26] but the contribution of the *effort* of teachers, parents, doctors, etc. in contributing to the skill, diligence and virtue with which a commodity is created. If these are somehow reflected in the price of the commodity, then they must also be a factor in the costs. Such a form of social accounting may be difficult to carry out, but this scarcely justifies the rigid theoretical distinction between productive and unproductive labour in the way that it was made by Smith and used subsequently.

The assumption of self-interested or even egoistic motivation

Although it is by now a commonplace that economics assumes that humans, in their economic activity and, indeed, in other spheres of activity, are primarily egoistic in their motivation and behaviour, this is an assumption that largely derives from the dominant conception of economic activity as oriented towards consumption. This is usually combined with an *atomistic* conception of society in which the individual is considered as the primary unit, not only ontologically but also epistemologically, so that we can only gain an understanding of the workings of the economy through understanding the aggregate of the workings of the individuals within it and their interactions with each other.

When one combines the psychological assumption of egoism with the epistemological assumption of individualism, the way is open for the construction of hypothetical models of economic behaviour in terms of individualistic utility maximisation. Adam Smith is the source of this conceptualisation of economic life, which has become dominant in economic thinking in the last part of the twentieth century. Its *locus classicus* is to be found in a famous passage:

> . . . man has almost constant occasion for the help of his brethren, and it is in vain for him to expect it from their benevolence only. He will be more likely to prevail if he can interest their self-love in his favour, and show them that it

is for their own advantage to do for him what he requires of them. Whoever offers to another a bargain of any kind, proposes to do this. Give me what I want, and you shall have this which you want, is the meaning of every such offer; and it is in this manner that we obtain from one another the far greater part of those good offices which we stand in need of. It is not from the benevolence of the butcher, the brewer, or the baker, that we expect our dinner, but from their regard to their own interest. We address ourselves, not to their humanity but to their self-love, and never talk to them of our necessities but of their advantages.[27]

It is puzzling that this is the same Smith who published *The Theory of Moral Sentiments* in 1759.[28] In this work, Smith develops the idea that a large factor in the formation of human moral attitudes is the growth of benevolent feelings towards others. He also lays some stress on the desirability of at least some of the other-regarding virtues, although placing, perhaps, most emphasis on prudence.[29] This book is, however, primarily about moral *attitudes* rather than *action*, and it is with the latter that *The Wealth of Nations* is primarily concerned. There may well be inconsistencies between these two books, but there is also a considerable difference in emphasis and it is the Smith of the later work whose opinions have most influenced economic theory.

Although the heritage of the egoistic utility maximiser has been taken up most strongly in the last fifty years or so, the classical and neo-classical heritage is more ambiguous. Ricardo largely accepts Smith's assumptions, but Mill and Marshall are much more cautious. Mill recognises higher forms of utility which include social pleasures, and stresses the growing interdependence of individuals under conditions of increasing prosperity.[30] Marshall emphasises mutual social dependency in a way that is missing in Smith and Ricardo.[31] The tendency in consumptionist economic thinking is that preference is determined by the individual subject without necessary reference either to other individuals or to any view of the common good. While it is possible for someone cognisant of the common good to act self-interestedly (he identifies his preferences with those of some collective such as his family, neighbourhood or nation), a person who is not must act self-interestedly in terms of his individualistic or selfish preferences and is thus motivated egoistically. In practice, modern economics has identified *preference* with *subjective preference* and thus with what individuals desire to consume (as revealed in the price which they are prepared to pay for a utility) and thus it is no exaggeration to say that the picture is one of egoistic motivation.

Marx does not explicitly operate with a model of egoistic motivation for two reasons. First, he is anxious to demonstrate the impersonal way in which a mode of production like capitalism determines the actions of individuals. Second, he does not believe that there is a universal human nature, but human characteristics, which are deeply affected by the mode of production to which they are bound. Given these qualifications, however, the model assumes egoistic motivation, without, however, attaching praise or blame to the individuals, both labourers or capitalists, who act according to the practical logic of the situation. In practice, this leads to individuals, as in neo-classical economics, 'dropping out of the picture' to be replaced by laws governing the circulation of commodities which are formally consistent with egoistic behaviour.[32]

The relative lack of attention they pay to factors of production that are not themselves directly involved in production

We have already seen that classical and neo-classical economics is largely based on subjectivism about preference formation and an individualistic epistemology of social explanation. These two assumptions are powerful enough to allow economists to generate predictive models of collective behaviour as aggregates of the behaviours of individuals. Such model-building assumes that economic activity is largely autonomous relative to other aspects of human activity. It is true that Marshall's definition of economic activity seems to preclude this, but if it is given a consumptionist interpretation it is easy to see that this is only an apparent inconsistency. For Marshall goes on to argue that as a science it makes a further crucial assumption:

> An opening is made for the methods and the tests of science as soon as the force of a person's motives—*not* the motives themselves—can be approximately measured by the sum of money, which he will just give up in order to secure a desired satisfaction; or again by the sum which is just required to induce him to undergo a certain fatigue.[33]

Economics thus uses money transactions as the measure of human behaviour. It follows that those transactions that do not have a monetary measure cannot be the direct study of economists.[34]

Any science has to select aspects of phenomena it wishes to describe and explain. Modern economics purports to study that aspect of everyday human life that involves monetary or exchange transactions. As such, it inevitably selects from the range of human phenomena and concentrates on one aspect. Such a procedure, although necessary if the aspect under consideration is to receive sufficiently thorough attention to advance our understanding, also carries dangers. The principal one is that of identifying an approach (a selective study of an aspect of a phenomenon), with a phenomenon itself. Thus the study of economics may lead one to believe that economic activity is an ontologically distinct sphere, as opposed to one that, for pragmatic epistemological reasons, is selected for special study.

There are two ways in which economic thinking has been affected by this approach. The first is through the creation of *homo economicus*, the creature exemplified in the quotation from Smith above, whose main, if not only, characteristic is that he is an egoistic utility maximiser whose preferences are formed subjectively. Even writers like Marshall, while they are anxious to keep such a gross creature out of their realistic description of economic activity, find it more difficult to keep him out of their equations, which inevitably simplify complex phenomena for the purpose of model-building. He also shows a tendency to appear in those areas that are not directly part of economic activity, such as in non-trading activities and the public sector.

Public choice theorists have been particularly active in promoting the study of the behaviour of institutions as the outcome of the egoistic behaviour of the individuals who inhabit them.[35] Like Smith, many modern economists and those social scientists influenced by economics, have found it difficult to separate human motivation and moral priorities into different compartments. Given the assumption, shared with Marxism, of the motivational priority of economic activity, it has seemed natural to import the motivational structures used to explain economic activity into non-economic activity, especially since it is implausible to suppose that human motivation and moral sensibility are compartmentalised into the different spheres of life studied by economists and other social scientists.[36] The second is to be found in the rigid distinction between spheres of economic activity and other forms of activity, as in the celebrated distinction made by Marx between economic *base* and non-economic *superstructure*, together with a one-way causal link between the former and the latter. It lives on in a less well-defined form in the distinction that we have already noted between productive and non-productive labour.

One result has been to neglect social and organisational structures and their possible effects on economic activity (see Chapter 5). If individual motivation and moral sensibility have to be understood in terms of the values and norms embodied in social relationships and institutions, then there can be no valid *a priori* assumption that egoism will form a satisfactory basis for the explanation of most behaviour *in any social context*, let alone that of economics.

It would be a gross oversimplification to say that economics has ignored the effects of social context and institutions. While it is, perhaps hard to discern such a sensitivity in the work of Smith and Ricardo, both Mill and Marshall refer to the effects of education on attitude and motivation and Marx refers to the 'animal spirits' that inform work when carried out in a workshop or field with other human beings or when employed on a variety of tasks.[37] The charge that these factors *are not sufficiently taken into account* is more difficult to refute, particularly in relation to the variety of different organisational forms that economic activity may take. This applies, not just to the organisation of a point of production like a workshop, but also to the way in which the management of an enterprise is conducted (whether, for example, there is a degree of self-government for the employees) and also in the generality of social relationships within the society in which economic activity is conducted (whether, for example, there are dense networks of social relationships or whether there are general habits of sociability and trust among the population).[38] A further and related question has already been touched on in relation to Marx's account of the relationships between economic and other forms of social activity, namely what influence does the economic play on these other forms? Often, there has been too little consideration of the relationship between the ways in which non-economic activities impact on economic ones.[39]

Finally, there is the effect that activities not directly concerned with production have on economic activity. It has been suggested that economics has tended to take it for granted that economic activity affects other forms of human activity. It is less acknowledged that this relationship may work the other way: that 'non-economic' institutions can affect the way in which economic activity is carried out. Smith and his followers draw attention to the importance of a legal system and defence in maintaining secure property relationships and contracts. Marx drew attention to these features of the superstructure in maintaining a dominant mode of production. However, less attention has been paid to the provision of education, housing, health care and leisure to the maintenance of economic strength, let alone the role played by families, churches, trade unions, clubs and charitable organisations. These are the social institutions through which 'non-productive' activity takes place.

Their 'thin' conception of the social institutions necessary to sustain successful economic activity

An abiding characteristic of economic thinking in the classical and neo-classical tradition is the discounting of *civil society*. Civil society includes: moral and religious customs; customs and institutions such as the festivals and ceremonies associated with a common cultural life; domestic institutions such as the family; 'intermediate' and more formal bodies not completely attached to the state such as churches, businesses, trade unions and voluntary organisations; corporate institutions that operate at a national or international level, such as trade union and business federations, world churches like the Catholic Church and political parties.[40]

It would be odd to ignore civil society in economies that are run for individual and social well-being or national strength. When consumption is the main aim, however, this is not so obvious, since it is far from clear that the presence of strong structures in civil society assists the development of markets. Indeed, there is a current not just of indifference to civil society, but of active hostility to it within sections of the tradition with which we are concerned.[41] The main reason is that it is assumed that markets, which are the principal institutions for the promotion of exchange and hence of consumption, function best when they are cleared of impediments that hinder the flow of information and deal-making. Since market exchanges are based on individual preference, institutions that hinder the scope for individual preference tend to hinder the effectiveness of markets. There is therefore, as O'Neill has observed, a tension between the atomised view of social relationships favoured by market theorists and a more molecular view favoured by those who see civil society having an important role in facilitating economic activity.

Even Marx should be admitted into the camp of those who discount the importance of civil society for economic development. This is not, perhaps, as strange as it might seem. For all its cruelty and injustice, capitalist economic development in its fullest form was necessary to its own demise, according to Marx and his followers. Pre-capitalist institutions such as the extended family, clans and guilds, had to be swept away in order that capitalism might fully develop. It is not surprising, therefore, that Marx discounted the importance of the institutions of civil society in contributing to capitalist economic development.[42]

The primary source of thinking about the importance of civil society for economic life is Aristotle, who emphasises the importance of the household as the basic unit of the economy. More recently, Mill and Marshall emphasised the importance of co-operation and trade unionism; List, morality and religion, together with association at the level of the community; Weber, religious beliefs and religious communities; Coleman, the sexual division of labour and Fukuyama, other-regarding virtues, such as trust.[43] But it is fair to say that this is a minority line of thinking in economic thought, which is hardly surprising given its generally consumptionist orientation.

CONCLUSION

Consumptionist economics and a conception of vocational education

This 'thin' conception of the social institutions necessary to sustain capitalism has had a great influence on the predominant conception of vocational education associated with conventional economics. First, there is a relative emphasis on deskilling, as the efficient use of capital is thought to involve an intense application of the process division of labour rather than mental or manual dexterity.[44] Second, and somewhat in contradiction, it is thought that vocational education and training occurs as the result of decisions of individuals and firms based on economic self-interest. Both calculate the discounted benefits of decisions to invest in training, treating such investments as a form of capital investment (hence the term 'human capital theory' for this approach), based on calculations of future earnings (individuals) and profits (firms). It is difficult, if not impossible, on this view for intermediate or state institutions to second-guess rational decisions made in market conditions, and so it is better that vocational education and training is run without state intervention. The individualistic nature of the vocational and training systems (VETs) developed on this basis stands in contrast to those based on more collective forms of decision-making.

These five inter-connected ways of looking at economic activity lead to a conception of vocational education which has the following features: (a) productivist in the narrow sense, because it is unclear how investment in the non-productive sector can contribute to the profitability of capitalist enterprises; (b) training, rather than education-oriented, since enterprises are concerned with specific skills for specific tasks, rather than 'polyvalent' abilities applicable in a variety of enterprises or even activities; (c) skill rather than virtue orientation, since labour is considered to be the responsibility of the individual and individual decisions are based on a calculation of financial benefit on an individual basis, rather than on the choosing of, in some sense, a vocation or way of life; and (d) individualist rather than collectivist, since it is assumed that the labour market will at the very least be primarily general, rather than occupational or internal and, more likely, will be relatively weakly oriented towards specific occupations.

Notes

1 A. Marshall (1890) *Principles of Economics*, eighth edition, London, Macmillan, p. 12.
2 See, for example, J. M. Keynes (1973) *The General Theory of Employment, Money and Interest*, second edition, London, Macmillan, p. 104.
3 Adam Smith (1981) *The Wealth of Nations*, Indianapolis, IN, Liberty Fund, p. 330.
4 Although he appeared to think that some forms of the good life were superior to others, see David Ross (1995), *Aristotle*, sixth edition, London, Routledge, Chapter VII; Aristotle (1988) *The Politics*, Cambridge, Cambridge University Press, e.g. Bk. III, Bk. VII.
5 Aristotle (1925) *Nichomachean Ethics*, London, Dent, 1925, VIII, 9, 1160a 10–30, p. 208.
6 Aristotle (1988) op. cit. Bk. I, 9, pp. 12–14.
7 J. O'Neill, *The Market: Ethics, Knowledge and Politics*, London, Routledge, p. 28.
8 See Keynes, op. cit. Chapter 23; Smith, op. cit. Bk. IV, Chapter VIII.
9 F. List (1991) *The National System of Political Economy*, NJ, Augustus Kelley.
10 For an account of List's influence on Japan, see J. Fallows (1994), *Looking at the Sun*, New York, Pantheon Press. For the Listians in the Soviet Union, see R. Szporluk (1988) *Communism and Nationalism: Karl Marx versus Friedrich List*, Oxford, Oxford University Press.
11 See Marshall, op. cit. p. 633 and his comment on p. 644:

> The Germans are fond of saying that the Physiocrats and the school of Adam Smith underrated the importance of national life; that they tended to sacrifice it on the one hand to a selfish individualism and on the other to a limp philanthropic cosmopolitanism. They urge that List did great service in stimulating a feeling of patriotism, which is more generous than that of individualism and more sturdy and definite than that of cosmopolitanism.

> See also J. S. Mill (1994) *Principles of Political Economy*, Oxford, Oxford University Press, p. 302

12 Mill, op. cit. Bk. II.
13 For example, Marshall, op. cit. Chapters 11–13.
14 Keynes, op. cit. pp. 373–374.
15 I share the view of Robinson that *value* as an economic concept has no clear application. See Joan Robinson (1962) *Economic Philosophy*, London, Penguin, Chapter 2. Marshall, although he uses the term *value*, can be interpreted as referring to cost in most places. One of the problems with the labour theory of value is that value seems to be determined in a circular way. Something has greater value because it embodies more labour. Because it embodies more labour it costs more. But there is no reason why, within certain limits, Ricardo's beaver skins shouldn't be cheaper than deer skins, even though they require more labour to produce, if they are less useful than deer skins [see Ricardo (1951) *On the Principles of Political Economy and Taxation*, Cambridge, Cambridge University Press, Chapter 1]. Ricardo's account only works if we assume that labour is *per se* valuable and that society is organised in a more-or-less egalitarian way so that all labour is remunerated to the same degree *pro rata*. On the other hand, one can acknowledge the link between labour and price taking into account skill, diligence and social inequality, thus making the link between effort and cost less of a metaphysical one.

16 Smith (1981) op. cit.; Marshall, op. cit.; Marx, op. cit. The latter treats skill as labour power previously expended in an educational process.

17 For example, List, op. cit. p. 81.

18 For a detailed challenge to this view, and an examination of the actual conditions of Smith's example of pin making, which clearly shows the inaccuracy of Smith's account, see G. Williams (2000) *Wealth Without Nations*, London, Athol Books.

19 Ricardo, op. cit. Chapter 31; Marx, op. cit. Volume 1, Part 4.

20 Marshall, op. cit. pp. 213–214.

21 Mill, however, maintains that profit-sharing can affect the morale of workers in such a way as to increase the quality of what is produced (op. cit. p. 145).

22 Smith, op. cit. p. 330.

23 Smith, op. cit. p. 331.

24 Keynes, op. cit. Chapter 10.

25 Mill, op. cit. p. 390.

26 Cf. Marshall, op. cit. Book VI, Chapter VI.

27 Smith, op. cit. Bk I, Chapter 2, pp. 26–27.

28 Adam Smith (1984) *The Theory of Moral Sentiments*, Indianapolis, IN, Liberty Fund.

29 Smith (1984) op. cit. Part VI, Section 1.

30 Mill, op. cit. Bk. IV.

31 As O'Neill, op. cit. p. 36, points out, however, Marshall's formal definitions of utility are largely subjectivist in character.

32 See M. Verdon (1996) *Keynes and the Classics*, London, Routledge.

33 Marshall, op. cit. p. 13.

34 This is not to say that economists' assumptions concerning motivation cannot be imported into the study of other areas of and given a non-monetary measure of subjectively determined utility [see Orchard and Stretton (1994) *Public Goods, Public Choice and Public Enterprise*, London, Macmillan].

35 See Orchard and Stretton, op. cit.; A. Maynard (1985) 'Performance Incentives in General Practice' in *Health, Education and General Practice*, George Teeling Smith (ed.), Office for Health Economics, pp. 44–46.

36 This is partly the reason why it is so difficult to reconcile the account of moral sensibility described in Smith's *The Theory of Moral Sentiments* with the account of motivation in *The Wealth of Nations*.

37 Marx, op. cit. p. 341, p. 694.

38 These attributes are often taken to be the main characteristics of social capital; see J. S. Coleman 'Social Capital in the Creation of Human Capital', *American Journal of Sociology*, 94, Supplement S, pp. 95–120; F. Fukuyama (1995) *Trust*, London, Penguin.

39 It is inevitable that the matter is put in this way, but I do not mean to imply the very thesis that I am trying to argue against, namely that one can make hard-and-fast distinctions between economic and non-economic forms of activity. I maintain that it is only legitimate to separate economic from other forms of activity if one is doing so for a particular purpose in a particular context.

40 Most theorists of civil society do not distinguish analytically between these different levels, but the distinctions are important for discussions in later sections of this book.

41 See, in particular Smith (1981) op. cit. Volume I, Bk. I, pp. 135–159; Volume II, Bk. V, especially pp. 758–786.

42 A. Gramsci (1971) *Selections from the Prison Notebooks*, London, Lawrence and Wishart, on the other hand, attaches great importance to civil society in capitalist Western Europe, attributing its political stability to the institutions of civil society.

43 Cf. M. Weber (1958) *The Protestant Ethic and the Spirit of Capitalism*, New York, Scribner; J. S. Coleman, op. cit.

44 This view is particularly strong in the work of both Smith and Marx.

5 Conceptualising economic life
Part two: Listian political economy

INTRODUCTION

The aim of this chapter is to present an account of economics that takes the development of the common good as a primary economic objective. The *locus classicus* of this conception is Friedrich List, whose political economy can best be seen as an extension of the Aristotelian view into modern conditions, involving market economies, technological innovation and nationalism. List was an economist not merely of the common good but of industrialisation in the period of German unification. Most commentators have emphasised his role as an economist of national industrialisation, which is an important aspect of his work. However, his account of the 'productive powers' that underlie economic activity are important in grasping the value he attached to well-being, both as an end and a further means of economic activity. There is one important omission in List's account, which is the internal political context of economic activity. Marx emphasises a point about politics that was already clear in Aristotle's *Politics*, that conflicts arise within civil society concerning different conceptions of the good. Vico emphasises the economic side of this conflict and this analysis was taken further by Marx, resulting in a view of the *irreconcilability* of economically based class conflict. List, with his strong emphasis on the importance of social solidarity for economic well-being, pays no attention to this feature of political economy. However, not only is it necessary to do so, it is also possible to arrive at a clear view of economically based class conflict as an engine of economic progress that is, at the same time, a means to the development of social solidarity that economists of the common good have sought to emphasise. This chapter will then close with a reappraisal of Vico in the light of List's general outlook.

CLASSICAL AND LISTIAN POLITICAL ECONOMY

List's political economy makes a break with the view of man as nothing more than a rational utility maximiser. He did not deny that the rational aims of economic behaviour were growth and prosperity, both for society and the individual, but he did deny that human behaviour could be sufficiently explained as utility maximisation. Contemporary economic theorists have got into difficulties about this point, either assuming that the utility model only works in economic contexts or seeking to buttress it with a richer account in terms of the other-regarding virtues and habitual, trustworthy behaviour.[1] The first solution suffers from pyschological implausibility, the second is incoherent. One cannot be a self-interested utility maximiser and practice other-regarding virtues;[2] only if utility-maximisation were heavily circumscribed by social considerations would this modification make sense. But such a change would lead to the wholesale revision of the moral psychological assumptions underlying most economic thinking, not a mere tinkering at the edges.

National and cosmopolitical political economy

List opens his criticisms of Adam Smith by asserting that the geopolitical context that Smith assumes for his economic model is unrealistic. Smith assumes a cosmo-political world economy where all nations are at peace, trading freely with each other.[3] The reality was, according to List, that the world was made up of a major manufacturing and trading empire (Great Britain), a nascent major manu-facturing economy (the United States), various emerging national economies and numerous subnational economies.[4] Apart from Britain, no other economy was capable of successful trading in manufactured goods on world markets. Neither was the assumption of world peace realistic. In part, the success of the British economy in the world was, as List saw, due to the presence of a powerful navy able to protect trade routes and open up new markets. Elsewhere he drew attention to the self-serving character of this assumption; to see the world economy as cosmopolitical suited the contemporary British interest very well. From this perspective, Smith is seen, not so much as a founder of a value-free social science, but as an apologist for British economic interests. List also drew attention to the fact that the free traders very often did not practice what they preached, for example in placing tariffs on the importation of cheap Indian clothing into the home market.[5]

Economies, asserted List, need to be seen in their political context if their relative successes and failures are to be understood. The early part of the *National System* is devoted to arguing this point through a series of case studies which are designed to show that it is only when a polity becomes a geographically substantial nation-state that it can become, and remain, a successful manufacturing and commercial entity. The Hanseatic League and the Italian city-states failed to last because of the development of trade barriers by nation-states, their own inability to promote and take advantage of free trade at appropriate times and their small size relative to their rivals.[6]

> Venice, although mistress of some provinces and islands, yet being all the time merely one Italian city, stood in competition, at the period of her rise to a manufacturing and commercial power, merely with other Italian cities; and her prohibitory commercial policy could benefit her so long as whole nations

with united power did not enter into competition with her. But as soon as that took place, she could only have maintained her supremacy by placing herself at the head of a united Italy and by embracing in her commercial system the whole Italian nation. No commercial policy was ever clever enough to maintain continuously the commercial supremacy of a single city over united nations.[7]

The Belgians and Dutch succeeded in developing their economies to the extent that, united, they formed a substantial agricultural and trading entity.[8] Subsequent division led to their losing the critical mass that had previously made them successful. The polities and nations that enjoyed and continue to enjoy long-term political and economic success are those that become nation-states: England, France and the United States for example. Each of these societies took a different route to economic success, but they all succeeded because they managed to deploy extensive resources to create markets for their manufactures, first internally, then externally. Crucial to their success during the infancy of their manufacturing industries was the imposition of tariffs on manufactured goods until such a time as those industries were strong enough to compete on international markets. In some cases, notably that of England, the successful international projection of military, particularly naval, power was critical to the extension and domination of overseas markets. In the case of France, the vigorous development of infrastructure and the shelter of England's continental blockade during the Napoleonic wars were critical.[9] Those nations that remain disunited, such as Germany, were doomed to be dominated by larger, more viable economic powers until they, too, succeeded in uniting into one nation-state.

Lest it be thought that List is nothing more than a political economist of the nationalist era, it is worth pointing out the importance that he attached to the development of the European economy. Although a great admirer of Napoleon's efforts in developing French industry he thought that the 'continental system' had serious defects which to some extent discredited it. First was the way in which it was used to further French economic interests at the expense of those of the other European nations. List thought that European economic union, if it was based on the free and equal association of nation-states, would not only allow industry to develop on a European-wide basis, but would lead to political peace as well, through the elimination of the ruinous balance-of-power wars that England had promoted to further her own pre-eminence. List was one of the earliest advocates of European union.[10]

For List, then, economic objectives were bound up with political ones. Secure nation-statehood could not be secured without protection for industrial development. Industrial development could not occur outside a political entity at least as powerful as a small nation-state and, preferably within the context of a continent-wide economic and political union, of which the United States was an example and Western Europe a potential example.[11] In this context, List used his case studies to illustrate how the active involvement of the state had promoted the economic development of Britain, France and the United States. The idea that consideration of economics is to be detached from that of politics, as Smith and his followers advocated, is not only false, but self-serving to the interests of the 'insular supremacy'. List, then, was a *political* economist *par excellence* in the sense that he placed national political economy in an international political context.

The theory of values and the theory of productive powers

List is known, if at all, for his advocacy of protectionism, economic nationalism and state direction.[12] However, his most important theoretical contribution was, perhaps, the most neglected, namely the *theory of productive powers*, the development of which he considered to be fundamental to economic success within the political perspective outlined above. The orientation of classical political economy is towards the aggregation of exchange values, particularly consumable ones. The type of moral psychology that is best suited to the production and consumption of exchange values is that of self-interested individualism, essentially oriented to the short, rather than the long term. First, it is more difficult to calculate long-term than it is short-term advantage, second, as Smith's contemporary Hume observed:

> Men are not able radically to cure either in themselves or others that narrowness of soul which makes them prefer the present to the remote. . . . All they can do is to change their situation and render the observance of justice the immediate interest of some particular persons and its violation their more remote.[13]

Such a perspective is, perhaps, suited to an economy whose aim is the short-term maximisation of personal consumption, the perspective which List rejected. This is not to say that he was not interested in prosperity, but rather that he saw material prosperity as a necessary, but not sufficient, condition of individual and social well-being. There is a fundamental difference of perspective on human nature between the classical economists and List. Despite Smith's apparent emphasis in the *Wealth of Nations* on the social nature of humanity and our desire to be approved of by our fellows, the vision in that book is quite different. Smith's apparent recognition of man's need for social esteem is, more fundamentally, an emphasis on the desire to impress others through displays of wealth and power.

List, however, retained the Aristotelian perspective of seeing humans as, first and foremost, social and political animals to whom social recognition and approval is a fundamental good. It follows that, within this perspective, the preservation and development of society in its broadest sense is a human goal. And, to the extent that economic endeavour is necessary to achieve it, it is to be subordinated to the development of the society rather than the desires of individuals. List recognised that Smith did have some conception of productive powers, but, he thought, they were too narrowly defined. Smith, for example, had a clear idea of human capital, which are the useful abilities of members of a society and, as such, part of its fixed capital, but he did not consider the institutions, customs, practices, habits and beliefs of a society as any part of its general stock.[14] Smith did, therefore, have a theory of productive powers, concerning those parts of the general stock which can be utilised to produce values. What he lacked is an account of how that stock and, in particular, the human part of fixed capital, is not only reproduced, but maintained and enhanced from generation to generation. Fukuyama has recently pointed out this omission in classical and neo-classical economics, regarding it as a defect, but his conception of *social capital* defined as spontaneous sociability and trust, although a major departure from the classical conception, still falls far short of the Listian notion of productive powers, which includes Fukuyama's narrower notion of social capital.

What, then, did List mean by productive powers? He certainly included all that Smith identified as part of the general stock which can be used to create values, including individual human abilities. Unlike Smith, however, he was unwilling to make a firm distinction between productive and non-productive aspects of the economy, particularly between productive and non-productive labour (see below). The productive powers of an economy are its *potential* for the creation of value, and to the extent that this resides outside the immediate process of production, in the external conditions that make production possible, the productive–non-productive distinction is unhelpful. List emphasised the importance of renewing workers not just physically as Smith and, later, Marx did, but spiritually as well. Likewise, the reproduction of the labour force is not merely a physical, but a spiritual matter and one moreover that should take into account the further development of productive powers. List expresses this point in a characteristically trenchant fashion.

> The man who breeds pigs is, according to this school [i.e. that of Smith and his followers], a productive member of the community, but he who educates men is a mere non-productive. The maker of bagpipes or jews-harps for sale is a productive, while the great composers and virtuosos are non-productive simply because that which they play cannot be brought into the market. The physician who saves the lives of his patients does not belong to the productive class, but on the contrary the chemist's boy does so, although the values of exchange (viz. the pills) which he produces may exist only for a few minutes before they pass into a valueless condition. A Newton, a Watt, or a Kepler is not so productive as a donkey, a horse or a draught-ox (a class of labourers who have been recently introduced by M'Culloch into the series of the productive members of human society).[15]

He continues,

> The errors and contradictions of the prevailing school to which we have drawn attention, can be easily corrected from the standpoint of *the theory of the productive powers*. Certainly those who fatten pigs or prepare pills are productive, but the instructors of youths and of adults, virtuosos, musicians, physicians, judges, and administrators, are productive in a much higher

degree. The former produce *values of exchange*, and the latter *productive powers*, some by enabling the future generation to become producers, others by furthering the morality and religious character of the present generation, a third by ennobling and raising the powers of the human mind, a fourth by preserving the productive power of his patients, a fifth by rendering human rights and justice secure, a sixth by constituting and protecting public security, a seventh by his art and by the enjoyment which it occasions, fitting men the better to produce values of exchange.[16]

Included in the concept of productive powers is, then, not only the fixed capital of an enterprise, but also fixed capital that contributes indirectly to the creation of value such as transport infrastructure and health care. To the extent that these cannot be provided by a nascent capitalist economy, they must be provided by the state and List extolled those whom he considered to be far-sighted leaders for promoting infrastructural developments such as internal communications.[17] But the state has a more extensive role than this; it can also actively promote economic development and expand particular industries as did France under Colbert and England during the Elizabethan and Stuart periods.[18] The provision of a properly administered system of law and democratic institutions are also important. The first renders an environment of stability for the long-term development of industry possible, the second provides the preconditions for the development of the spirit of enquiry, which, List believed, is essential to the entrepreneurial spirit.

But List also located productive powers in civil society, in moral customs and in institutions such as churches and guilds, for example. Through such bodies, national characteristics favourable to the development of the economy can be nurtured and built up from generation to generation. Morality based on other-regarding virtues such as loyalty and trustworthiness and self-regarding virtues such as prudence and endurance jointly allow for the setting up of long-term, large-scale enterprises and reduce transaction costs. Religion contributes in much the same way, but also promotes the striving for perfection that is necessary for the achievement of excellence in some branches of industry and in the development of machinery and technique. National characteristics born of association at the level of village and town constitute an important part of this social capital. Writing of Germany after the devastation of the Thirty Years War, List remarks:

> Only one thing the Germans had preserved; that was their aboriginal character, their love of industry, order, thrift and moderation, their perseverance and endurance in research and in business, their honest striving after improvement, and a considerable natural measure of morality, prudence and circumspection.[19]

However, even these characteristics could not by themselves promote national economic revival. List goes on:

This character both the rulers and the ruled had in common. After the almost total decay of nationality and the restoration of tranquillity, people began in some individual isolated circles to introduce order, improvement, and progress. Nowhere was witnessed more zeal in cherishing education, manners, religion, art and science; nowhere was absolute power exercised with greater moderation or with more advantage to general enlightenment, order and morality, to the reform of abuses and the advancement of the common welfare.[20]

The contrast between the theory of productive powers and the theory of values was developed by List through an analogy. In the short-term, a family which uses its landed wealth to gain more money-wealth will be better off than one which invests with a long-term goal in mind; it will possess more exchangeable values. However, within a generation or two, the long-term investor will not only be prosperous, but will have gained the means of further extending that prosperity, while the family which attends only to short-term gain will find that 'stupidity and poverty must increase with the diminution of the shares in the landed property' which, since it will not have been invested in, will become less and less productive.[21]

The one puts out his savings at interest, and keeps his sons at common hard work, while the other employs his savings in educating two of his sons as skilful and intelligent landowners, and in enabling the other three to learn a trade after their respective tastes; the former acts according to the theory of values, the latter according to the theory of productive powers.[22]

One of the weaknesses of both conventional and Marxist economics is their inability to provide a convincing explanation for technological innovation. Both the *Wealth of Nations* and *Capital* have little to say on this matter, although Marx was, of course, acutely aware of the *effects* of technology on the economy. By placing productive powers at the centre of economic discussion and locating the success of capitalism in their development in a national context, List helped to clarify the role of technological improvement in economic development. First, it is important for a nation to draw on what List calls the 'aboriginal' qualities of a people, in the case of the Germans the 'honest striving for improvement' that he recognised as a national asset. Second, there is a sense of national purpose; the idea that economic development is a long-term process which may require long lead times to bear fruit. Third, there is the dynamic that arises from the development of cities and the concomitant development of greater individual freedom, which allows innovation to flourish. Finally, there is the reciprocal pull between town and country so that innovations based on the freedom to think creatively which are available in an urban environment, create the technology available for the further development of agriculture, which in turn can support a larger, urbanised population. There are, therefore, in List's concept of productive powers, the materials for an account of the conditions under which technological innovation can take place.

On the face of it, List made a radical break with classical political economy in emphasising the complexity and ramifications of productive powers. His account is further subversive of conventional economics in that it broadens its focus beyond the theory of the production of values, to the *preconditions* for the production of values, which include virtually all aspects of human society. Without discounting those parts of the discipline which have this narrower focus, it is fairly clear that a Listian discipline of economics would not just be a science of political, but a science of social economy as well. Two questions need to be asked about the viability of his conceptualisation of economics. First, is it as innovatory as it seems? Second, can his insights be better accommodated within a conventional framework?

It has been argued by Gide and Rist that the contrast between values of exchange and productive powers is unhelpful because the only way to measure the strength of productive powers is by measuring the values of exchange that they actually produce.[23] A policy aimed at increasing productive powers would aim at increasing values of exchange and vice versa. Therefore the idea of productive powers is implicit in the conceptualisation of the economy as values of exchange. The apparent persuasiveness of this argument rests on the reflection that just as we tell whether or not someone is strong by his ability to carry out actions that require strength, so we judge the productive powers of an economy by its propensity to produce exchange values. But it does not follow from this that a man's strength is nothing more than the sum of his actions. It is a necessary condition for us to describe him as strong that he performs acts that require strength. This does not, however, exhaust what we mean when we describe him as strong. His potential for acting is not described in terms of the actions that he has already performed, but in terms of what it is reasonable to expect that he will do in the future. This is List's point, that we can only judge the long-term success of economic endeavour if we are able to judge its long-term potential. And its long-term potential cannot be extrapolated from its current production of values of exchange alone. The theory of productive powers makes the long-term assessment of capacity an indispensable feature of judgements of economic strength and it cannot be gauged solely from present production of exchange values.

It has also been argued by the same authors that List was unfair to Smith; the latter did have a theory of productive powers.[24] But this is mistaken. He paid tribute to Smith's innovations and noted that he mentioned the importance of productive powers, even quoting him to that effect. List's quotation was, however, both inaccurate and overgenerous. Although Smith wrote that the annual labour of every nation is the fund which originally supplies all its wants and necessities, for him the productive powers are those of labour, not society.[25] The general thrust of *The Wealth of Nations* is to emphasise the productive power of labour, on the one hand through division of the labour process and, on the other, through the skill with which it is applied. The moral and social context of the deployment of labour, to which List attached such great importance, is largely missing in Smith. Naturally, Smith was not committed to the absurd view that economies could operate outside any social or moral context nor to the view that there are no non-economic preconditions for economic growth. Indeed much of *The Wealth of Nations* is devoted to the claim that certain preconditions are necessary, namely the absence of regulation by such bodies as guilds and the presence of laws that allow men the security to enjoy the fruits of their labour. But the general thrust of Smith's work is to withdraw the state and conventional moral notions from economic life. On the one hand, the state should ensure conditions that allow for open markets and fair competition, on the other hand, individuals should proceed on the basis of a rational calculation of self-interest. So far from advocating the building up of productive powers as a socio-moral force in the manner of List, Smith worried that the division of labour would lead to what we would now call the 'dumbing down' of the workforce, for which a minimal educational provision, partly provided by the public, would supply a partial remedy.

> . . . the understandings of the greater part of men are necessarily formed by their ordinary employments. The man whose whole life is spent in performing a few simple operations . . . has no occasion to exert his understanding or to exercise his invention in finding out expedients for removing difficulties which never occur. He . . . generally becomes as stupid and ignorant as it is possible for a human being to become.[26]

In these circumstances, the state can provide for basic education

> . . . by establishing in every parish or district a little school, where children may be taught for a reward so moderate that even a labourer may afford it; the master being partly, but not wholly paid by the publick; because if he was wholly, or even principally paid by it, he would soon learn to neglect his business.[27]

There are some reasons for thinking that, not content with making the rational calculation of self-interest the sole motivating force in economic life, Smith toyed with the idea, at least in *The Wealth of Nations*, of making it the driving force in non-economic life as well. In the quotation above we are a long way removed from List's qualities of 'honest striving for improvement' which he saw as such an important factor in economic improvement.

Second, what of the idea that List's insights can be incorporated within the theoretical assumptions of conventional political economy? Fukuyama, although he aims to supply what he sees is defective in classical political economy through the development of a concept of social capital, fails to see that his attempt to do so results in an incoherent moral psychology. Fukuyama's concept of social capital is much narrower than List's concept of productive powers but is, arguably, incorporated within it. If Fukuyama's innovations are incapable of being incorporated into the conventional model, then *a fortiori* the same is true of List's much more wide-ranging modifications. Fukuyama argues that classical political economy is 80 per cent accurate, but requires the addition of the concept of social capital in order to explain the differing levels of success in different types of capitalist economies.[28]

The missing 20 per cent concerns the social environment within which economic actors operate and the most important feature of this is *trust*, which Fukuyama defines as: '. . . the expectation that arises within a community of regular, honest and co-operative behaviour, based on commonly shared norms on the part of other members of that community'.[29]

Trust develops where other-regarding virtues such as kindness, sociability, honesty and fidelity are valued and developed; it is their byproduct. Long-term projects can only be secured through trust; as Hume pointed out, if we are to attend to our long-term interests we must put them in the hands of those who make them their immediate interest and this means trusting someone who takes his obligations to his fellow humans seriously. We take on such obligations not so much to impress others, but so as to be well-regarded as useful and decent members of society.

But this is precisely the assumption about human nature that Smith rejects, and classical economics has largely rejected it ever since. Smith refers to self-interest underlying 'a bargain of any kind' and his suspicion of social association which is not bound by ties of self-interest is evidenced in his treatment of such institutions as guilds and apprenticeships (to which institutions Fukuyama attaches a good deal of importance) and in his inability even to trust schoolteachers with the proper discharge of their duties if they receive a regular, publicly paid wage.[30] Fukuyama's concept of social capital cannot operate as a bolt-on amendment to the moral psychology of conventional economics; it entails a fundamental complication and revision of the model if it is to be coherent. List supplied that complication by allowing us to see economics in a different light through his emphasis on productive powers and the preconditions for their development.

In two important respects, the theory of productive powers goes well beyond the concept of social capital. First, List took seriously the idea that humans are political animals, that although they can exist outside a political framework, they need to be completed by one in order that their energies be fully harnessed. For List, the state does not merely provide the framework for the orderly conduct of economic activity, it expresses the spirit and aspirations of a nation and contributes to a nation's striving for power, influence and prosperity, through giving economic activity a central direction and by providing the infrastructure that the private sector does not have the resources or interest to provide. Second, because people feel themselves to be part of communities and nations, they work for the common good, not just for themselves and their immediate associates, and this means that they wish to take into account the needs of future, as well as currently existing generations. This is the point of the familial analogy that List employs to explain the idea of productive powers; investments are made for generations to come, not just for the immediate future. In this attitude there are echoes of Burke's claim that society is an unwritten contract between past, present and future generations.[31] The theory of productive powers is, then, a radical conceptual innovation in economics which has since been largely neglected in the classical tradition. Attempts, such as those of Fukuyama, to graft it or aspects of it on to the conventional model, are confused and contradictory. It is now appropriate to ask what relevance this innovation has to modern conditions.

LISTIAN SOCIAL CAPITALISM IN MODERN CONDITIONS

List's most obvious relevance to current conditions is that he arguably provides the theoretical underpinning for the 'social capitalism' that modern Germany, Scandinavia and the Pacific Rim countries in their different ways exemplify. All these countries take social capital seriously, including that which is embodied in the institutions of civil society; in all of them the state plays some role in the direction of economic activity, in many cases through the mediation of corporate entities in civil society such as businesses and trade unions, and in all of them economic life is directed to a conception of the common good as well as to individual prosperity. It is a consequence of these features of social capitalism that economic activity at all levels has a longer-term orientation than in individualistically based capitalist economies, based on a Smithian moral psychology.

Although acknowledging no debt to List, Hutton is perhaps the most eloquent exponent of social capitalism in the United Kingdom. His idea of stakeholding embodies a political conception of economic life that would have appealed to List.[32] Likewise, his emphasis on the long-term nature of successful economic activity has strong Listian overtones. Hutton, like List, recognises that the sources of human motivation are more complex than was recognised by Smith and his followers and, in particular, that a sense of inclusion and participation is vital to the psychic well-being of the great majority of people and hence to their ability to perform well as economic actors.[33]

Political economy and the politics of interest

List was a political economist who advocated social inclusion as a precondition of economic success. He had an acute recognition of the way in which conflicts of interest shape economic and political affairs. But, for him, these conflicts occurred largely *between* rather than *within* polities. As an economist of nationalism, List took little or no account of social and, in particular, class conflict in economic development and the formation of policy, although he *was* acutely aware of the regional dimension of national politics. In part, this omission is one of emphasis; unlike other political economists, List was concerned to stress the advantages that can be gained from national co-ordination rather than intra-national conflict. He had a repugnance for the opinions of Malthus which involved mass starvation as a means of population control.[34] This is quite consistent with his identification of the importance of the other-regarding virtues for economic development and his recognition that man's self-esteem depends to a considerable extent on social approbation.

Nevertheless, in so far as List was a *political* economist, he paid insufficient attention to class conflict *within* developing capitalist societies. Conflict of this kind was very much part of economic development of early nineteenth-century Germany, complicated by the fact that Smith's old adversaries, the guilds, were still very powerful.[35] There is, however, an apparent problem in associating a Listian perspective with an acknowledgement of class struggle. As Smith recognised, in a situation of class conflict the strong will prevail and mould the polity and economy to their own interests. In the atomised society that he advocated, combinations of employers would be almost inevitably successful, held in check only by a population with a modest education. He could not contemplate a vigorous development either of the state or of employee-based economic institutions within civil society, because he thought that the pursuit of individual self-interest through the agency of corporate or state bodies would be inimical to the operation of a market economy.[36] A Smithian account of class conflict, if incorporated into a Listian perspective, would destroy it by undermining the alternative moral psychology on which List wished to ground his economic theory. On the other hand, conceptualising class conflict on a Marxist basis also brings problems. Marx recognises that different social interests are involved in capitalist production and explains in great detail where, in the process of production, the basis of a conflict of interest lies. However, he believed that these differences are fundamental and irreconcilable and, due to the internal dynamics of a capitalist economy, are bound to sharpen until a point is reached where the system is no longer viable. Again, the incorporation, unadulterated, of Marx's insights would imply the ruin of a political economy that associated success with social cohesion.

And yet any political economy worthy of the name has to take into account conflicts of point of view in general, and conflicts of economic interest in particular. How can this be done within a Listian framework without destroying it? It is necessary to recognise, first of all, that conflicts of economic interest are not necessarily only the expression of individual short-term economic interest, nor of aggregations of such interests. They may well be expressive of the desire to maintain a common life or security for future generations. Secondly, it is necessary to recognise that, in different contexts, social groups may co-operate, trading off suboptimal but better than minimal solutions against the background of a perception of mutual common good. Such an account of class and economic conflict is quite consistent with an Aristotelian view of the social nature of man and Aristotle himself recognised the role that conflicts of interest played in political life.[37] What is required, then, is an account of economic and class conflict that satisfies these requirements. Such an account can be found in the work of Vico.

Vico on class conflict

Vico's writings on class conflict in antiquity have been largely neglected, despite their obvious influence on Marx. His conceptualisation of class conflict may, however, provide a solution to the problem posed in the previous section, namely how to incorporate an *intra-national* dimension of economic conflict into a Listian perspective. Vico's account, based on his mythic conception of the history of the gentiles, is centred around what we would now describe as the idea of having a stake in one's society. This stake is bound up closely with material interest, but is also connected with the desire for dignity and respect as a member of society. In Vico's account, the *famuli*, those who left the primeval forest as refugees after the formation of the first permanent settlements, lived as virtual slaves of the original city dwellers, with no civil rights, including no right to marry. Later, they acquired what he calls *bonitary* rights to enjoy some of the fruits of the land that they worked, as long as their masters allowed them to. Later still, struggle led to *quiritary* right, whereby the plebeians (descendants of the *famuli*) were allowed lifetime possession of the land but remained intestate, their land reverting to the nobles after their death. Finally, the plebs achieved the right of *connubium*, that is, the right to legally marry and to pass on property to their descendants; in effect they became citizens.[38] It is to this growing social inclusion of the plebs into ownership, citizenship and religious practice in common with the nobles, that Vico attributes the success of the Romans.[39] Vico's account of class conflict, suitably amended to take account of modern conditions, satisfies the conditions for incorporating an account of intra-national political conflict into a Listian inclusive perspective. It sees the class conflict as one for social inclusion as well as material security; it does not see it as a zero-sum game, but as one open to outcomes that all can see as beneficial, and it recognises that people associate in corporate groups with their own sets of values in order to further their interests.

Are there any analogies with the class struggles of antiquity that would enable us to better understand modern political and economic conflict as a struggle for social inclusion? I would like to suggest that there are. The development of the working class in Western Europe has been marked by conflict over the expansion of an economic and social stake in their societies that has taken different forms in different nations, but within which can be discerned certain common patterns. A working class without any security of employment or social security, but with freedom to move and to change employment, is similar in relative status to Vico's *famuli*; the modern equivalent might be the newly urbanised proletariat of England in the nineteenth century, which aroused the fears of Malthus and others. The development of trade union recognition and an element of social security are analagous to the bonitary right, while the growth of a stake in the society through the attainment of the vote, of employment rights and indirect ownership through pension and insurance funds, can be likened to the quiritary right acquired by the plebs.

Finally, the development of forms of ownership and control through a system of partial industrial democracy, through municipal and co-operative ownership, through works councils and employee representation on boards of directors might mark the advent of the modern equivalent of *connubium*, whereby full inclusive citizenship is obtained for those who depend on their labour for their upkeep. Seen through this perspective it is no accident that one of List's spiritual heirs, Konrad Adenauer, a co-founder of a political movement that takes the idea of economic development in the context of social inclusion very seriously indeed, should have been crucial in the institution of the practice of *Mitbestimmung* or co-determination in German enterprises, an innovation which placed a proportion of employees on the supervisory boards of larger firms.[40] This measure, as Osterheld argues, gave Germany a measure of success and stability unknown in other western countries for more than twenty years.[41]

List's political economy is crucial for an understanding of the success of modern capitalism beyond the United Kingdom and the United States. Suitably amended with Vico's account of class conflict, it will enable us to better understand modern 'social capitalist' economies.

Notes

1 'In matters such as buying and selling, or deciding what and how to produce, we will do others more good if we behave as if we are following our self-interest rather than by pursuing more altruistic purposes.' Samuel Brittan, quoted in John Kay, 'Staking a Moral Claim', *New Statesman*, 11 October 1996, p. 18. See also Francis Fukuyama (1995) *Trust*, London, Penguin.
2 See Chapter 6 for a fuller account of the difficulties involved in trying to do this.
3 F. List (1991) *The National System of Political Economy*, NJ, Augustus Kelley, Chapter XI. First published 1841.
4 As D. Levi-Faur (1997) 'Economic Nationalism: From Friedrich List to Robert Reich', *Review of International Studies*, 23, 3, 359–370, p. 367, points out, however, List advocated a system of international trade regulation similar to GATT [see List (1983) *The Natural System of Political Economy*, London, Frank Cass, p. 126].
5 List (1991) op. cit. pp. 42–43.
6 Ibid. Chapters I, II.
7 Ibid. p. 10.
8 Ibid. Chapter III.
9 Ibid. Chapters VI, XXXV.
10 Ibid. p. 421.
11 J. Fallows (1994) *Looking at the Sun*, New York, Pantheon Press, emphasises this aspect of List's thought. He argues that one cannot assess the rationality of an economic policy without first noticing what *ends* it seeks to serve. If the ends are national power rather than consumer spending, it is perverse to criticise an economic policy on the grounds that it is adopting means inappropriate to ends that it has not chosen (pp. 183–185).
12 W. Hutton (1995) *The State We're In*, London, Penguin, p. 267; Fukuyama, op. cit. p. 217.
13 David Hume, *A Treatise of Human Nature*, Bk. I, Part II, Section VII, p. 100 of Henry D. Aitken (ed.) (1948) *Hume: Moral and Political Philosophy*, Hafner.
14 Smith (1981) *The Wealth of Nations*, Indianapolis, IN, Liberty Fund, p. 282.
15 List (1991) op. cit. p. 142.
16 Ibid. pp. 143–144.
17 Ibid. Chapter VI.
18 Ibid. Chapters IV, VI.
19 Ibid. p. 81.
20 Ibid.
21 Ibid. pp. 138–139.
22 Ibid. p. 139.
23 Charles Gide, Charles Rist (1948) *A History of Economic Doctrines*, London, Harrap, footnote 3, p. 281.
24 Gide, Rist, op. cit. footnote 2, p. 282. Levi-Faur, op. cit. p. 363, also emphasises the importance of mental capital in List's conception of productive powers, while failing to

take sufficient account of the importance of the social capital which, for List, is the necessary medium of existence for an individual's mental capital.

25 Smith, op. cit. Volume I, p. 10.
26 Smith, op. cit. Volume 2, Book V, Chapter 1, p. 782.
27 Ibid. p. 785.
28 Fukuyama, op. cit. p. 13.
29 Ibid. p. 26.
30 Ibid. Chapter 18.
31 Edmund Burke (1986) *Reflections on the Revolution in France*, London, Penguin, pp. 194–195.
32 Hutton, op. cit. esp. Chapter 12.
33 Ibid. Chapter 7.
34 List, op. cit. p. 129.
35 Richard Biernacki (1995) *The Fabrication of Labour: Germany and Britain, 1640–1914*, San Francisco, CA, University of California Press, pp. 259–312.
36 See, for example, Maynard's comments on general practitioners: Alan Maynard (1985) 'Performance Incentives in General Practice' in *Health, Education and General Practice* George Teeling Smith (ed.), Office for Health Economics, pp. 44–46.
37 Aristotle (1988) *The Politics*, Cambridge, Cambridge University Press, especially Books III and IV.
38 G.Vico (1968) *The New Science*, Cornell University Press, pp. 214–219.
39 Ibid. p. 422.
40 For a detailed account of this development, see Wolfgang Streeck (1992) *Social Institutions and Economic Performance*, London, Sage, Chapter 5. Streeck's book also contains a valuable account of the *Handwerk* or artisanal sector of the German economy, which also contains a significant element of employee self-government (op. cit. Chapter 4). For a more recent appraisal of *Mitbestimming* see *Mitbestimmung und neue Unternehmenskultur*, Hans Böckler Stiftung 1998, by the same author.
41 Horst Osterheld (1996) 'Konrad Adenauer' in Hans Klein (ed.) *The German Chancellors*, Berlin edition q, p. 21.

6 Moral education and work

INTRODUCTION

Implicit in the account of political economy developed in the previous chapter, with its emphasis on the formation and development of social capital, is the role of morality in economic activity. If education is a preparation for life and vocational education is a preparation for economic life (broadly conceived in the sense of the previous chapter), then moral education is an essential part of vocational education. More generally, moral education has an important part to play in any form of education because preparation for life involves engagement with other human beings. Since morality is concerned with the way in which we treat others and the way they treat us, it follows that not only is moral education a central part of education, but that it is also to a large extent, social and practical in character, involving our growing ability to situate ourselves and to act in relation to the well-being of others.

The moral aspect of vocational education has been somewhat neglected by philosophers of education. This is partly because they have largely confined their attention to moral education during the period of childhood and adolescence rather than young adulthood. However, preparation for life does not finish with the completion of compulsory education, but continues into and beyond the period of initiation into adult life. During this period moral education continues to be very important, not just for personal relationships of a sexual nature, where it has an obvious role, but also for relationships with fellow-workers in the broadest sense.[1] It is particularly surprising that the very influential virtue–theoretic approaches to moral education that now play a great role in philosophical reflections on moral education have little or nothing to say about this aspect.[2]

Of course, if these arguments are right, morality and moral education should play a role in economic activity, however conceived. But the issue is sharpened somewhat by a consideration of economic activity as having the common good and human well-being or *eudaemonia* as one of its principal aims. For this suggests that considerations of morality are a central part of economic activity, not merely in the way that it is conceived (although this is important enough), but also in the way that it is carried out. For *eudaemonia* is an intrinsic good, worth pursuing in itself, not as an end-state of economic activity, but as something disclosed within it. *Eudaemonia* is thus partly achieved through the successful *outcome* of economic activity, through, for example, the achievement of rich and satisfying forms of personal life, which themselves consist of activities, but also *intrinsically* through the pursuit and enjoyment of worthwhile work activities. There can be an immanent spiritual significance in the practice of work, as an aspect of the use of our active powers.[3] In this respect, work might be seen as having an intrinsic value in relation to the release of our active powers in the pursuit of something that is itself intrinsically valuable (social and personal well-being). In this sense, the pleasure derived from work is not merely an aspect of the sensual excitation derived from mental and physical activity but from enjoyment of the pursuit of something valuable.[4]

If the morally appropriate ends of action are the pursuit of well-being in the context of the society of other human beings, then it is quite natural to conceive of morality, at least in large part, as the exercise of virtues, and moral education as their development.[5] Virtues in this sense are settled dispositions of character for whose *exercise* we are responsible. To some extent, we are also responsible for their *development*, although the fact that education is often necessary to develop them suggests that this is only true up to a point.[6]

A VIRTUE–THEORETIC ACCOUNT OF MORAL EDUCATION AND WORK

Moral education in childhood proceeds through conditioning and, later, training to increasingly reflective autonomous action, that is, action for which a person bears responsibility. Someone who has acquired settled modes of response and acting should be able to exercise them in increasingly complex situations where choices have to be made, and effort exercised, in order to achieve individually and commonly held goals.[7] These constitute those features of character that we consider under the aspect of virtue.[8] But the other side to moral growth that we need to consider in relation to activity generally, and work in particular, is that people also become autonomous in the distinct, but related, sense that they are able to both choose personal ends and means worthy of achieving those ends.

They become aware of the different ways in which a worthwhile life can be realised within their political community, for example, through becoming an artisan, a professional worker, or through bringing up a family, and are able to choose means appropriate to achieving such ends, each of which is a proper means of self-realisation.[9] Moral education does not then just consist in developing those character traits, but also in developing the ability to choose a worthwhile mode of life and appropriate and acceptable ways of achieving it. While the first is not obviously a part of vocational education, although I will show that it should be, the second and last is more clearly so, since it is a precondition of choosing a mode of life and an occupation that one is presented with meaningful choices and has the ability to exercise them. This is part of what is sometimes called *prevocational* education and, for an autonomous citizen, is a presupposition of choosing the means towards such an end, which will largely consist in the prerequisites for and pursuit of occupational formation in the chosen field.[10]

One problem in this discussion is the relationship between intrinsic and extrinsic goods. It seems as if the pursuit of both is self-contradictory, but this need not be so. It need not be the case that something that is valuable in itself, is of no value in relation to that which it is done for. Nor need it be the case that something which is done for the sake of an end is of no value in itself, even if the end intended does not come about. The pursuit of material well-being through consumption as a primary economic aim makes this difficult to see clearly, since it is often the case that we do often only attach value to economic activities like making, buying and selling in so far as they promote the maximum amount of consumption, which is itself seen as an intrinsic good.

The key problem is the elevation, in our kind of society, of consumption as an aim of economic activity *largely to the exclusion* of other aims. But one need not dismiss it entirely as a legitimate aim of economic activity to see that it needs to take its place alongside other aims, notably that of promoting well-being.[11]

Economic activity can do this by allowing and promoting activities that are themselves intrinsically valuable, in that they offer the opportunity for the exercise of both self- and other-regarding virtues and in the sense that, properly conceived, consumption itself can be seen as a means to the intrinsic good of well-being, that is, to the instrumental promotion of activities that themselves have an intrinsic worth. The ends for which work is carried out, or the moral constraints under which economic activity is undertaken, are also important considerations when one considers the worthwhileness of particular occupations. An occupation, say farming, can be undertaken only for the sake of profit, without any consideration for the physical environment, human health or the welfare of animals. A concern with the aims of and constraints on one's chosen occupation is, arguably, an important matter in the moral formation of a future worker. These considerations encapsulate some of the major problems of modern societies in relation to their economic life. First, how is work to be made valuable and satisfying? Second, how can it be managed in such a way as to promote economic efficiency (productivity, profitability and quality) in a way that satisfies moral sensibilities and takes due account of the long-term good of society? Third, how can consumption be managed and directed so that it promotes, rather than undermines, human well-being? Consideration of the importance of morality and moral education to economic activity thus brings us to the heart of some of the most perplexing problems that modern societies face.

Ethical and meta-ethical aspects of moral education

So far, little has been said concerning the specific virtues required by economic activity. This is for a good reason, namely that the answer varies according to the economic aims espoused by societies and the relative weightings that are attached to them. I have tried so far to establish that consideration of the virtues required for successful economic activity, and for the pursuit of the common good, is essential if we are to determine what elements of moral education are most appropriate to vocational education. This in turn depends on what a society is prepared to regard as unconditional goods that are worthwhile pursuing, which, as we saw, need not exclusively be material utilities.

Thus, it is evident that different societies may have different conceptions of well-being. It follows that one cannot assume that their perceptions of the virtues that constitute well-being or the means to its realisation, will be the same. Thus, if well-being is solely identified with consumption, then the virtues to which most importance is attached will be those which promote the production, circulation and consumption of goods and services. Diligence, prudence, competitiveness and hedonism will all, in different measure, and in different contexts, tend to be highly valued.[12] More generally, we would expect a relatively high weighting to be attached to self-regarding virtues exercised in short time-frames, namely those in which it is possible to form reasonable expectations of positive relationships between individual effort and material rewards.

One complicating factor here is that the aims of economic activity need not be exclusive and even that the prioritisation of one may lead to the more active promotion of another than had been realised. For example, a man concerned about whether he has received the grace of God may so act in this life as to make his election a palpable reality. By acting as if one were a member of the elect, he thus demonstrates that he is. So the self-regarding virtues of diligence and prudence may be directed towards an end that is not obviously economic, namely one's salvation beyond this world. The exercise of these virtues may, however, have the direct, practical effect of promoting accumulation and growing material prosperity in this life.[13] On the other hand, the other-regarding virtues of trust and sociability, which arise from the everyday associative life of a society and of strong institutions of civil society, may have the effect of promoting long-term economic projects resulting in material prosperity.[14]

We can conclude, then, that there are internal, as well as empirical, relationships between the aims of economic activity, social conceptions of well-being and the particular mix of virtues that are valued in any particular society. A society that values trust will tend to have trustworthy relationships within it. One may expect this to be empirically true and, if false, because of some major interfering factor. It is also part of our *concept* of trust that it involves the development and sustaining of relationships that involve trust. We have also seen that the relationships between the virtues and economic well-being are not simply related as means to contingent ends, since the ends identify the permissible means. Furthermore, the exercise of a given combination of virtues for a given non-economic end, may involve the realisation of a different, economic one as a by-product. Specifically, the pursuit of forms of individual or social well-being which are not directly tied to consumptionist ends may result in more successful achievement of those ends than the pursuit of a conception of well-being that values such ends above all others.

Different societies may promote quite different sets of virtues or permutations and weightings of the same and similar virtues, according to the conceptions of well-being that they endorse. A *meta-ethical* conception of morality as the promotion and exercise of virtue is compatible with widely differing *ethical* conceptions of which virtues it is desirable to maintain and promote in different societies.[15] The promotion and maintenance of those virtues is, in turn, dependent on moral education. Finally, any society has to take account, over the medium to long term, of the less-immediate or unintended consequences of the conception of morality that it promotes.

It will become clear later in this book that if one endorses a conception of well-being that foregrounds other-regarding virtues associated with sociability, trust and a concern for the long-term viability of a society, then not only are there certain consequences for moral education, but there are consequences for the 'backgrounded' aims of well-being as well, and in particular for the availability of goods and services for consumption.

DEVELOPING THE VIRTUES AS A PREPARATION FOR LIFE-IN-WORK

It is generally accepted that the virtues are developed in practical contexts.[16] Training, instruction and imitation play important roles in early moral education, as a child learns to react to the perceptions of others of its behaviour and as it learns to take responsibility for its actions. As it learns to live in a socially more complex world than that of immediate family relationships, these processes themselves become more complex and are, in turn, gradually and partially replaced by more reflective forms of action.

Moral education at school

The home and the family, together with the immediate environment of the home, provide an essential context for early moral education. However, when a child goes to school it gets its first large-scale encounter with the number and complexity of human relationships to be encountered in later life. First, and most obviously, a child will have to learn to form work and play relationships with other children, often of different backgrounds and temperaments. Second, it will have to form relationships with other adults, notably the teachers who will be most closely involved with its own education.

The particular environment of the school is worth reflecting on in this connection. During the early years of schooling, children come to realise that their actions have consequences both for themselves and for other people and that they are responsible for their actions. They learn more and more about the demands that the adult world makes on them as children. However, what they learn about what demands the adult world will make on them as future adults, is necessarily more limited. It was argued in Chapter 3 that education has three main aspects—liberal, civic and vocational—and that these are closely connected with each other in various ways. In the earlier years of schooling, these tend to be less readily differentiated than they become later. Moral education is a strand in all three of them.

Among other things, most state education systems aim to inculcate their future citizens with the characteristics that tend to be most prized by the society or, perhaps by the ruling groups in that society, for the station in life for which they are likely to be destined. A society, therefore, that aims to perpetuate a strong class structure and relatively low levels of social mobility will tend to promote different forms of moral and citizenship education for different groups of future citizens.[17]

One might therefore expect that the aims and practice of moral education will differ in various ways according to the social characteristics of those being educated. In particular, those destined for work in subordinate positions will not be encouraged to develop great ambitions on the personal side of their lives, nor will they be encouraged to develop their autonomy to its fullest possible extent.[18] Some self-regarding virtues will be encouraged: prudence and diligence, for example. Among the other-regarding virtues, obedience and loyalty to country and to social superiors will be deemed appropriate.

A society which is less organised on hierarchical lines, but which also values interdependence, will place different emphases on moral and civic education. It may well encourage a greater degree of autonomy and, while placing some emphasis on prudence and diligence, may also encourage independence of thought and personal ambition to a greater degree. The mix of other-regarding virtues is also likely to be different, including loyalty to a wider range of people and institutions than in the former example. Trustworthiness will be developed as an attribute of independent action rather than merely as an aspect of obedience. The choices that can be made will excite different reactions among the readership of this book. It will be evident enough from what has already been said where my sympathies lie, but for the moment, I want to develop a case about the normative role of schools in what is sometimes called 'socialisation' rather than be directly prescriptive about it. It is unavoidable though, for a society that pays close attention to its education system, to engage in the moral formation of its future citizens or subjects in ways that encourage the growth of desirable traits and the discouragement of undesirable ones. Even a society that deliberately neglects this task is doing so to some extent, either by indicating that the characteristics of a significant number of its citizens are of no consequence to it, or through implicitly encouraging diversity through default, allowing civil society to play a more direct role than the state in socio-moral formation.

This aspect of education takes place in different ways. First, through the practical arrangements of *schooling*; through making it possible for a community of teachers and pupils to work safely, harmoniously and productively together through the provision of a normative framework for the conduct of daily school life. Second, through foregrounding those parts of the curriculum in which moral implications are highly significant in a practical sense, for example, team games and religious worship. Third, through emphasising certain aspects of those areas of the curriculum where moral issues are introduced *vicariously*, for example through the study of history, literature and religion.[19] Finally, it may do so by explicit moral formation through religious and moral instruction or even 'critical thinking' classes.[20] While it is true, as Ryle and others have argued, that morality is neither a body of knowledge nor a discrete practice that can be taught to children by an 'expert' it is, nevertheless, true that teachers have an important influence on their pupils' moral development while at school, perhaps *the* most important influence.[21] They do this in the following ways: through being moral examples; through the provision of advice in practical moral situations and through explicit instruction in and inculcation of moral rules and higher level moral principles such as the categorical imperative or Hobbes' superordinate Law of Nature.[22] A teacher cannot usually either provide an example of super-erogation nor show pupils how to be supererogatory in their moral lives. It is arguable, however, that a school can, through the means given above, provide an atmosphere in which the supererogatory is expected.

Thus, by fine-tuning different aspects of schooling for different classes of pupils, societies can go some way towards producing different socio-moral attributes in different classes of future citizens. This does not, of course, mean that they can guarantee to produce such attributes in individuals, nor that they can guarantee that pupils will leave schools with a tidy set of 'desirable' beliefs. It does not even mean that they will not be able to exercise choice, at least to a limited degree, concerning the kind of life that they would wish to lead.[23] Nevertheless, a state which sets out to influence its citizens will have an effect, and one of the areas of life in which this will be felt most profoundly will be at work.

The scope and limitations of school-based moral education

However, although schools provide an important context for moral and civic education, through providing a variety of opportunities, both practical and vicarious, for moral engagement, they also have severe limitations, particularly in relation to work-related moral education.

A young person's moral sensibilities grow through educational and social experiences that are both practical and vicarious. The practical experiences gradually encompass a greater variety and complexity of moral situations in which action and appraisal are required. Thus a growing child comes to be aware of and respond to a family, a neighbourhood, schools of growing size and complexity, together with some of the agencies of civil society such as clubs, associations and churches. In all these situations, a capacity for acting with growing responsibility and for acquiring those virtues that are communally valued, is developed. The changing contexts in which action takes place are also important for moral development, since both action and appraisal have to be appropriate to the demands of particular situations and contexts.

Vicarious moral experience is important because it allows for an indirect experience of moral situations that might be relevant and it also allows for reflection on action in a more detached way than is often possible in everyday life. It also helps to make young people sensitive both to the uniqueness of particular situations with respect to their moral characteristics, but also to the fact that there may not be one right way for everyone to act in such circumstances.[24]

Important and indispensable though these educational experiences are, they are radically incomplete in one respect. There is an important sense in which children, and even adolescents, although they are acknowledged to be responsible for their actions, are not fully autonomous. That is to say, they are not yet fully free to make irrevocable life choices on their own, neither are they held fully to account for their actions as members of a moral community. This only becomes possible when they take on those positions of adult responsibility which fully reflect their account-ability for major decisions concerning their own lives, for their responsibility for the welfare and even the lives of other human beings, and for their contribution to social well-being through economic and domestic activity.

However, adolescents' decisions regarding the kinds of occupations that they wish to follow are inseparable from decisions about the kinds of persons that they want to be. Thus, one's decision to follow a technical, caring, artistic, craft, professional, domestic, charitable or manual occupation is not simply a decision about which skills one wishes to acquire in order to take part in the labour market, but it is a decision about the kind of life one wishes to lead, the values one wishes to espouse, those attributes of one's character that will be most developed. It is impossible for schools to form these attributes, and for teachers to provide an exemplar for anything other than teaching itself, because of the particular kind of environment that a school is.

One very significant role that schools can have, however, is in getting pupils to seriously consider the ramifications of their putative occupational choices, such as the moral qualities desirable, not only to practise a trade in the technical sense, but also in dealing with fellow workers, customers, suppliers and the wider public. Furthermore, pupils can usefully be introduced to the need to reflect on the broader role that occupations play in the well-being of society, and in this respect, closer engagement with employees and with workplaces is an important aspect of the prevocational education that can take place in schools.

Specialist technical schools are not an ideal environment for all aspects of vocational education; it is precisely because of their relative disconnection from the workplace that they find it difficult to motivate adolescents who want to get to grips with the challenges of adult life.[25] This is not to say that schools cannot have a very valuable vocational role. The development of autonomy involves questions of choosing ends in life that reflect what one wants to become. Schools can provide some of the material for reflection on this for adolescents from the ages of between 12 and 14 up to 15 and 16 years of age, through the provision of generic introductions to different occupations. Such schools tend to be more effective if they are staffed with teachers with the appropriate occupational experience, and if they have close links with local and regional economic activity.[26] They cannot provide the full sense of urgency and engagement, however, nor the real exemplar of senior colleagues fully engaged with the demands of the workplace, that work-based vocational education can provide.

This element of seriousness in adult life, the fact that there is often no one else who can take responsibility for one's actions or shortcomings, marks it off from the period of upbringing, which, in our society, now extends into late adolescence and early adulthood. Entry into adulthood involves responsibility in family life, often as a parent or as someone primarily responsible for the welfare of another and as someone with an occupation, where one's contribution to a common enterprise affects its success and the welfare of colleagues who share in it. Thus, not only does the level of seriousness change (the relative 'vicariousness' of life during the period of upbringing and schooling is shed), but the contextual nature of life changes, particularly in the immediacy and urgency of one's dealings with fellow human beings who are to some extent dependent on oneself.

The fact that one is autonomous with respect to important choices in life, that one has to earn the trust and respect of others through one's actions, makes the necessary moral education that has preceded this point something radically incomplete. All that one has accomplished up to this point is now put to the test in the complex situations of adult life. But this has implications for the community of work, social, associational and domestic life that a young adult is in the process of entering. A new worker is expected to be loyal, reliable and prudent (and maybe a great deal more) in his dealings with others at work and in the social and associ-ational activities bound up with work.[27] In acquiring these attributes he needs guidance, though of a different kind than that encountered at home and school and in the neighbourhood.

In these circumstances, the crucial figures are friends and senior adults, experi-enced in the occupations which the young person is entering. Sometimes these are relatively formal relationships, as in the provision of work-based vocational education and training or through the exercise of management responsibilities. At other times they are more informal and come about through friendship, companionship and the camaraderie of working in a team of mutually dependent human beings. One crucial difference between these work situations and those of school life is that in the latter case, the stakes are often far higher. One's workmates' well-being, livelihoods and even lives may depend on one's own sense of responsi-bility and ability to make sound judgements. The early years of work and domestic responsibility are therefore of critical importance in reaching moral maturity, let alone wisdom and experience.[28]

These considerations have important consequences for the organisation of work and for the continuing education of more experienced workers. The work-place, as the site of continuing moral growth, is only likely to be effective in that role if it, and the work which it supports, are themselves able to provide sufficient scope for the young worker to mature morally. A workplace where responsibility is abstracted from all aspects of one's labour, where there are no opportunities for the acquisition of new abilities and little opportunity for working as a team or in situations where friendships can develop, is not going to provide that kind of possibility for moral growth. Neither is it likely, from the point of view of the enterprise, to engender a sense of personal responsibility, loyalty or ambition in its employees.[29] The organisation of work is also important from the point of view of the continuing vocational and moral growth of more experienced and senior workers. For these, whether they work informally, or in a more formal managerial or tutelary role with younger workers, need themselves to prepare and to be prepared for providing for the workplace education of younger workers.

For some of these roles, only informal preparation is possible. It is through working with others and through encountering and overcoming problems collectively that one gains the ability to be calm and patient and the capacity to endure and to co-operate with others on their solution. These sorts of experiences provide the background for inducting less experienced workers into the exigencies of the work process and of working with others. As Wolfgang Streeck puts it:

> Industrial training is not just the acquisition of manual and mental skills but it is also, and increasingly needs to be, a process of socialization in work-related values, in a culture and community of work in which extra-functional skills like reliability, the ability to hold up under pressure, and solidarity with others working at the same tasks are highly regarded and rewarded. To internalize value orientations, at work and elsewhere, people need role models; teachers however, can serve this function only to a very limited extent and only for a very few, selected roles. Unless one aspires to be a teacher oneself, work-related skills and orientations are acquired not from professional teachers but from more experienced peers in a place of work where technical competence can be blended into, and transmitted together with attitudinal discipline and diligence.[30]

These remarks of Streeck's provide some indication of the complexity and richness that induction into a demanding occupation can provide and the ramifications of work-based training and education will be explored more fully in Chapter 7. Suffice it to point out at this stage that more experienced workers will need to fit into at least some of those roles, both formal and informal, that can be characterised as follows:

- *Exemplar*—someone who provides a daily practical example of what it is to be a good worker.
- *Mentor*—someone who provides a programme of structured guidance to the work environment and the activities within and associated with it.
- *Teacher*—someone who provides a more formal programme of instruction, training or guidance in some aspect of the work process.
- *Manager*—someone who has a formal role in organising the work and attending to the welfare of younger and/or more junior workers.
- *Friend*—someone who enjoys a personal relationship with a fellow worker and supports that person through bad, as well as good, experiences.

Last, but not least, there is a vital, but often neglected, *civic* dimension to occupational formation. All occupations are morally significant, first in the standards of probity with which workers deal with customers, suppliers and the public, second in the wider effects that the occupations themselves have on society. An occupation pursued solely for short-term profit without consideration for others or for social well-being is, whatever its immediate financial benefits, harmful in the long term both to workers employed in it, and to the society in which it is practised. For this reason, it is important that workers enjoy a degree of occupational autonomy so that they can set standards for individual behaviour and so that they can help in determining socially acceptable ways in which their occupation is practised. These concerns can be pursued through trade unions, occupational associations and, where the socio-political circumstances allow it, through the governance of enterprises (see Chapter 14).

CONCLUSION

The choice of primary occupation is one of the most important that people can make. It is not just a technical decision about how best to gain an advantage in the labour market (even if some people represent it to themselves as such), but, to a certain extent, a question about the ends in life that one wishes to adopt and thus, the kind of person that one wants to be. The decision entails developing the kind of occupational virtues that are esteemed in the chosen vocation and integrating those with one's life objectives more broadly conceived.

Schools have a critical role in carrying forward the moral formation begun at home and in preparing young people to make sensible and reflective choices about their major life objectives and occupations, based on their interests and developing sense of what is worthwhile in life. They can even, to a certain extent, give them a sense of what it means to make such a choice. They cannot, however, provide a sense of the urgency and seriousness of direct engagement with an occupation, nor with the technical, social and moral demands that it makes. Nor can they provide the experiences that lead, in due course, to a worker taking on a tutelary role for younger workers.

We can conclude, then, that the workplace is an essential location for the validation of life choices, for the acquisition of technical skills in conditions where they are to be applied seriously, in forming young people into the values, disciplines and virtues that are prized in a particular occupational context and in making them aware of the social ramifications of their chosen occupation. Moral education cannot therefore end with the period of compulsory schooling. Its completion takes place at work and continues for a very long period. Allowing young people to leave school without adequate preparation for an occupation, or any meaningful opportunity to follow one, is therefore not only a serious dereliction of society's responsibilities for young people, but a way of storing up very serious social trouble for the future.

Notes

1 It is, of course, an insight of Rousseau in *Emile* that this sentimental education continue into young adulthood. Rousseau, however, seems to think that in other respects, moral education is pretty well completed by the eve of adulthood. Even literature affords

relatively little reflection on the role of morality at work, let alone moral education in the workplace. J.-J. Rousseau (1762) (1966) *Emile ou l'Education*, Paris, Editions Flammarion. A notable exception is the work of D. H. Lawrence (see, for example, *The Rainbow*, London, Penguin).

2 See, for example, D. Carr (1991) *Educating the Virtues*, London, Routledge 1991; David Carr, Jan Steutel (eds) (1999) *Virtue, Ethics and Moral Education*, London, Routledge.

3 See, for example, the account of Levin's participation in the harvest in *Anna Karenina* [Leo Tolstoy (1954) *Anna Karenina*, London, Penguin].

4 See the discussion of the source of pleasure in N. Dent (1984) *The Moral Psychology of the Virtues*, Cambridge, Cambridge University Press, who does not place the emphasis that I do on the pleasure that arises from the pursuit of activities that are themselves intrinsically valuable. Dent, however, implicitly recognises the value of means as well as ends when he argues (p. 114) that practical reason involves deliberation about means as well as ends. If some means are excluded as legitimate ways of achieving ends on moral grounds, then this suggests, at the very least, that means are not morally neutral.

The idea that pleasure and intrinsic good might arise from work will only seem bizarre to those who adopt an attitude to human activity on an analogy with Aristotelian physics, that we are naturally at rest and require an extrinsic utility to galvanise us into activity; the 'marginal utility of work' described in Marshall's *Principles of Economics* and implicit in the work of Smith [see M. Verdon (1996) *Keynes and the Classics*, London, Routledge.] However, if it is normal for humans to exercise their active powers, if only for sense gratification, then the 'inertial' state is not normal and we must assume that humans take pleasure in activity and have a propensity towards it. As Verdon has argued this is the assumption of Keynes and it can also be found in Marx. Even the 'realistic' Marshall recognises it.

5 By this I do not mean that deontological, affective, perceptual or utilitarian considerations are to be entirely disregarded, but rather to foreground that aspect of morality which is most related to action and therefore to the issues which I wish to consider.

6 This is particularly true of the conditioning and training stages of moral education [see C. Winch (1998) *The Philosophy of Human Learning*, London, Routledge, Chapter 14].

7 Ibid.

8 Some features of our character are not under our control and can only partly be developed into dispositions through education, for example, *sociability* as opposed to shyness.

9 Aristotle's discussion, with a much more structurally simple and homogeneous community in mind, is, in places, much more restricted as to the different modes of life that a *citizen* may pursue, and suggests that different modes are appropriate to different stages of life [Aristotle (1988) *The Politics*, Cambridge, Cambridge University Press, Bk VII, p. 9]. The position that I am adopting is, however, that citizenship can be exercised in both a more functionally diverse and a more inclusive way than Aristotle was prepared to contemplate [see also J. O'Neill (1998) *The Market: Ethics, Knowledge and Politics*, London, Routledge, Chapter 2].

10 For an account of prevocational education, see H. Entwistle (1970) *Education, Work and Leisure*, London, Routledge, Chapters 7 and 8.

11 Aristotle argues that physical well-being is a condition of *eudaemonia*, even though the good man can make the best of poverty and disease (*Politics*, Bk VII, p. 175).

12 For a discussion of prudence, see Smith (1984) *The Theory of Moral Sentiments*, Indianapolis, IN, Liberty Fund, Part VI, section 1.

13 Cf. Max Weber (1958) *The Protestant Ethic and the Spirit of Capitalism*, New York, Scribner, Chapter V.

14 F. Fukuyama (1995) *Trust*, London, Penguin, however, thinks that these other-regarding virtues can exist in a non-problematic way alongside the self-regarding virtues of acquisitiveness and competitiveness developed to a high degree in the same individual, a dubious assumption.

15 See, for example, Nietzsche's (1954) celebration of archaic or Homeric virtues over those valued in the Christian tradition in the *Twilight of the Idols*, in *The Portable Nietzsche*, edited and translated by Walter Kaufman, London, Penguin.

16 The *locus classicus* for this claim is to be found in Aristotle (1925*) Nichomachean Ethics*, London, Dent, pp. 28–29.

17 See A. Green (1990) *Education and State Formation*, London, Macmillan; A. Green (1996) 'Education and the Development State in Asia' in Centre For Labour Market Studies, MSc in Training, *Module 3*, Units 1, 2, pp. 251–270.

18 In other words, the range of possibilities deemed by society for them to be acceptable to choose will be relatively limited (see the discussion of autonomy in Chapter 3).

19 All three of these are collectively described by the title 'hidden curriculum' although some aspects may be more hidden than others.

20 Cf. R. Paul (1990) *Critical Thinking: What Every Person Needs to Survive in a Rapidly Changing World*, Rohnert Park CA, Centre for Critical Thinking and Moral Critique.

21 See, for example, David Carr (1991) op. cit.

22 Immanuel Kant (1959) *Fundamental Principles of the Metaphysic of Ethics*, London, Longmans; Thomas Hobbes (1968), *Leviathan*, London, Penguin.

23 It is important to realise in this connection that even a fairly class-bound education system may open more opportunities to a child brought up to a very restricted view of his possibilities by the inward-looking nature of his family and community.

24 Cf. Winch, op. cit. Chapter 14; Evan Simpson (1989) *Good Lives and Moral Education*, New York, Peter Lang; Peter Winch (1972) *Ethics and Action*, London, Routledge.

25 See Wolfgang Streeck (1989) 'Skills and the Limits of Neo-Liberalism', British Socio-logical Association, *Work, Employment and Society*, 3, 1, March, pp. 92–101.

26 Cf. Entwistle, op. cit.; Michael Sanderson (1994) *The Missing Stratum: Technical Education in England 1900–1990*, London, Athlone Press.

27 By 'associational' activities, I mean those ties which may involve friendship, but which are organised on a more formal basis, often, but not always, with a serious purpose in mind, such as a trade union branch.

28 One of the great contemporary difficulties of induction into domestic responsibility is precisely this lack of supporting structures within family, community and civil society that used to be part of young people's practical 'on the job' preparation for these responsibilities (see Chapter 11). In what follows, however, I wish to concentrate on this induction in the workplace, while recognising its importance in domestic life.

29 This may, of course, from a particular narrow and focused view of the objectives of the enterprise, be a quite desirable situation. It is less clear that this is so when one takes a broader view of economic objectives (see Chapters 10 and 11).

30 These characteristics are sometimes assimilated to skills (cf. Wolfgang Streeck op. cit.). If the above analysis is right, however, they are moral attributes of doing certain kinds of things well.

7 Vocational education and vocational training

An examination of the conceptual relationship

INTRODUCTION: THE IMPORTANCE OF TRAINING IN EDUCATION GENERALLY

Any discussion of the nature of training in vocational education is going to be affected by previous thinking about this subject. Unfortunately, much of the discussion of training in the philosophy of education has been bedevilled by a very one-sided view of what it amounts to. This view has made it difficult for philosophers of education to take training seriously and hence to take the role of training in workplace and vocational education seriously. There is a historical account to be given of the difficulties involved in accepting the educational value of training that will be tackled in the next section. At this point, however, we can start by pointing out that very often *training* is confused with a quite different process known as *conditioning*.[1]

Conditioning involves the development of a set response in an organism to a stimulus in such a way that the organism concerned reacts in the same way in the same set of circumstances in the future. Examples are the salivation of a dog on hearing a bell, the running of rats through a maze or the pecking of pigeons to elicit food.[2] Human beings can also be, to a certain extent, conditioned. It is of the nature of training, however, and particularly of the training of people, that they are taught to respond *flexibly* and under their own volition, to a *variety* of stimuli. Naturally, the boundaries between rigid training and conditioning are not always clear and may be set in different places for different purposes, but the general distinction is clear enough and, in practical terms, most training is quite palpably not conditioning.

Let us look first at the training of animals. The flexibility of animal training can be seen, for example, in the actions of a sheep-dog, who has not only to respond to instructions, but to make assessments of situations, to respond flexibly to the evolution of those situations and to deal with a wide range of non-identical cases. The relationship between animal and human in this situation depends on communication, but only in a very limited way. There is a complexity and variety in the animal's actions that is just not present in conditioned behaviour.[3] The training of humans, however, involves language in a much more thoroughgoing way. A human can be taught *why* they are being taught, the *point* of a training activity, *why* it is being carried out in a particular way, and the part that the trainee can play in making it effective. In addition, the use of language to give complex instructions, explanations, encouragement, reproaches and praises exceeds anything that is possible in commerce between human trainers and animal trainees.

This is not to idealise all training. It can be good or bad, restrictive or enabling, well or badly executed. The key point is, though, that it is often qualitatively different both from conditioning and from even the more complex forms of animal training. Can anything be concisely said that differentiates conditioning from training? There are a number of points which, taken together, serve to demarcate the two kinds of process, although there will inevitably be borderline cases:

1   Conditioning is an involuntary process; one can resist it up to a point, but one is not an active participant in it when it is effective; it works best when one is passive. This is not true of training. If it is to be *successful* rather than *adequate*, it requires that the trainee has some commitment towards the process.
2   Training usually involves the *confident* and *unhesitating* mastery and application of technique, or confident judgement.[4] In demonstrating these qualities, someone who has been trained shows that they are active masters of the skill or technique that they have been trained in.
3   Training involves varying degrees of *autonomy*. Someone who has been trained needs to know when to apply the technique, in what manner and to what degree, given the particular circumstances that obtain at the time. Someone who has been conditioned merely acts in relation to a stimulus.[5]
4   Training often involves propositional knowledge as well as technique. In order to exercise judgement in the application of technique, varying degrees of knowledge are required. Successful conditioning does not require knowledge, but merely the elicitation of a narrowly prescribed range of appropriate behaviour.

These features may be present in varying degrees in trained responses. When they are present to a small or non-existent degree, then we are inclined to say that the process is one of conditioning rather than training. When they are present to a high degree, we are inclined to say that the training leads to the development of high levels of skill and, maybe, knowledge on the part of the trainee.

THE RELATIONSHIP BETWEEN EDUCATION AND TRAINING

The relationship between education and training is usually misdescribed, at least in the dominant Anglo-Saxon manner of thinking about these things, in terms of a contrast of incompatibles. If one has been trained in X, one has not been educated in X and vice versa.[6] In a trivial sense this is true, since education and training are different processes. As was argued in Chapter 3, education is concerned with preparation for life, whereas training is concerned with the inculcation of technique, so training cannot at the same time be education. But while this is uncontroversially true, it misses a central point: that the two concepts operate at different levels.

Education is usually a long-term process that involves the acquisition of knowledge, skill and understanding. The acquisition of *particular* knowledge, skill and understanding may, however, involve a certain degree of training. To deny this would be tantamount to denying that training could have any role to play in the acquisition of anything humanly useful, which is absurd. The two kinds of process are of a logically different order, but relate to each other in quite specific ways. Education may consist of episodes of training, but is not training itself. An episode of training may contribute towards education, but is not a complete education in itself. Sometimes vocational education is called 'training', but that is usually for one or both of two possible reasons that do not compromise the analysis offered here.

1   That because of its historically low prestige, forms of vocational and professional education are assigned the low prestige title 'training'.
2   Some forms of vocational education, particularly those implicated in low-skill activities, give little scope for judgement, craft knowledge or broad knowledge about the activity in which one is being formed, but consist solely of inculcation in a restricted and relatively easy-to-master set of techniques.

Historical misunderstandings of training and work

As was mentioned earlier, many of the common misconceptions about training stem from misunderstandings about what actually happens when someone learns in a work or work-related environment. The characteristics of work and work environments vary enormously and have done so historically; it is very difficult and usually unsafe to make simple generalisations about them. Given this variety, it is also difficult to generalise in a simplistic manner about the kinds of teaching and learning that take place in such environments. Modern thinking about the issue, particularly in the UK and other anglophone societies, has tended to assimilate work-based teaching and learning activities with training.

In order to understand it, we need to consider the ways in which economic development and the industrial revolution occurred in Britain during the seventeenth, eighteenth and nineteenth centuries and, more specifically, the influential account of how it occurred in the work of Adam Smith and Karl Marx.[7] Put briefly, Smith and Marx describe the onset of large-scale capitalist production in terms of the *division of labour*, particularly the process division of labour. The creation of any artefact requires a number of discrete activities which can be distinctly specified. Typically, artisanal production, such as was found in the mediaeval and early modern guild system of manufacture, was relatively *holistic*.

Although there were inevitably divisions between some parts of the process of creation as a whole, when one conceives of this as ranging from the appropriation of raw materials and the construction of tools of work, to the final finishing of the product, artisanal production tends to concentrate large segments of the creation of a product in the hands of one person, or a small team of people. An artisan is someone who not only carries out and controls a large part of the process, he may also conceive and plan what is to be carried out as well. An artisan is likely to have, not just a number of skills considered aggregatively, but a considerable degree of autonomy over exactly what is produced and how.

There are obvious problems with adapting artisanal forms of manufacture to conditions of large-scale production. These relate to the diseconomies of scale involved in distribution and collection among large numbers of artisans, the difficulties of employing capital efficiently when it is distributed among many small units of labour and, from the point of view of a holder of capital, the lack of control over the manufacturing process that is likely to result from such disaggregation. From the mediaeval period onwards, therefore, the factory system of production developed.[8] At first, this involved the concentration of artisans in one place, each pursuing their trade individually, but the capitalist benefiting from economies resulting from bulk buying of raw materials and reduced costs of transport and distribution. Note that, at this point, artisanal involvement in design had already probably disappeared, since the capitalist was likely to hold plans for the production of items on a large and uniform scale.

Early factory production evolved into a system whereby each artisan gradually reduced the range of processes in which he was specifically involved. Eventually this range narrowed until each worker was occupied with a particular individual process, involving one particular skill. Although this might be a skill that was difficult to acquire, the introduction of machinery to carry it out would reduce the worker to a supervisor of machinery, according to the standard account to be found in Smith, Ricardo and Marx. Although this is a considerable oversimplification of complex historical processes and also a simplification of what is involved in the use of industrial machinery, let us accept it for the moment as the dominant and most influential account of what happened.[9] The next step was the development of the production line, in which the processes were carried out in a linear fashion step-by-step until the manufacturing process was completed under close supervision. The ultimate development of this system is known as *Taylorism*, after the American industrial psychologist Frederick Taylor, who advocated a strictly controlled production process, governed by a regular tempo of work, with processes broken down into their minimally viable components, strictly supervised by line management.[10]

Taylorist methods give us the dominant image of the industrial age: manufacturing operates in a way already prefigured by Marx.[11] Work is reduced to one simple, repetitive, process requiring little or no skill, for the greater good of the manufacturing process as a whole. The dehumanising potential of manufacturing using the division of labour was already recognised by Smith, writing in the last quarter of the eighteenth century.[12]

In these circumstances it is hardly surprising that the dominant form of preparation for work was thought to be training for a few simple operations. It would hardly be exaggerating to say that, in the Taylorised workplace, training could often amount to little more than conditioning.

Given the relatively low skill base of British manufacturing during the late eighteenth and early nineteenth centuries, the emerging system of mass education had little concern with developing economically relevant skills. What were regarded as the virtues of docility and reliability formed an important part of moral education for the mass of future workers who could then be trained on simple tasks in the workplace.[13] It is not surprising that liberal educators came to associate training with mindless forms of activity, at least in the workplace. However, training *as such* began to acquire a poor reputation in whatever context it took place. Moreover, the spread of progressive forms of liberal education during the course of the twentieth century, undermined training activities associated with the acquisition of skills in the primary school and this decline reached a climax with movements which became influential in the late seventies and early eighties of the twentieth century, which sought to remove training elements from the acquisition of numeracy and literacy.[14]

This historical legacy has deeply affected attitudes towards training at both school and work. Training has come to be seen as a dehumanising kind of quasi-conditioning process. Indeed, writers on training often take Taylorist industrial training as a paradigm for training in general.[15]

VOCATIONAL EDUCATION AS FORMATION:
A PRELIMINARY SKETCH

This brief outline of the development of Taylorism and the way in which it came to be accepted as representative of the modern capitalist workplace, accounts in part for the poor reputation that training has among educators. Enough has been said, however, to suggest that the forms of training associated with Taylorist production processes are largely peculiar to those processes. Even Taylorised workplaces are often more complex that the simple model suggests and a description of the production line and the manual procedures associated with it are not the whole story.[16] The key to understanding a work process and the human relationships within it rests on an understanding of what Marx called the *forces of production*, the totality of the way in which human relationships are organised within a system of production.

Furthermore, the persistence of various kinds of artisanal occupation throughout the period of the industrial revolution, up to and including the present time, has been associated with very different forms of vocational preparation. Although these are often known by the generic name 'training' in the UK, they are, in fact, often very different from the processes described above. The term 'formation' is a better way to characterise many of these processes because they involve, in some sense, the making of a person into a worker, that is a human being with particular skills, attitudes and virtues. The commonest model of formation is to be found in the institution of *apprenticeship*, which dates from the mediaeval period. Apprenticeship was associated with state-regulated trade associations, the *guilds*, which regulated all aspects of a particular trade. The general model of apprenticeship is the attachment of a youth to an experienced artisan who teaches him the elements of the trade or craft, while the worker gradually comes to carry out more and more of the work process. Within this general model can be discerned different forms of practice. For example, many kinds of apprenticeship involve a formal element of instruction and practice, sometimes leading to certification, as well as the serving of a minimum amount of time as an initiate. Second, apprenticeship offers, to varying degrees, an extended social and moral education. The apprentice may learn of the history, traditions and values of the guild he is entering, either formally or informally. He will be inculcated into the rituals that govern the guild and its work practices and will, through working with others, acquire the social and craft virtues associated with successful practice of the trade.[17]

Apprenticeship is not the only model of formation, but it is one of the most historically persistent.[18] There are other models, such as different forms of on-the-job instruction and training, the use of an older worker as a mentor, and more formal instruction outside the immediate work environment. All these different approaches can be combined with each other, either in or outside the apprenticeship context, to varying degrees.

The evolution of high-skill approaches to the running of advanced economies has tended to accentuate the move away from the conditioning type of training associated with Taylorism to more complex kinds of vocational education. These typically involve *polyvalent skilling* (a worker possesses a related group of skills that can be applied in a variety of different tasks in the workplace), *deep skilling*, where a worker acquires fundamental principles of a trade or craft, which can be augmented as different applications of the fundamental principles emerge, and *redundant skilling*, where the worker applies skills that may be required in circumstances that do not yet obtain.[19] Formation may consist of the following connected elements in varying degrees.

First, there is a *prevocational* element (see Chapter 3), much of which takes place during the phase of compulsory education. Second, there is a *theoretical element*, where the scientific, technical historical and economic aspects of an occupation are introduced to the student. This usually takes place outside the workplace. Third, there is practice skill-formation, which may take place outside the workplace. Fourth, there is an on-the-job element, which includes instruction and skill-formation in the context of the work process, under the instruction of a senior worker. Fifth, there are the social and moral elements of learning to operate within the workplace as part of a team of fellow-workers. Sixth, there is an element of coming to organise one's affairs and those of the enterprise or trade that one is involved in. Each of these elements is present to some degree in many modern types of formation.

One of the key features of the modern large-scale enterprise and workplace is the need for management. Many of the specialised functions in the modern economy are not concerned with the direct production of goods or delivery of services, nor with activities peripheral to these functions, such as distribution and delivery. They are concerned with the control and organisation of workers involved in the direct activities of production and servicing, with the financial, informational and legal control of the enterprise and with strategic direction. These functions are usually known under the generic title of 'management'.[20]

There are certain features of the formation of managers that make it distinct from those of people involved in some of the other core functions of an economic process. First, there are generic functions concerned with the ability to operate successfully in a commercial marketplace and to organise the work of subordinates. Second, there are more specific functions concerned with the legal, financial, personnel, informational and computational, advertising and marketing aspects of running a commercial business, not to mention specific functions associated with the type of business that is being managed. Management education and development are properly seen as kinds of formation, although their specific form varies from country to country and from culture to culture. Prominent features of management education include traditional liberal education, professional vocational education (see Chapter 8) and various forms of adult pedagogical technique which encompass the socio-moral as well as the practical–technical side of formation. These include such practices as mentoring and team-building and have certain formal similarities with apprenticeship.

COMPETENCE BASED EDUCATION AND TRAINING

Competence Based Education and Training (CBET) is currently influential in the US and the UK, particularly, but not exclusively, in vocational contexts. It is seen as an alternative to vocational education based in educational institutions and to formational kinds, such as apprenticeships. The key idea is that one can be accredited for the competent performance of an activity in a work setting. The accreditation follows an assessment procedure which tests the assessee's ability to perform a variety of tasks in the workplace. The claimed virtues of CBET are, first, that it focuses on what workers need to do in the workplace and not on superfluous extras; second, that it gives them credit for what they already know, without their having to go through a further, unnecessary, period of training or education in order to gain recognition for their abilities.

It can be seen from this brief description that the term 'Competence Based Education and Training' is something of a misnomer. The competence is based on performance defined in a circumscribed way, namely the ability to perform a task according to certain specifications on a particular occasion. The phrase 'education and training' is misleading because the point of CBET is precisely to decouple assessment from education and training. Indeed, a large part of the point of this approach is to provide a system of accreditation that is removed from prior education and training.

CBET is thus symptomatic of a commitment to identify vocational education and training with forms of low-level training, rather than formation. The reason is that the emphasis rests on the behavioural characteristics of an individual rather than a more holistic measure of ability.[21] It is important to see that there really is a difference between the two and that it is a difference that matters for many occupations, particularly complex ones. One can most easily identify workplace competence in those cases where ability to carry out the job can be fully specified in terms of individual behavioural characteristics. The kind of job for which this can be done most easily is that of the operative on a Taylorist production line, whose sole occupational role is to carry out a limited number of actions within a limited number of contexts.

Why, then, are other kinds of occupation not so easily specifiable in CBET terms? The main reason is that they are much more complex, but this in itself does not tell us much. It is not simply that many occupations require workers to do a number of different things, but also that the *kinds* of things that they are asked to do are unsuitable for assessment of this kind. More particularly, workers are required to carry out tasks that involve *prior* judgement of the most appropriate actions to take, *ongoing* assessment of the task as it is carried out and *reflection* on its nature and how it can be improved. In addition, many occupations require an ability to work with other people under a varied set of conditions. These features mean that many workers need knowledge that is closely integrated with their practical abilities.

This is so, even for relatively straightforward cases:

> A carpenter or mechanical fitter needs to know which type of metal screw to choose for each job; screws come in a myriad of different lengths, diameters, threads, heads (flat, round, Philips, etc.) and in different metals (brass, steel, chrome, etc.). If a final assessment of capabilities had to wait until the candidate had used each type in the course of his normal work in front of his supervisor, and had done so properly on a sufficient proportion of repeated occasions, it would take a very, very, long time for him to be judged as qualified.[22]

It is, therefore, very difficult to describe competence in terms of a relatively small number of discrete tasks, precisely because the contextual features of work situations mean that tasks require prior judgement and the ability to reflect during and after the carrying out of a task. To extend the example in the quotation, it may turn out that the fitter encounters an unforeseen problem during the course of a job and has to adapt his original plan. Reflection post-task may lead him to conclusions about how he will go about similar tasks in the future.

To train someone to be competent in the sense of 'able to perform as an X' where X is the space to be occupied by the name of an occupation, is then, to give them a range of abilities mental, moral and physical. This is true even for minimal competence, let alone for the highly skilled worker who strives for excellence in everything that he does.

ASSESSMENT IN VOCATIONAL EDUCATION

It follows that judging competence for all but the simplest of occupations is likely to be a very complex and time-consuming task, particularly if it is carried out according to the principles of CBET. Even then, it is likely to suffer from problems of validity and, possibly, reliability. As has already been noted, CBET is more of a system of *accreditation* than of *training*, even though it is often introduced as a new form of training policy. However, before we go on to look at the details, it is worth noticing that CBET accreditation, because it relates to *whether or not* someone can carry out a certain task rather than *how well* they are able to do so, is limited as a form of accreditation, particularly when employers are interested in the *degree* of competence of a worker. Although CBET-based forms of accreditation like NVQs have a hierarchy of levels relating to the complexity of the skills assessed, these levels do not have a provision for assessing proficiency *within* that skill level. For example, NVQ level 1 says whether or not someone can carry out basic activities in a field, not how well they are able to do so. Thus one very important dimension of occupational assessment is excluded from the outset.

Validity is another major problem with CBET accreditation. If the skills required to work within an occupational area cannot be summarised in terms of a limited set of discrete skills, as the CBET approach suggests, then to what extent can CBET-characterised competences be meaningfully assessed? If they cannot be, it is hard to see the point of CBET, since its claimed merits are as an accreditation approach, rather than as a form of training. In order to answer this question, it is necessary to take a closer look at assessment and its relationship to education and training.

THE GENERAL RELATIONSHIP BETWEEN TEACHING, LEARNING AND ASSESSMENT

One currently influential philosophical account of criterion-based assessment is that it cannot achieve its objectives of giving a reliable and valid summation of what someone knows.[23]

Reliable assessment inevitably simplifies what is to be assessed and renders it of limited validity. On the other hand, attempts to produce criteria that are valid run into intractable problems. These are related to the kinds of consideration that Prais draws our attention to in the quotation above. Any specification of criteria tend to limit the competence or knowledge assessed to a procedural sequence tied to a particular context. The ability of the worker in the example can be specified in terms of his ability to carry out certain tasks, but in doing so, one misses the holistic character of work within the occupation and fails to pick up the skilled and knowledgeable worker's ability to make contextually appropriate judgements. For much the same reason, any attempt to assess a candidate through an examination fails to encompass their full range of knowledge, let alone their ability to apply it contextually.[24] The only kind of assessment that can be attempted, on this argument, is of a form whereby an assessor who is personally knowledgeable about the candidate is able, over an extended period, to gain a picture of the candidate's knowledge and abilities in their contextual employment. Any other kind of assessment is bound to miss the target that it sets itself.

The strength of this argument is that it draws attention to the fact that no system of assessment can be perfect. However, it is doubtful that defenders of assessment have ever claimed that it could be. Assessment procedures are always a compromise between the requirements of validity, reliability, time and expense.[25] But it does not follow from this that formal procedures are of no value. Indeed, the argument misrepresents what assessment sets out to do, together with the purposes of examinations.

Why is assessment necessary? The answer to this question was first given by Anthony Flew. If a teacher is teaching a subject matter to a pupil he will, if he is serious about what he is doing, take care to get it right. In this case, he will seek to ensure that the formal activity of teaching leads to the characteristic results of teaching, namely that the pupil learns what the teacher teaches. He needs to do this in order to know whether and to what extent he has been successful. Not to worry about these matters would be to betray a lack of concern about whether one's teaching had achieved even a minimal degree of success. Anyone who putatively performs an activity without any concern for whether or not he achieves a minimal degree of success, is not seriously carrying out that activity. Therefore, a teacher who taught but had no interest whatsoever in assessment would not, in any serious sense, be teaching. Assessment is therefore an essential aspect of teaching.[26]

The argument does not require that a system of assessment be perfect, nor even that it necessarily be formal, but it does require that it focus on whether or not skill, knowledge or understanding has actually been gained. It would not be sufficient, for assessment purposes, that some external sign that learning had taken place be present, such as a look of enlightenment on the face of a student.[27] There are a variety of ways in which assessment can be carried out, but inevitably, vocational assessment needs a more complex arrangement than conventional academic assessment, if the occupational tasks being assessed are more complex than the Taylorist practices described earlier.

Academic assessment is primarily concerned with whether or not propositional knowledge has been acquired, together with a judgement as to whether or not that propositional knowledge can be suitably organised for a particular purpose and communicated intelligibly. Examinations or some other form of written assessment are usually sufficient for such a purpose. Examinations are particularly important because, properly administered, they take account of the fact that a formal assessment cannot usually assess all the knowledge that may have been acquired. Instead, the aim is to sample that knowledge through the unseen selection of particular aspects for study, thus obliging the student to have a grasp of the whole body of knowledge if he is to have a reasonable prospect of being successful.

Vocational assessment is also likely to require some theoretical element of this kind, for the reasons advanced by Prais above. The carpenter in the example needs to show examiners his ability to choose the right kind of screw for the job, even if he is not actually at that moment confronted with a task that requires that screw. He also needs to be able to display the kind of task-specific competence that is tested through NVQ-like procedures, which, in this context, may take the role of practical examinations or may be required *in addition to practical examinations.* However, this may not be enough if the work role demands other qualities such as patience, diligence, ingenuity in unusual situations, the ability to work well with others in a variety of conditions and so on. In these circumstances, the candidate needs to display the ability to apply what has been learned in a variety of specific contexts and this can best be done through a period of extended probation in the work situation, before full accreditation takes place.[28]

The answer to the kind of objections made against criterion-referenced assessment by Davis is, then, that in the case of propositional knowledge, validity is secured by a properly administered examination procedure. In many systems, a large proportion of the propositional knowledge tested is not specific to a particular occupation, but is more general and might be regarded as part of a liberal curriculum.[29] Where such knowledge is not occupation-specific it is not necessary to make a further assessment in practical contexts. Where it is, however, a practical examination can be provided, together with a probationary period, which should satisfy the most demanding of assessment sceptics. This is, in fact, precisely the kind of accreditation procedure that is adopted in Western European countries, such as Germany.[30]

These procedures also supply an answer to Davis's worries about the validity of criterion-referenced assessment procedures, on the grounds of their being insufficiently context-specific. Most occupations require a considerable amount of common knowledge and skill, such as literacy and numeracy. These are assessed as part of the process of vocational accreditation and are therefore, partly at least, assessed in occupational contexts. Therefore, if schools and vocational colleges are teaching such material with insufficient thoroughness for it to be appplied in occupational contexts, this will be detected through occupational assessment procedures, and this very fact exerts a certain amount of pressure on prevocational schools to do their job properly. Davis's arguments should not lead us to abandon formal assessment, but rather to make it even more rigorous where this is necessary, for example, when examination procedures are relaxed so that candidates are only required to know thoroughly a part of the syllabus. We can conclude that (a) assessment is an essential part of vocational formation, (b) that it needs to take a variety of forms, including extended exposure to the occupational situation, and (c) that it is, in part, a further assessment of what has been learned in prevocational educational situations.

We are now in a better position to provide an overall evaluation of CBET. It has been noted that it is primarily an accreditation procedure, rather than vocational formation. As such, it focuses on a very limited aspect of assessment, namely the successful performance of a range of centrally specified, occupationally specific tasks. It is not designed to assess either knowledge in breadth (through an examination) or knowledge in depth (through extended workplace application). It is therefore only suitable (if indeed it is even suitable for this) for occupations that require limited propositional knowledge, little variety in work tasks and little need for occupationally specific moral virtues.[31] In addition, by posing as a form of training when it is a form of assessment, the conceptual connection between teaching, learning and assessment is exploited in a very unhelpful way.

While one can be taught without assessment procedures, this is usually taken as a sign of the relative unimportance of what is taught, for reasons advanced by Flew and outlined above. Traditionally, liberal political theory has emphasised assessment as a means of ensuring that education takes place, without specifying how that education should take place.[32] Now, although assessment cannot take place without there being some material which is assessed, and, therefore, at least implicitly, some form of curriculum, nothing very specific or systematic is required. The arrangements made, as envisaged by Mill and Smith, may well be piecemeal. Because CBET does not require any specific form of training, it is left to market providers to ensure the degree of preparation necessary for passing the accreditation procedures. Much is therefore left to the workings of a market in training and therefore, to the assumption that users' (trainees' and employers') knowledge of who are good and bad providers of training will be made available to potential trainees. One can, however, assume such knowledge only in the perfect markets of neo-classical theory. The imperfect market of Austrian economic theory is unable to provide such knowledge.[33] First, without a unitary independent assessment body there is no guarantee that assessment bodies in competition for students will not subtly lower their standards. It is no good claiming that knowledge of such distortions will always enter the public domain if one holds, at the same time, that the knowledge distributed through the marketplace is imperfect. Second, indirect measures of assessment, such as client satisfaction are both unreliable and invalid.[34]

CONCLUSION

The place of training in a modern economy

It has been argued in this chapter that not only is training a key feature of education, it is much more complex than conditioning. Second, it was argued that vocational education is better seen as formation rather than low-level training. Some historical reasons why it has been thought to be the latter were suggested. An educative model of vocational education has been outlined, together with the kinds of assessment procedures that belong with such a model. CBET models are more suitable to the kind of low-level skill training that a formational model tries to move beyond.

Notes

1 See C. Winch (1998) *The Philosophy of Human Learning*, London, Routledge, Chapter 5 for a further explanation.
2 David Lieberman (1990) *Learning*, CA, Wadsworth.
3 Cf. Winch, op. cit. Chapter 5.
4 As David Beckett (1998) 'Anticipative Action and its Contribution to an Emerging Epistemology of Practice', *Proceedings of the Annual Conference of the Philosophy of Education Society of Great Britain*, pp. 209–222 points out, some forms of training that involve reflection on practice do not always result in unreflective action.
5 An unintentionally amusing example is given by Lieberman, op. cit. p. 336, of the expectation that successfully conditioned rats would not be able to run through the bottom of a flooded maze. The fact that they swam presumably showed that the conditioning process, as originally envisaged, was unsuccessful.
6 Peter Abbs (1987) 'Training Spells the Death of Education', *The Guardian*, 5 January, is a typical example of this approach. R. F. Dearden is much more cautious but nevertheless thinks that training can subvert education [Dearden (1984) 'Education and Training', *Westminster Studies in Education*, 7, pp. 57–66, esp. p. 64].
7 A. Smith (1981) *The Wealth of Nations*, Indianapolis, IN, Liberty Fund; Marx (1970) *Capital*, London, Lawrence and Wishart.
8 See List's account of the Hanseatic League's factories in London and Novgorod [List, (1991) *The National System of Political Economy*, NJ, Augustus Kelley, pp. 15–16]. First published 1844.
9 See, for example, Marshall's account of the introduction of machinery into watchmaking for an appreciation of the complexity involved [Marshall (1890) *Principles of Economics*, eighth edition, London, Macmillan, pp. 213–214].
10 Frederick Taylor (1911) *The Principles of Scientific Management*, New York, Norton.
11 Karl Marx (1970) *Economic and Philosophic Manuscripts of 1844*, edited with an introduction by Dirk Struick and translated by Martin Milligan, London, Lawrence and Wishart, pp. 106–119.
12 A. Smith (1981) op. cit., Volume 2, Book V, Chapter 1, p. 782, quoted in Chapter 5.
13 Andy Green (1996) 'Education and the Development State in Asia' in Centre For Labour Market Studies, MSc in Training, *Module 3*, Units 1, 2, pp. 251–270.
14 See, for example, Nigel Hall (1988) *The Emergence of Literacy*, London, Hodder; Frank Smith (1985) *Reading*, Cambridge, Cambridge University Press.
15 Cf. Robert Dearden (1984) op. cit.
16 Geoff Mason, Bart Van Ark, Karin Wagner (1997) 'Workforce Skills, Product Quality and Economic Performance' in A. Booth, D. Snower (eds) *Acquiring Skills: Market Failures, Their Symptoms and Policy Responses*, pp. 177–197.
17 Pat Ainley, Helen Rainbird (eds) (1999) *Apprenticeship: Towards a New Paradigm of Learning*, London, Kogan Page. See in particular the contribution by Linda Clarke 'The Changing Structure and Significance of Apprenticeship with Special Reference to Construction'.
18 Clarke (1999) in Ainley and Rainbird (1999) op. cit.
19 See Geoff Mason, Bart Van Ark and Karin Wagner (1997) op. cit. on multi-skilling, Wolfgang Streeck (1992) *Social Institutions and Economic Performance*, London, Sage, on polyvalence and redundancy; David Ashton, Johnny Sung (1997) 'Education, Skill Formation and Economic Development: The Singaporean Approach' in Centre For Labour Market Studies, MSc in Training, *Module 3*, Units 1, 2, pp. 351–372, on deep skilling.
20 A good general account of the various functions of management can be found in Marshall, op. cit. Book VI, Chapters VII, VIII.
21 Cf. Terry Hyland (1993) 'Competence, Knowledge and Education', *Journal of Philosophy of Education*, 27, 1, 57–68.

22 S. J. Prais (1991) 'Vocational Qualifications in Britain and Europe: Theory and Practice', *National Institute Economic Review*, 136, May 1991, 86–89, 87.

23 See Andrew Davis (1998) *The Limits of Educational Assessment*, Oxford, Blackwell.

24 According to Davis, assessment procedures focus on 'thin' procedural knowledge rather than 'thick' contextual knowledge (Davis, op. cit. Chapters 2, 5.)

25 Robert Dearden (1979) 'The Assessment of Learning', *British Journal of Educational Studies*, 27, 2, 111–124. Prais, op. cit.

26 Anthony Flew (1976) *Sociology, Equality and Education*, London, Macmillan, p. 89.

27 See John White (1999) 'Thinking About Assessment', *Journal of Philosophy of Education*, 32, 2, 201–211, for an argument along these lines.

28 Prais, op. cit. This can also be done concurrently, through the induction of the trainee as an apprentice, where he spends a lot of time applying newly acquired knowledge and skills in a work-specific context.

29 Prais, op. cit.; also David Matheson (1999) 'Lifelong Learning and Economics in Switzerland' in *Education as a Commodity*, Nafsika Alexiadou and Colin Brock (eds), John Catt Educational, 1999, pp. 135–148.

30 It should also be pointed out that examination and assessment are carried out by independent bodies so as to ensure the integrity of the assessment process (Prais, op. cit.).

31 See Howard Gospel, Alison Fuller (1998) 'The Modern Apprenticeship: New Wine in Old Bottles?' *Human Resource Management Journal*, 8, 1, 5–22 for examples of how different trades view NVQ procedures relative to more traditional forms of assessment.

32 See, for example, John Stuart Mill (1974) *On Liberty*, London, Dent, p. 160; Smith (1981) op. cit. p. 786.

33 For a defence of the 'Austrian' view of educational markets, see James Tooley (1998) 'The Neo-liberal Critique of State Intervention in Education: A Reply to Winch', *Journal of Philosophy of Education*, 32, 2, 267–282.

34 For an argument to this effect, see Winch (1998), 'Markets, Educational Opportunities and Education: Reply to Tooley', *Journal of Philosophy of Education*, 32, 3, pp. 429–436.

8 Learning in the workplace[1]

INTRODUCTION

So far, we have looked at the relationship between education and training, and have observed that this relationship is a complex one, in which training plays an important part in educative processes, including vocational educational processes, without necessarily supplanting their specifically educational features. It is now time to look more closely at workplace learning to see exactly why the *conditioning* model considered in the previous chapter is so inadequate. The issue is complicated by the variety of different accounts of workplace learning on offer, all of which have certain inadequacies, some of these greater than others.

Workplace learning contexts have distinctive characteristics that distinguish them from child-rearing and schooling contexts. While it is extremely difficult to either distinguish workplace from non-workplace learning contexts in a hard-and-fast manner, the distinctive characteristics need to be dwelt on. Associated with this issue is the *diversity* of such contexts, which also makes it extremely difficult to generalise about them.

Perhaps the most important feature of workplace learning is that it takes place in contexts which are practical in the sense that they are directed towards some other primary end than learning, namely the production of some good or service. The second most important feature is that the learner is almost invariably an adult, rather than a child. The first feature has the important consequence that successful learning matters in a quite immediate sense, since a consequence of failing to learn is likely to be failure in the production of what is aimed for. This has the further result that success or failure in learning has more or less immediate consequences for colleagues whose well-being is also bound up with the success of the work process. It has no less important consequences for customers, clients, patients, etc. who are the recipients. The pressurised nature of the work environment means that whenever the work process is itself complex, much of the learning needed to acquire competence has to be done in conditions that in some way realistically represent the working environment, while shielding the novice from the worst consequences of not carrying out the work with full competence. Workplace learning is thus often associated with a related form of simulated environment, or *practicum*, in which it is possible to take risks and make mistakes which would be disastrous in the workplace. The relationship between the theoretical, simulatory and fully practical aspects of workplace learning is of the greatest consequence for its success.

The fact that *adults* rather than children are the learners also has important consequences. For one thing, learning to operate successfully in a workplace environment requires the development of the social and moral capacities of trainee workers (see Chapter 6) as well as their abilities to work with materials and artefacts. Second, it presupposes that trainees already have a level of autonomy and responsibility which affects the way in which they learn and can be taught. Finally, the trainee is in the workplace usually as the result of a choice, rather than as a result of compulsion. Thus, although workplace education is part of preparation for life, the voluntary nature of the choice made has an impact on what kind of preparation it is possible to ask someone to undertake. Both of these considerations: of the practical and pressured nature of the workplace as a learning environment on the one hand, and of the adult nature of the learner on the other, need to be borne in mind when we consider theories about the nature of workplace learning.

There are various theories of workplace learning. It will be proposed that it is futile to seek for an overarching theory, but that its complex and contextually specific nature needs to be understood before we can properly appreciate the importance of planning for different kinds of learning for vocational education.

THEORIES OF WORKPLACE LEARNING

Workplace learning as training

In Chapter 7, accounts of workplace learning as a form of conditioning were dismissed as inadequate for the great majority of cases. It was noted, however, that there has been a persistent tendency in the literature to pay insufficient attention to the differences between conditioning on the one hand, and training on the other. The invalidity of the conditioning model leaves it open as to whether it is possible to adequately account for workplace learning in terms of *training*.

The key feature of conditioning is the loss of independence of the organism to be conditioned. Behaviour is 'shaped' according to a routine and the response to the shaping is rigidly circumscribed by the shaping process. Conditioning in its purest form does not allow for any flexibility in either stimulus or response. Behaviourist experiments on animals in laboratory conditions are the purest examples of learning-as-conditioning. However, once the environment is not a laboratory, it is less possible to control all the factors that may contribute to either stimulus or response. Neither should we assume that animals subjected to conditioning always behave predictably. The workplace is not a laboratory, so is not an appropriate location for a pure form of conditioning. However, it is possible to maintain that in Fordist/Taylorist production conditions, stimuli and responses will have little scope for variety and will hence approximate to conditioning, but the characteristics of humans that make them different from rats make this claim implausible. Even on a highly Taylorised production line there is social interaction during the working day. Furthermore, workers bring their sensibilities, values, memories, hopes and expectations into the workplace, and these have an effect on how well they learn in a way that is difficult to account for in a conditioning schedule. If workers are treated as if they were no more than a complicated rat, their active co-operation is not likely to be engaged and dissociation, both cognitive and moral, from the workplace task is likely to result. Conditioning is not an adequate account of how learning in adults takes place except in very limited conditions concerned, for example, with the recuperation of autonomic or semi-autonomic physiological functions after accident or injury, or in other highly specialised circumstances. Even here, the active co-operation of the patient is likely to be a factor in success. Attempts to apply it to workplace learning with normal adults are likely to end in disaster.

Ryle distinguishes between 'training' and 'drilling' (which he equates with conditioning) and argues that the results of training are the building up of intelligent capacities, whereas the use of the latter results in the establishment of habits.[2] Training, argues Ryle, may partially consist of drills, but is not to be identified with them. Examples of drilling include, for example, learning multiplication by rote rather than calculation, and learning to slope arms correctly. These contrast with the training that is necessary to handle multiplication by calculation or to become proficient in marksmanship and map-reading.

Ryle's concept of drill is probably nearer to what it is possible to do to get people to learn routines in unvarying situations and is hence something more than conditioning in that it presupposes a degree of participation and involvement in the activity. His concept of training captures the active and autonomous result of those processes that actively engage the abilities and capacities of the learner, while at the same time subjecting him to the authority of the one imparting knowledge or skill. As in drill, practice and repetition are essential to the process, but the ability to handle information, weigh the different elements that are relevant to a decision, or to engage in dialogue with others, cannot be inculcated through drill alone. Furthermore, the results of training in complex activities are not necessarily predictable. For example, a soldier trained to manoeuvre will use map-reading skills to assist him in the achievement of objectives. Those objectives may have been set by the trainer, but it is quite possible that the soldier has the freedom and the ability to choose how to achieve those objectives in different ways and hence may well use those skills in an unpredictable, but practically rational, manner. The Rylean model of training promises, then, to account for how people acquire practical ability in difficult tasks in complex conditions.

To summarise then, training in Ryle's sense involves the acceptance of authority, the inculcation of routine and the development of flexible and variable ways of achieving goals through the development of specific abilities like calculation and map-reading. These forms of practical knowledge are necessarily complex, since they are exercised in situations that are always, in some sense, unique. Hence they involve the integration of abilities with the recognition of situations in which they can be exercised (that this is an appropriate situation for using multiplication), the adaptation of abilities to specific situations (choosing the right kind of screw for a particular woodworking operation), the involvement of skill and knowledge from related areas (the recalculation of distance, using a map of a different scale) and the negotiation of what are the appropriate procedures with others involved in a task (arguing that the use of the map rather than dead reckoning is most appropriate at this point). One does not have to agree to Davis's argument that nearly all useful knowledge is interconnected, rather than narrowly procedural, to appreciate the fact that the flexible and intelligent application of know-how is, in most cases, of more use than the performance of narrowly circumscribed routines. It looks, then, as if Ryle's account of training bids fair to provide us with the beginnings of an account of many kinds of workplace learning.

The Rylean version of training is much more realistic than anything offered by scientific behaviourism, however it has a serious limitation. The problem is that it emphasises practical knowledge to such an extent that the role of propositional knowledge in occupational learning is largely ignored. A Rylean could protest that this is unfair; Ryle explicitly acknowledges the role of propositional knowledge in the acquisition and possession of skills. A child learning to play chess may, but need not, consciously learn the rules and memorise them before putting them into practice in playing. But he need not, and, in any case, when he comes to play the game fluently, may well no longer be able to cite them. This does not mean that he no longer knows that a checkmate position is one where the threatened king cannot move out of check in one move, simply that this knowledge is embodied in his playing of the game or in his judgements as a spectator.[3]

Thus, in playing chess or map-reading, I display propositional knowledge behaviourally through playing chess or navigating. Furthermore, the process of acquiring these skills may well involve instruction and memorisation, together with the conscious articulation of propositional knowledge, as I make the first hesitant steps in the acquisition of a skill. Thus, I may say to myself 'that symbol means a windmill, therefore there should be a windmill one mile to the northwest over the brow of that hill'. Later, I will not do this, but will go ahead on the assumption that I will find a windmill there.

Nevertheless, there are aspects of Ryle's account that cause unease. It is true to suggest, as Ryle does, that the conscious articulation of propositional knowledge may drop out of the picture as a skill becomes embedded. The examples just given exemplify this well. It is also true that someone who does not consciously articulate the proposition may still, in a formal sense, be said to know that such-and-such a symbol signifies a windmill, even though he may not be able to describe the symbol. The problem is that Ryle's model works well for certain cases but not for others. It is a particular problem for our concerns, because the complex workplace skills in many modern processes involve a far greater contribution of technical, propositional knowledge than do activities like map-reading and chess-playing which, while often intricate and subtle in their detailed practice, nevertheless can be described constitutively through a relatively restricted set of propositions.

Many modern work processes involve a large body of technical knowledge derived from science which, furthermore, does not remain static. While much of this knowledge may be absorbed into contextually sensitive practical knowledge, it may well be that full possession of the technical knowledge requires articulation in some form or other, particularly when relatively unusual or new situations are encountered. Sometimes occupational problems will require fairly explicit processes of reasoning in which key technical propositions serve as hypotheses to be tested. When the work process involves more than one person it may be necessary, when determining courses of action through deliberation, to rehearse and discuss propositions to determine what the relevant hypotheses are, or what the most likely source of a difficulty is. In modern complex forms of activity, it may well be that a certain amount of 'redundant' skilling is built into training, that is, skills that are potentially useful in the workplace. Here the acquisition of such skills may well not have the opportunity to bed down into implicit activity and may exist for a while as an amalgam of technical propositional knowledge and relatively unformed practical skill. We can conclude then, that practical know-how, although it may account for an important aspect of many forms of workplace learning, is not adequate as a complete account.

Workplace learning as the application of theory to practice

Technical knowledge is sometimes contrasted with practical knowledge. Oakeshott is representative of those who make a strong contrast between the two. Ryle, as we have seen, is careful not to exclude propositional elements from practical knowledge. Oakeshott, on the other hand, reduces the acquisition of practical knowledge to a highly sophisticated form of imitation and assimilation.[4] Technical knowledge, on the other hand, is acquired through instruction, rote learning and reading. It is then applied normatively, the propositions learned serving as *rules* for or constraints on the carrying out of the activity.[5] The mechanical application of a recipe would be an example of applied technical knowledge in this sense. If we contrast a cook who has *practical* knowledge of how to make a dish with one who has technical knowledge, the contrast will, perhaps, be clearer. The 'practical' cook will not only be able to assemble and prepare ingredients, use timings and make measurements, but will be able to do these things in ways which the 'technical' cook cannot. He will probably have an intuitive grasp of quantities, he will have skills in assessing the quality of ingredients which are not available in recipe books, and he will, above all, be able to make changes to the way he cooks through his knowledge of the success of previous cooking of this particular dish. He will also subtly modify his recipe to take into account this previous experience and the context of the current exercise in terms, for example, of the known tastes of guests or customers. The 'technical' cook on the other hand, will only be able to apply the recipe learned from a book or other source in a rigid and contextually insensitive manner. The 'practical' cook will also quite likely have learned his skill through a process of apprenticeship, through which practical knowledge is absorbed through a prolonged process of working with a master practitioner.

A major problem with this picture is that it is a contrast of caricatures.[6] It is possible to find examples of both kinds of learning and practice in a variety of different workplace situations. One problem is that it is a poor representative of the *actual* relationship between theory and practice. The second is that neither of these models is particularly desirable for most forms of workplace learning. The kind of relationship between master and apprentice that Oakeshott describes is extremely important in a wide variety of occupations, and there is no doubt that a significant non-discursive and imitative element is present in a lot of learning that takes place through this kind of relationship. Oakeshott appears to place a great emphasis on the ability of a master to communicate with his apprentice through facial expression and gesture, and for the apprentice to have an intuitive grasp of what it is that the master wishes him to do. There is little doubt that, as such a relationship develops between learner and teacher, the implicit element in the communication between them will become more established, at least in some areas of their work together, particularly, for example, when skills are being consolidated and/or refined.

There are, however, going to be many occasions, particularly at the beginning of learning, where verbal instructions will accompany more implicit forms of teaching, and where it may also be necessary to formally test technical knowledge. This is particularly likely to be the case in those situations where the master is also a qualified workplace teacher, part of whose task it is to see that theoretical elements of an apprentice's formation are properly integrated into practice.

The model of acquiring technical knowledge described by Oakeshott would be of little value in most cases. Since he does not even describe most cases, his account of technical learning is seriously misleading. However, in seeing that it is, we will also come to understand that simple models of learning in which theory is acquired, which is then put into practice, fail to capture the subtlety and complexity of workplace learning in many contexts. To see this, it is important to examine the kind of technical knowledge that is likely to be of use in workplace situations.

In this respect, the 'cookbook' analogy is misleading. A recipe is *largely* a set of *instructions* rather than propositions. In other words, it tells the reader what to do. In this sense it is not theoretical knowledge at all, but a set of prescriptions that may or may not have been derived from a theoretical basis. Someone who is following a recipe is not putting theory into practice but is following instructions. *Theory* can be described as the propositions that provide a warrant for practices. Instructions, like recipes, are most useful for those who have a *poor* theoretical grasp, since they are for those who do not have at their disposal sufficient theoretical knowledge to enable them to construct or to justify their own practices. Theory comes in a wide variety of forms, but for our purposes, I will concentrate on empirical propositions that may serve as warrants for certain practices.

It is now well understood that theory in this sense usually exists in a complex logical structure and that one significant way of mapping theoretical knowledge is through exploration of the range of generality of different theoretical propositions. This model works well for theories that are derived from the natural sciences. In these cases, the theory usually has an axiomatic and deductive structure. Typically, the kind of theoretical knowledge relevant to technical and professional work in many kinds of scientifically based occupations, while derived from very general propositions in, for example, physics or biochemistry, is less general and is usually selected for its relevance to the task. This is not to say that only knowledge that is *directly* relevant to the workplace is selected, but it is likely that, as a body of knowledge, it will not explicitly draw upon a thorough grounding in the most fundamental principles of theoretical knowledge on which it itself depends, but will be a selection of intermediate, or derived, knowledge, which is more directly relevant to the occupation concerned; this could be called 'applied theoretical knowledge'. The more abstract and wide-ranging this is, the more applicable it is likely to be to a range of technical processes that ultimately depend on such theoretical knowledge. One may contrast, for example, the theoretical knowledge of electronics required by a computer hardware engineer with that required by a car mechanic who has to repair vehicles fitted with modern electronic devices like engine management systems. The more well-grounded and relevant such knowledge is in a worker, the greater his ability to judge when and what part of it is applicable, and to use it to support and justify his practice. The less well-grounded and relevant that knowledge, the more reliant the worker will be on rules derived from instructional manuals.

The example itself illustrates the growing importance of applied technical knowledge in modern work. It also raises questions about the amount of applied theoretical knowledge that it is appropriate to give to workers. This is not just a question of how theoretical their job is (contrast the inventor with the repair operative), but also a question of the degree of knowledge and skill that is thought to be constitutive of the occupation. Whatever the degree of this knowledge, however, it should be fairly clear from the account given, that the way in which theoretical knowledge enters working practice is not through an instructional manual, except at the lowest levels.

It is far more likely that someone with a reasonable degree of technical knowledge will be able to make independent judgements within work situations precisely because he will have guidelines and justifications for constructing his *own* solution to a problem. Putting the matter in this way also illustrates the limits of *only* learning the applied theoretical knowledge necessary for an occupation. It is precisely because *theory* is *not* a set of instructions that it cannot be straightforwardly put into practice. It has first got to be recognised as *relevant* to practice and one has to be engaged in practice to some degree before theory can be recognised as relevant to practice. This suggests that the relationship between theory and practice in learning to master an occupation is likely to be complex. If one cannot practice without theory, and if theory is useless without knowledge of how to apply it, then the two have to be introduced very carefully in order to ensure that they support each other.

The theory–practice model does, then, appear to capture some of the most important aspects of workplace learning, but it is still subject to some serious criticisms that vitiate it as a *general* theory of workplace learning. First, theory often does not take into account the contexts in which it is meant to apply. The model allows for the adaptation of theory to practice, but, when thought through, this concession obliges us to modify the account. As it is discovered that theory needs to be modified to take account of practice, this has a consequence for the theory. At the very least, the original theory is not directly applicable in the context in which it has to be modified before it can be applied. Since it is unlikely that this will only be one context, a more general point is likely to hold, namely that theoretical knowledge, even applied theoretical knowledge in the sense explained above, needs to be contextualised before it can be used. The relationship between theory and practice is more of a dialectical one than is sometimes acknowledged (Oakeshott, for example, does not take account of this).[7] Applied theoretical knowledge and practice need to be mutually reinforcing.

Second, technical theory does not take into account the social and moral nature of the workplace and the need to work effectively with others. This point is closely related to the one already made, placing emphasis on the social aspect of work. It is, however, an extremely serious point for anyone who wishes to take into account both the constraints and the opportunities provided by working with other human beings. If theory prescribes practices that the social group in the workplace finds morally unacceptable, or merely inimical to customary modes of operation, then those advocating the application of this particular theory will need to take account of these factors before they can successfully apply the theory. The third point is recognised by Oakeshott, namely that certain aspects of practice, even if they have a theoretical *rationale* need to be acquired through practice and some form of learning by example. In other words, even the formulation of the *contextual* application of theory fails to capture the fact that large aspects of the practice may be only accessible through some form of learning by participation, theory playing a relatively subordinate role. Finally, there are many practices that are not based on a clear theoretical model at all, but rely instead on socially distributed propositions and skills whose mastery depends on participation in an extended form of life. Sturt's account of the traditional wheelwright's trade captures this kind of knowledge, not usually found in epistemology textbooks, very well. Not only is the totality of the wheelwright's knowledge difficult to capture, because of its social and geographic distribution, both in its theoretical and practical aspects, but the very notion of a totality of such knowledge is problematic, because of the vagueness of its own boundaries.[8]

Workplace learning as the acquisition of practical wisdom

Given the difficulties of showing that an account of the contrast and relationship between theoretical and practical aspects of workplace learning is adequate, it is tempting to reconstrue this relationship as something different, namely as practical wisdom or *phronesis*. The Aristotelian *phronesis* model goes some way towards capturing the complexity of practical learning and works well with some aspects of activity. Moral learning, for example, which enters virtually all aspects of life, cannot take place through the study of moral textbooks. Although, as Hobbes argues, instruction in certain precepts may be an important feature of early moral learning, it cannot be the whole thing.[9] It has already been argued that the putting of rules into practice can only issue in unskilful performances if not supplemented by a deeper practical understanding. The deeper practical understanding in morals comes partly from vicarious experience but, more significantly, from engagement in authentic situations where moral considerations are salient. Since not only is each individual and each situation unique, it is extremely difficult to prescribe, even on a contextualised theoretical basis, what is the right thing to do. It may also be the case that what is right for one person is not for another.[10] Moral learning is, then, extremely difficult to conceptualise on a theory–practice model of any kind; the acquisition of moral wisdom has to be primarily practical, depending on one's social engagement and increasingly mature reflection on that engagement. Unfortunately, although the notion of *phronesis* is very good at capturing key features of moral education, its extension as an account of learning in other contexts is less clear. For, although the theory–practice relationship is difficult to formulate in a satisfactory enough way to account for the huge variety of workplace situations, it is difficult to dispense with the distinction in accounting for a wide variety of forms of workplace practice and learning. Even if one accepts, as I do not, Carr's characterisation of certain kinds of professional occupations as pre-eminently moral in character,[11] it is difficult to see that traditional professions, such as medicine, religion, law and teaching, can be accounted for without a description of their theoretical basis. Perhaps *phronesis* works best for teaching, but even here, the claim that there can be no worthwhile theory of pedagogy is highly controversial; it may be a highly contextualised and culture-specific theory, but still a theory for all that.

The other problem with a *phronesis* account of workplace learning relates to the social dimension in which practical skill is acquired. Such an account does not preclude some theoretical distillation of practical wisdom; one may, for example, give general characterisations of what, say, courage looks like in different contexts or one may use Aristotle's doctrine of the mean as a general guiding principle (although it is not applicable to all virtues), but it is primarily a theory of learning through practice in which theoretical propositions are, in the main, *post hoc* generalisations. However, much practice involves the ingestion of those practical maxims that are the common currency of the occupational group and the learning of these maxims and the putting of them into practice is a key aspect of occupational formation. Teaching, again, provides a good example of this. Take the question of how teachers come to understand what it is realistic to expect of their pupils. They will have their own ideas about this in relation to the children in their classes, but these will be affected by views that are extant within their school, their profession and the wider community about what it is realistic to expect. At one level, these ideas might have a seemingly credible academic currency through the work of researchers into psychometry or verbal deficit theory.[12] At another, they may exist in simplified and distorted form, mixed with less theoretical popular ideas about the abilities of certain groups, as professional 'common sense' or implicit world-view in Gramsci's sense.[13] Classroom or staffroom common sense will embody practical maxims gained from collective experience, but these will be filtered through academic theories about educational achievement, often distorted.

Whatever, one may think about the character and the quality of the common sense thus developed, the important point about it for this discussion is that it is not only derived from reflection on the individual experience of teachers, but also from socially diffuse professional collective norms and experience, which are ingested during initial and later training, through socialisation into the occupational group and through daily interaction with pupils and colleagues. It is therefore seriously misleading to describe the practical wisdom of teachers as if it were acquired solely through individual experience. Not even practical moral wisdom is a purely individual achievement. Although each individual must come to act virtuously in his own circumstances, it does not follow that the assumptions on which he bases his actions and judgements are solely based on individual experience, rather than collective assumptions about what is and is not acceptable behaviour, about the moral psychology of different kinds of individuals and the different weightings given to different kinds of circumstances. Much is the same for specifically occupational forms of practical wisdom which, of course, have a moral aspect.

So practical wisdom has a social and occupational dimension and cannot be understood except in relation to it. But once we accept this, then we have to acknowledge that, in many cases, there is an element of *technique* in it, in the sense that theory is, consciously or unconsciously, being applied to practice, even if it is through the operation of a highly implicit form of 'common sense' in Gramsci's use of the term.

The problem that lies behind trying to characterise workplace learning as the learning of theory and its application to practice on the one hand, and as the acquisition of practical wisdom on the other, is that neither works as a 'one size fits all' model of what is bound to be a very diverse and complex set of phenomena, in which, in some occupational contexts the theory–practice model may offer a better overall fit than a practical wisdom model, and vice versa.

Workplace learning as acquisition of the ability to engage in 'reflective practice'

The model of learning described as 'reflective practice' pioneered by Donald Schön is often used as a recommendation for the kind of ongoing learning that should take place in professional contexts.[14] Schön's account suggests that those who acquire mastery in their occupational contexts are reflective; that is to say, they have the ability to reflect in action, in circumstances where detachment and conscious ratiocination may not be possible, but sensitive appreciation of and adjustment to the nuances of the individual situation might.

Schön's account captures important elements of practical wisdom, especially the nuanced and subtle response that arises from 'reflection-in-action' which contributes to the tacit knowledge that underlies successful practice. In this sense, Schön, drawing on Ryle and Polanyi, is working out their descriptions of tacit knowledge in the epistemology of various professional practices.

There are two important aspects of workplace learning that are not given due emphasis in Schön's work. The first is that *reflection-in-action* is overindividualised, in the sense that it is made to seem as if it is primarily the individual worker alone who is learning in the work situation. This is very often not true, since the ability of a worker to learn through collective action, through the observation of the action of workmates or through *ad hoc* commentary criticism and encouragement, is also crucial to the achievement of mastery. Reflection-in-action, in so far as it describes a mode of workplace learning, needs to be expanded to take account of the social contexts in which learning very often takes place. This is associated with Schön's tendency to overtheorise the process by describing it as a process of theory construction and the worker as a researcher in action.[15] There are situations where it is appropriate to describe action as encompassing reflection, and the reflection itself as a process of theory construction and testing. For example, a mechanic will often frame a series of hypotheses concerning a defect in an engine, and will go on to test each of these in a hypothetico–deductive manner. A further stage might be the framing of probabilistic hypotheses related to the defect, weighted according to different models of vehicles.

In these cases, it is proper to describe the process of occupational thinking as one of theory construction and testing, because it may well be that this is exactly how the mechanic conceptualises the process himself. In certain circumstances, he may even verbalise the process as he carries it out, and will quite likely do so if, for example, he is working with an apprentice. It would be misleading, however, to describe all processes of learning on the job in this way. For example, Polanyi's account of the shifting of kinaesthetic attention from the object that one holds, to what it is in contact with, in the process of learning to use an implement, is not always captured by an account in terms of theory construction and testing, although there are circumstances when it might.[16] Lying behind Schön's thinking at this point appears to be the idea that learning can be modelled on unconscious theory-building on Chomskyan or Fodorian lines. The incoherence of this conception has been justly criticised by others.[17]

The second criticism of Schön's account rests on his inadequate recognition of the importance of *post hoc* reflection, or what he calls 'reflection-on-action'. It is not that he takes no account of it, rather that he takes insufficient account. Developing moral sensibility depends crucially on an ability to ask oneself: 'Why did I do that?' and this is a characteristic of someone who is serious about the moral standing of their past actions.[18] One often learns to do this through being questioned about one's actions and later learning to do so oneself. Much the same point can be made about workplace learning generally, which as we have seen in Chapter 6, has a strong moral element anyway. It is also very often the case that reflection-on-action is a collective process carried out by the work team, or by the team in conjunction with management and/or clients. Schön's account places too much emphasis on the individual and his alleged implicit theory-building activities. In this respect, he belongs to a tradition of thinking about learning that goes back to Rousseau, which places considerable emphasis on the unconstrained autonomy of a solitary or near-solitary individual in learning in practical situations.[19]

CONCLUSION

There is no one theory of workplace learning that is capable of encompassing all the relevant cases. The relationship between so-called technical rationality and practical wisdom is closer than is sometimes acknowledged, particularly in the more science and technology-based forms of work found at the turn of the twentieth century. The contrast between a technical–rational and a practical–rational model of workplace practice is misleading if it is pushed too far. Many modern work processes require the application of theory to practice, but do so in a social and moral context which requires that the relation of theory to practice is reflexive, that is to say, applied theoretical knowledge has to be linked to the context of its application if it is to be useful, and this contextual application necessarily involves the deployment of skill and practical wisdom, which in turn have ramifications for the theoretical base on which the practice is based. The analogy between learning to be a morally mature individual and learning to be a skilled worker can only be carried so far before it becomes misleading. The workplace is a major site of moral concern which cannot be ignored in any worthwhile account of workplace learning. But the learning of routines, skills and processes is not just a matter of morality, it is often a matter of applying theoretical considerations to work; this is not true of learning to be good.

Furthermore, the social nature of workplace practice, always important, has, if anything, become even more significant in the last few decades. There are a number of reasons for this. First, the hierarchical managerial model associated with Taylorism in manufacturing industries has been steadily losing ground, to be replaced by more co-operative and team-based forms of working.[20] Second, even where Taylorism remains entrenched, it is recognised that the delegation of responsibility to line workers has tangible benefits, for example in the incremental improvement of the production process.[21] A third and related point is that modern manufacturing processes require extensive teaching and learning in order for firms, especially at the high value-added end of the market, to maintain a competitive edge through the deployment of skills that may be redundant in one context but vital in another; this learning is often team-based.[22] A more general point here is that, as has often been pointed out, the demands for new learning that modern technological innovation imposes, means that there is an inevitable growth of interdependence in the deployment of complementary skills whose totality is collectively owned. These skills are most successfully used when there is a thorough *collective* knowledge of the context in which they are deployed.[23]

We can conclude from this discussion that workplace learning, if is to be successful, is likely to be context-specific, rather than the application of an overarching theory. It is likely to include the following elements: social and moral learning; an articulation of the relationship between theory and practice; specific, contextualised practice and a reflective element. A proper understanding of the weighting of each and the specific relationships between them will depend on particular cases.

Notes

1 This section owes a particular debt to the writings of Paul Hager and David Beckett, who have both made significant contributions to our understanding of the nature and problems of workplace learning, see Hager (1999) 'Know-How and Workplace Practical Judgment', *Proceedings of the Annual Conference of the Philosophy of Education Society of Great Britain*, pp. 21–34; Beckett (1998) 'Anticipative Action and its Contribution to an Emerging Epistemology of Practice', *Proceedings of the Annual Conference of the Philosophy of Education Society of Great Britain*, pp. 209–222.

2 G. Ryle (1949) *The Concept of Mind*, London, Hutchinson, pp. 40–41. Oakeshott, however, is less cautious and suggests that practical knowledge can neither be taught nor learned, existing only in practice. See Michael Oakeshott (1962) *Rationalism in Politics*, London, Methuen, pp. 10–11.

3 A similar view can be found in the work of Jean Lave.

4 Oakeshott, op. cit. p. 8.

5 Ibid. p. 7.

6 To be fair to Oakeshott, he does emphasise that all activities require both technical and practical knowledge; problems arise through his separation of the two kinds, if this is meant to be more than a distinction between two aspects of an integrated form of knowledge.

7 I am indebted to Stephen Norris for this point.

8 For a good account of the implications of Sturt's description, see C. A. Macmillan, (1982) *Women, Reason and Nature*, London, Macmillan, pp. 48–52.

9 T. Hobbes (1968) *Leviathan*, London, Penguin, Chapter 26.

10 Cf. Peter Winch (1972) 'The Universalisability of Moral Judgments', in *Ethics and Action*, London, Routledge.

11 D. Carr (1999) 'Professional Education and Professional Ethics', *Journal of Applied Philosophy*, 16, 1, pp. 33–46.

12 On psychometry, see Stephen Wiseman (ed.) (1973) *Intelligence and Ability*, London, Penguin; on verbal deficit theory, see Basil Bernstein (1973) *Class Codes and Control*, Volume I, London, Paladin; for an account of the evolution of popular ideas about children's abilities, see J. C. B. Gordon (1981) *Verbal Deficit*, London, Croom Helm.

13 See A. Gramsci (1971) *Selections from the Prison Notebooks*, London, Lawrence and Wishart; Wilfred Carr (1995) *For Education*, Buckingham, Open University Press, Chapter 3.

14 See, for example, Donald Schön (1991) *The Reflective Practitioner: How Professionals Think in Action*, Aldershot, Avebury.

15 Ibid. pp. 68–69 for example.

16 M. Polanyi (1958) *Personal Knowledge: Towards a Post-Critical Philosophy*, London, Routledge, pp. 49–68.

17 See, for example, G. P. Baker and P. M. S. Hacker (1988) *Language, Sense and Nonsense*, Oxford, Blackwell, Chapters 7, 8.

18 Cf. Christopher Winch (1998) *The Philosophy of Human Learning*, London, Routledge, Chapter 14, esp. pp. 163–166.

19 For example, J.-J. Rousseau (1762) (1966) *Emile ou l'Education*, Paris, Editions Flammarion, pp. 232–235 on the Montmorency incident.

20 Linda Clarke and Christine Wall (1996) *Skills and the Construction Process*, Bristol, Policy Press on the construction industry; G. Mason *et al.* (1997) 'Workforce Skills, Product Quality and Economic Performance' in A. Booth and D. Snower (eds) *Acquiring Skills: Market Failures, Their Symptoms and Policy Responses*, pp. 177–197; W. Streeck (1992) *Social Institutions and Economic Performance*, London, Sage; P. Thompson *et al.* (1995) 'It Ain't What You Do, It's the Way that You Do It: Production Organisation and Skill Utilisation in Commercial Vehicles', *Work, Employment and Society*, 9, 4, pp. 719–742 on motor vehicle manufacturing; Geoffrey Hodgson (1999) *Economics and Utopia: Why the Learning Society is Not the End of History*, London, Routledge, Chapters 8 and 9 for a more general and theoretical account.
21 Cf. Peter Wickens (1995) *The Ascendant Organisation*, New York, St Martin's Press.
22 Streeck, op. cit. Clarke and Wall, op. cit.
23 Hodgson, op. cit. Chapters 8 and 9.

9 Two rival conceptions of vocational education

INTRODUCTION

In this chapter, two alternative 'ideal types' of vocational education will be outlined: one derived from the consumptionist tradition of Adam Smith, the other from the social and national tradition of political economy to be found in the work of Friedrich List. This discussion follows closely on the outline of the two distinct traditions of political economic thinking found in Chapters 4 and 5. Smith wrote fairly extensively about both education in general and vocational education in particular in *The Wealth of Nations*, but List did not write at length about educational and training matters, although his work is pregnant with educational and training implications that I will try to draw out from the main body of his work. I will then consider what the issues separating them are, and what the implications of those differences are for a modern economy.

THE DIVISION OF LABOUR

Smith is well known for his identification of the principle of division of labour as an engine of economic progress. It is less clear, however, that he had an unambiguous idea of what exactly it was, and this in turn has a bearing on his views on education and training. He fails to distinguish between the following, holding them all to be characteristic features of a modern economy.[1]

(1) The first is between different kinds of production (e.g. manufacture and agriculture; between ladies' shoe manufacturing and gentlemen's).[2] Such a division has obvious advantages in terms of economies of scale and the making use of a competitive advantage in a certain geographical area (e.g. proximity to running water for water-powered machinery), but does not, of itself, have any implications for the way in which any specific production process is organised, or for the division of labour in any other sense. As List pointed out, this kind of specialisation leads to symbiosis; the concentration of machinery-making in urban areas allows for the development of agricultural machinery, which increases production so as to support a greater urban population.[3]

(2) The second is between different stages in the production process (e.g.

pin-making). This is run together with (1) at the beginning of *Wealth of Nations* and is the distinction for which Smith is, perhaps, most famous. The breaking down of a production process like pin-making may lead to a better use of the same material and human resources and hence to more rapid and cheaper production. If less labour is put into the manufacture of a pin, then it will cost less. The greater availability of pins in the marketplace will also tend to bring the price down. By breaking down the labour process in this way, the skill required in manufacturing processes is diminished. This happens in two ways: first, by the disarticulation of a series of skills, each worker does not need to be either multi-skilled or to be able to manage the articulations between each part of the process. (List was to point out, however, that this articulation would itself require complex co-ordination and, although he does not spell it out, it requires the development of a cadre of management to oversee that articulation—the 'line managers'.) Second, because the simplification of the process as a whole and the fact that one person can perform one operation many times, rather than many operations a few times, it becomes possible to allow one person to operate a piece of machinery that carries out, or assists in carrying out, that same operation many times over.[4]

(3) Finally, Smith distinguished between the *invention* of a process and the machinery for putting that process into effect (like the manufacture of watches), from putting that process into effect as in (2). This particular distinction between mental and manual labour is an extreme one. On the one hand, there is the purely cerebral activity of invention, which, according to Smith, involves 'deep thought'; on the other, the manual carrying out of the process foreshadowed by the inventor. Although we have already seen that Smith was committed to reducing the individual skill content in a production process, we can see, with this example, that he does so in an extreme way. Not only is the process of production voided of skill, but so also are the means of creating and improving it; the line workers are agents for carrying out the process of production, but they have no role in inventing or improving the artefact. This feature of Smith's account perhaps gave most weight to Marx's account of alienation. Through becoming divorced from any creative activity in production, man loses his species essence, which is to plan and to make according to a plan.[5]

There is, however, no logical reason why a line worker should not be an inventor or an improver, Smith just did not seem to attach any significance to his acting in this role. The role of invention, too, seems to be one of making a qualitative leap from no artefact to artefact, rather than the slow application of incremental improvements to both the product and the process of its manufacture.[6] The example does not explain Smith's relative inability to account for technological development through his economics, but does show that he seemed to work with a somewhat limited idea of technological innovation and how it comes about. Although the divorce of physical from mental work in the division of labour in the second sense is not a logical consequence of the process division of labour, it appears to follow naturally from it if one assumes that the mental component of labour is the *prior planning* of an activity. (This appears to be Marx's as well as Smith's view, although it is noticeable that it was not apparently shared by Gramsci.[7]) If, on the other hand, one assumes that there is an intellectual or mental component to everyday work processes, then it by no means follows that the process division of labour implies the total divorce of mental from physical activity. By 'mental' is not meant an internal, discrete thought process which is itself a kind of quasi-action, but the aspect of human activity that allows us to attribute understanding, diligence, care, forethought, and so on, to an activity, as well as more abstract activities like forming plans 'in one's head'. All of these are, in a sense, as we have seen in Chapter 8, 'mental' activities although it is a mistake to think of the latter as always something purely solitary and non-discursive, or as something isolated from prior activities such as teaching and practice.

The idea that this does always follow has led to the view of human manual work under conditions of the division of process-labour as something that has no mental component, and thus to the mistaken view that the role of machinery in a total work process is simply to substitute for the human element, rather than to alter the relationship between people and the process of work and, indeed, the character of the work process itself.[8] Picturing human labour as qualitatively no different from animal or machine labour makes it difficult to see how this could be so; how, for instance, the introduction of new machinery in building may allow for new methods of production and new skills to facilitate those methods. Neither does it allow for the way in which incremental improvement may arise from the involvement of workers in the application of a technique in a work process. Smith's account also appears to completely miss the *formational* element in vocational education, even in occupations which rely heavily on the process division of labour, as did watchmaking in the eighteenth and nineteenth century.

SMITH, EDUCATION AND TRAINING

Smith developed quite systematic views about education in general and vocational education in particular. Three factors appear to have influenced his views. First, his view of man in the *Wealth of Nations* as a rational egoist. Second, his view of the guilds and apprenticeship and, more generally, professional associations, as obstacles to economic development. Finally, his perception of the deleterious effects of the division of labour on the abilities of workers. Smith deals with both elementary and vocational forms of education in the *Wealth of Nations*. I will look at his views of elementary education first.

Smith believed in a universal primary education which was not completely run by the state. There is no evidence to suggest that he thought that, for most of the workforce, education was necessary beyond that stage. This is not because he did not think that some occupations were complex and required formation, training or practice (see the example of agriculture), but because he thought that the division of labour would render such formation unnecessary for most people. The division of labour, according to Smith, as we have seen in Chapter 5, has deleterious effects on the intellect of the workforce.[9]

Shackleton points out that Smith realised that this outcome will outweigh the benefits that the division of labour brings to society, and so he prescribed education as a remedy. In addition, education allows for the development of a society alert enough to examine critically the claims made by self-interested bodies and individuals. This aspect of Smith's views of education relates to broader aspects of his political economy and, in particular, to the idea that corporate bodies and combinations of powerful individuals, acting in the interests of their members, could gain excessive power and disrupt the workings of the market.[10]

Unlike modern advocates of markets, Smith appears to take the view that elementary education can only to a limited extent be left to the market. He is clear that the failure to educate the lower classes will lead to adverse effects for the society as a whole and insists that becoming educated is not a market choice, but a necessity which should be backed up by regulation and sanctions.

> The publick can impose upon almost the whole body of the people the necessity of acquiring those most essential parts of education by obliging every man to undergo an examination or probation in them before he can obtain the freedom in any corporation, or be allowed to set up any trade either in a village or town corporate.[11]

According to his egoistic account of motivation, however, it would not do for the state to provide a full salary for teachers, as they would then have no incentive not to neglect their duty.[12] The elementary system envisaged by Smith is regulated by the state, but only partly financed by it. It has, as its primary aim, the preparation of citizens able to provide some resistance to the power of commercial combinations.[13]

When we turn to his account of the appropriate form of vocational education for the mass of the common people, we find that his suspicion of corporate bodies led him to view some kinds of educational institutions with considerable suspicion. This was true of the old universities and of guilds (with their associated system of apprenticeship), which he argued acted to control the labour supply and to bid up the price of labour. There were, then, two reasons why extended education would be unnecessary for the mass of the people, at least as far as their ability to contribute to economic life is concerned. First, elaborate and long-drawn-out approaches to vocational education and training distorted the working of labour markets. Second, because advances in the division of labour rendered the skills that they developed redundant in most cases.

Since people act out of individual self-interest, then it may be in their interests to set up institutions which interfere with the workings of the market. Employer combinations, trades unions and occupational guilds are all examples. Smith is especially hostile to the guilds and their system of vocational education. He sees apprenticeship as promoting idleness, economic conservatism and the bidding up of labour prices beyond the market clearing rate.

The institution of long apprenticeships has no tendency to form young people to industry. A journeyman who works by the piece is likely to be industrious, because he derives a benefit from every exertion of his industry. An apprentice is likely to be idle, and almost always is so, because he has no immediate interest to be otherwise. In the inferior employments, the sweets of labour consist altogether in the recompense of labour. They who are soonest in a condition to enjoy the sweets of it are likely soonest to conceive a relish for it, and to acquire the early habit of industry. A young man naturally conceives an aversion to labour when for a long time he receives no benefit from it. The boys who are put out to apprentices from public charities are generally bound for more than the usual number of years and they generally turn out to be very idle and worthless.[14]

(It should be noted that Smith is talking here about a particular type of apprentice who most certainly could not be considered typical of the range of apprentices.)

One can see here key Smithian themes concerning self-interest, one's short-term conception of what it is, and, following from these, the need for rewards to be immediate if they are to promote industrious habits. In addition, he was sceptical about the need for skilled labour, arguing that the division between mental and physical forms of labour meant that the need for skilled labour would be relatively limited and confined to such tasks as invention, in contrast to the period preceding the discovery of the division of labour, when jobs like those of agricultural workers were relatively complex.

The first invention of such beautiful machines, [clocks and watches CW] indeed, and even that of some of the instruments of work employed in making them, must, no doubt, have been the work of deep thought and long time, and may justly be considered as among the happiest efforts of human ingenuity. But when both have been fairly invented and are well understood, to explain to any young man, in the completest manner, how to apply the instrument and how to construct the machines, cannot well require more than the lessons of a few weeks; perhaps those of a few days might be sufficient.[15]

Thus, the division of labour in senses (2) and (3) can be seen to have, among its other effects, the decline in a need for skilled labour, except certain kinds of mental labour, which would require very few people. This effect has another, for economists of liberal bent, pleasing consequence. Since there is no requirement for vocational education and training, there is no need to provide it either, so the inconvenient problem of providing public goods which cannot be provided through individual action is obviated.[16]

Unfortunately, as with his account of pin-making, Smith's account of watch-making, even when carried out under the process division of labour, bears little resemblance to the situation found in the eighteenth, and even less to that found in the nineteenth, century. Marshall, in his account of late nineteenth century manufacturing, looks quite closely at watch-making and finds that, although reliant on a process division of labour, manufacturing the components required a 'highly specialised manual skill, but very little judgement'. Those who finish and put together the component parts of a watch must always have a highly specialised skill. However, the introduction of machinery, while rendering many of the old skills obsolete, introduces a new factor into the division of labour, namely a less skill-specific set of abilities and an energetic sense of responsibility, which together 'go a long way towards making a fine character'.[17]

The example well illustrates the depth of commitment that is required in so many skills, even in a highly specialised process division of labour, when many components of a trade are mechanised. It also illustrates an important require-ment for effective thinking in this area, namely an appreciation of the detail of how a particular occupation is organised, rather than an *a priori* vision of how it should be organised, then translated into a pseudo-factual account, as we find in Smith, in order to develop a particular, tendentious, view of vocational education and training.

The outline of a Smithian system of vocational education and training can, therefore be summarised as follows:

1   The provision of a substratum of primary education to ensure basic literacy and numeracy.
2   The development of a higher system of education for those who are likely to be inventors and engineers (although even this is problematic).
3   The provision of On the Job Training (OJT) for unskilled and semi-skilled work when there is a market demand for the relevant products.

We can see how, in terms of the framework outlined in Chapter 7, Smith's account of occupations and the training required to carrying them out, need, in many cases, amount to little more than a conditioning in certain competences, particularly if the process division of labour is *Taylorised*, that is to say, the pace of work in a process division of labour is organised on a production line basis. In these conditions, jobs became reduced to largely automatic performances, and in fact many of these kinds of jobs are now performed by robots, which can carry them out more effectively. Interestingly enough, Taylor openly admitted that his innovations in manufacturing were based on a recognition of an antagonism of interest between the employer and the labourer, and that the production line was a means of securing the obedience of the labourer to the work process designed by the employer.[18] Taylorism can thus be seen as a logical extension of the process division of labour as conceived by Smith in the context of mechanisation and automation.

In this type of occupational context, the use of CBET (see Chapter 7) also makes more sense. In the Taylorist environment, with a rigid division between management, innovatory and assembly functions, assembly work allows for no exercise of initiative, nor does the context of work need to vary in any significant way. The range of competences necessary for any particular occupation can be easily specified, the simplicity of the tasks involved require little or no formal training, and assessment need not be complicated by such factors as the necessity for theoretical knowledge, or the need to use personal initiative.

VOCATIONAL EDUCATION AS PERSONAL AND SOCIAL CAPITAL FORMATION

An Adam Smith model of vocational education distinguishes between entrepreneurs, workers on the line, inventors and the professions. In the work of Marshall, we see the role of the entrepreneur as manager, and management as a separate occupational category, subjected to serious examination. According to Smith, the process division of labour led to a highly unnatural exercise of human powers; in recognising this, he anticipated Marx. In preindustrial times work required a wide range of different abilities and a high degree of skill and judgement. Writing of agricultural labourers, for example, he says:

> But the man who ploughs the ground with a team of horses or oxen, works with instruments of which the health, strength and temper, are very different upon different occasions. The conditions of the materials which he works upon, too, is as variable as that of of the instruments he works with, and both require to be managed with much judgement and discretion.[19]

This description looks like an example of practical wisdom (Chapter 8). Smith appears to have taken the view, and Marx to have followed him, that the development of industrial production leads inexorably to a decline in the need for either technique or practical wisdom as significant factors in the economy, except for very small groups of specialist workers. Marx explicitly states, for example, that a form of technical education that releases the active powers of workers, can only be contemplated in an alternative form of economic organisation to that of capitalism.[20]

It seems clear that Smith not only contemplated, but welcomed, the decline in individual ability that arose from rigorous application of the process division of labour. From a narrowly consumptionist point of view, this position has a certain plausibility. It was earlier argued, however, in Chapters 3 and 5, that there are alternative ways of organising economic life, which place greater emphasis on national, social or individual well-being. It will also be argued in Chapter 11 that, even on consumptionist criteria, this is a badly conceived strategy for a society in the long term. For the moment, however, the assumption will be made that there are meaningful alternatives to the Smith model of vocational education and that they are relevant both to wider economic goals and to a more sophisticated conception of the production of private, consumable goods.

This question cannot be properly answered without a further consideration of the key feature of Listian political economy. This puts the *development of productive powers* in the centre of economic concern, with at least as much importance as current production and consumption. This means that economic policy will be oriented to the long term. The concern with productive powers is also, in consider-able part, a concern with the continuing development of competitive advantage based on long-term socio-economic as well as material assets. List was clear that this requires both state planning and institutional preservation and development in changing circumstances. However, there is an internal logic to economic development that it must be the goal of economic policy to develop.

If productive powers are developed, this implies that the general education and skill levels of the population are increased. This means in turn that appropriate levels of skill are available to create certain kinds of goods and services, and that there are consumers who can purchase them. A couple of examples make this clearer.

(a) An illiterate and innumerate population cannot support a large printing and information diffusion economy. On the other hand, the existence of a numerate and literate population will create a demand for such products, not just for leisure consumption, but also as a way of improving production processes.

(b) An agricultural economy may support an industry producing agricultural machinery, agricultural chemicals and research stations, provided that there is sufficient knowledge within the agricultural sector to make use of the products available. Where there is such a population, it will itself create new demands.

Important as these considerations are, I wish to draw attention to them at the moment only in order to focus on the consequences of operating an economy that relies both on skilled, educated workers and on the production of high value-added, sophisticated goods and services. Central to the idea of work in such a context is that of seeing it, at least to a certain extent, as constitutive of what one wishes, as a human being, to be. One of the most important results of the individual exercise of autonomy is precisely the choosing of an occupation. Such a choice should be one that accords with one's individual conception of one's own well-being and, in the context of weak autonomy discussed earlier, should also involve, in some way, the development and release of one's active powers.

Choice of an occupation and choice of what one is to be and the goals which one wishes to pursue in life are, therefore, on this conception of an occupation, tightly bound up with each other. Essentially the notion of an occupation involves some kind of long-term commitment to a particular way of life. The idea of a vocation or 'calling' in life is central to this particular conception of vocational education. Occupations are classified in various ways, the classification relating, not only to the level of skill, knowledge and understanding involved, but also to such factors as the nature of professional formation, the strength of organisation of worker's interests, the social status of the occupation and the kind of pro-fessional closure operated to regulate the labour market. In this chapter I also wish to interpret the term 'occupation' in a very broad sense to include productive, but not necessarily directly remunerated, activities. Their lack of remuneration neither entails that they are not preceded by some form of vocational education nor that they should not be.

The first group of these activities are those that are perhaps most suitably known as *vocations*. They have two important characteristics. First, their prime goal is the well-being of other people. Second, it is difficult to achieve the highest standards of excellence without devoting a considerable amount of one's life to their dedicated pursuit. Among these vocations can be discerned: religious ministry, medicine and related occupations, teaching and child-rearing. There is a secondary kind of vocation which does not necessarily involve the well-being of others as a major goal, but the achievement of high standards in some recognised activity: various forms of literary, scientific, artistic, and aesthetic activity come into this category. Like the first group, they are characterised by the length of time and dedication necessary to practice them successfully. It is important to realise, however, that any occupation can become a vocation if it acquires, for the person who practices it, a primary focus *either* on service for others *or* on the trade itself, or for both.

There is a group of occupations, characterised as *professions* which, in important respects, overlap with the first group. The well-being of others is an important, but not the only, or even the prime, concern of this group which include law, engineering, accountancy and various technical occupations including work which involves, for example, housing, the environment and the maintenance of equipment and machinery. This group is characterised by the presence of at least some of the following: a particular type of formation which, increasingly, is to be found within post-compulsory higher education;[21] the presence of a body of applicable theoretical knowledge; the possession of *technique* closely related to the theoretical knowledge; some form of professional closure to regulate the labour market and to discipline members of the profession.

Next there is a group of activities known as *crafts* or *trades*, which include technical activities such as construction and maintenance of artefacts (these very often include a high degree of applicable theoretical knowledge), a high degree of autonomy in the design, as well as the production of the service or the artefact, close liaison with the customer and the requirement of a significant degree of practical wisdom because of the complexity of the work itself and the complexity of the social and/or physical environment in which it takes place. They all involve some form of vocational preparation, which can include, in different mixes, formal technical education, apprenticeship and on-the-job training. They also will, to varying degrees, require formal certification of competence before they can be practised. The term 'craft' or 'trade' includes an enormous variety of different occupations which embody various mixes of these characteristics. Thus, work at the 'technician' level usually and increasingly involves a high degree of applied theoretical knowledge, together with an extensive practical repertoire and a high degree of practical wisdom in order to operate in a complex environment. 'Craftsmen' very often require developed aesthetic sensibility and the ability to design, which is integrated with various complex practical activities that involve close practical acquaintance with the raw material worked upon.

Crafts such as furniture-making, pottery or landscape-gardening not only require a high degree of skill in execution, but also imply artistic judgement and a degree of autonomy in conception, as well as execution. The product of a craftsman may or may not be utilitarian in function, but it almost always has an aesthetic or even an artistic dimension to it.[22] In this sense, a craftsman designs and creates as well as makes. His role is to put into effect a plan which he has made and to modify that plan as he carries on with his work. As Marx might have said, in this way he is acting in a distinctly human fashion or in accordance with his species nature.[23] Naturally, his ability to plan will be constrained by commercial considerations; his client will very often give him specifications which he has to work to and, at the very least, in order for him to be able to survive from his occupation, he will need to take account of the needs and tastes of potential customers. A craftsman might work within a tradition of manufacture often centuries old, with its own lore, values and culture. These he needs to master if he is to be successful. He needs to know and to care about the materials with which he works. He needs to have a feel for what is right and appropriate in the aesthetic sense.

> A cabinet maker who is also a craftsman, will, generally, be horrified at the suggestion of using screws to secure joints even if the objection to using them has little functional relevance, and within limits, even if it is counter-functional. They will think of it as a kind of violation of their materials, for if they are a craftsman they will care for the wood in ways which are not reducible to its functional properties, although it cannot be entirely independent of functional considerations either.[24]

He also needs to know about the kind of people to whom he sells what he makes; their own values and traditions, as well as their needs and desires. The pursuit of a craft occupation can be deeply fulfilling and, some writers would argue, a vocation in itself, involving a process of self-realisation through the work.

Trades as opposed to crafts are very often indistinguishable from what I have called crafts, in terms of formation and certification, but they have certain characteristics that differentiate them from crafts. Trades such as plumbing, printing or bricklaying are more obviously utilitarian in nature and lack a significant degree of artistic scope or autonomy in conception when compared with most crafts, but may, nevertheless, demand high degrees of skill and a certain amount of knowledge. For this reason, they are often thought to demand *training* rather than education. Like crafts, however, they exist within traditions, often of great antiquity, with their own culture and values. Like craftsmen, tradesmen, if they are to be good at and respected for what they do, need to care deeply about the task in hand, about the materials they work with and about the people they work for. In addition, they need to be prepared and able to solve a series of practical problems, often of a quite demanding nature and this requires not only knowledge, skill and experience, but also a kind of intellectual resilience and persistence that allows them to triumph against often adverse conditions and circumstances.

Good tradesmen also develop ingenuity, or the ability to solve seemingly intractable problems with quite simple and effective solutions. It is notorious that there are tradesmen who have none of these things, but it is less often asked why there are so many lacking in these desirable attributes and whether or not the education and training they receive may not have some bearing on the quality of their work as tradesmen and their attitudes towards the trades that they practice. Craftsmen and tradesmen alike need a good grounding in both literacy and numeracy in order to solve the kinds of problems that characterise their trades and in order to administer their affairs. They, like those who follow a more overtly liberal route in their education, need such a grounding if they are to be effective. But they need more than this; an acquaintance and identification with the values, traditions and history of their occupations makes them what they are, people who take a pride in being tradesmen of a certain kind. Very often these aspects of formation have important practical effects. Knowing the history of one's trade, for example, enables one to solve practical problems that have their origins in work carried out earlier on the installations on which they are working. The resilience and ingenuity spoken of earlier does not just arise from personal characteristics, but also from working with more experienced tradespeople and acquiring the values and attitudes of mind as well as the procedures that allow seemingly intractable problems to become tractable. In these respects, the acquisition of applied technical knowledge is only a component of an educative process that must include an induction into both the formal and informal traditions and history of the trade. It must also include a work-specific moral formation and related development of practical wisdom that, while it builds upon earlier moral education, involves inculcation into the particular traditions of loyalty, respect, patience, persistence and so on, that characterise excellence within that particular trade. As argued in Chapter 7, the notion of competence as it is deployed in CBET is quite inadequate to characterise the complexity of this kind of vocational formation.

The occupational categories described above need to be distinguished from particular periods of employment that anyone engaged in them may be involved in. Naturally, there will occur employment-specific formation or short-term training, even within highly organised occupational and internal labour markets (see Chapter 10), but it is a characteristic of these types of occupation that there is a considerable 'front-loading' to their professional formation. Because of the complexity of the occupation and its traditions, together with the moral aspect of formation, which affects the formation of character, it is likely that vocational formation will occupy a significant part of an individual's early life. This does not, of course, preclude continued professional formation and job-specific training, but the lengthy and intense nature of the initial formation has profound implications for the much-vaunted idea of 'labour-market flexibility', particularly when it is applied to 'high-skill' occupations (see Chapter 10).

The Smithian training model or its modern counterpart, CBET, has few of these features, or, if it has them, does so to a limited degree. It is precisely these features of vocational *training* as opposed to vocational *education* that make it suitable for economies organised on a low-skill basis, which also rely heavily on 'flexible', largely general labour markets. The relationship between lack of skills and labour market flexibility, together with its implication for conceptions of the common good, will be examined more fully in Chapter 11.

It can now be seen how forms of vocational education that are predicated on a 'social capital' or 'productive powers' model of operating economic life have a significant liberal component. First, they are based on the idea of *autonomy*, a decision to engage oneself in one of them entails the choice of a significant way of pursuing the good within the context of the values and priorities of one's society. Vocational formation also gives one the means of pursuing that vision of the good, together with furnishing one with the means to pursue other aspects of the good in one's life, namely family, personal social and charitable objectives. Second, vocational formation in this sense entails features that are common to liberal forms of education, namely a strong and continuing grounding in literacy and numeracy and basic useful information about one's society. Third, like scientific forms of liberal education, formation in this sense also includes a considerable amount of theoretical knowledge, albeit *applied* theoretical knowledge. Finally, like liberal education, it includes a strong and continuing element of moral education, and, particularly in some occupations, a strong element of *aesthetic* education.

CONCLUSION

A comparison of the political economies of List and Smith (Chapters 4 and 5) suggests not only widely differing views concerning the way in which an economy should be run, but also concerning the development of vocational education and training (VET). How VET is seen is bound up with questions about how people are motivated, what kinds of social conditions are necessary to motivate them and the general relationship between economy and society. Therefore, the changing of a VET system, just like the changing of an education system more generally, is dependent upon and also has ramifications throughout society and politics. It cannot be a simple matter of a technical recipe to aid economic growth, but touches on the heart of what any society is about. To conceptualise an economy in the Listian way as a *political* economy, is to make vocational education a central feature of society and furthermore, a kind of vocational education which has strong liberal overtones, in contrast to the utilitarian, Smithian model.

In terms of the distinctions made in Chapters 7 and 8, the Smithian model conceptualises learning in terms of training or drilling for nearly all forms of non-professional employment, together with a traditional liberal education, supplemented by practically-based professional formation for the professions, inventors, proprietors and the leading strata of society. The Listian model would not be so directly prescriptive, but would involve different mixes of the different kinds of approaches to learning outlined in Chapter 8. For some, drilling or training would be most important. For most others, although training in technique would be important, so also would an element of theoretical education which would be contextualised within training in technique through simulation, but which would also be embedded in practice through real work situations, so as to develop both the elements of practical wisdom and the ability to reflect during and after work processes in order to further develop expertise. Such complexity would only apply to professional work on the Smithian model.

The institutional implications for vocational education on the Listian model are clear, even if the precise details for each occupation are likely to vary. Elements of college-based work that would encompass both theory and technique through simulated activity would be supplemented by periods of mentored and assessed work practice in the workplace, that would ensure the embedding and development of occupational knowledge through practice in realistic conditions.[25]

The choice of a particular form of vocational education and training is, then, a consequence of larger political choices concerning how society should be run and what conception of human flourishing should be pursued within that society. As to the institutional forms which such a liberal form of vocational education can take, there is no one answer, although the arguments of Chapters 6, 7 and 8, together with this chapter, suggest that a significant element of work-based learning is absolutely indispensable. Chapter 15 will be particularly devoted to this question.

Notes

1 These distinctions owe much to the work of G. Williams (2000) *Wealth Without Nations*, London, Athol Books, Part II.
2 A. Smith (1981) *The Wealth of Nations*, Indianapolis, IN, Liberty Fund, Chapter 1.
3 List (1991) *The National System of Political Economy*, NJ, Augustus Kelley, Chapter XX.
4 As G. Williams, op. cit. has convincingly shown, however, it is historically incorrect to suppose that the process division of labour arose under free market conditions. It was, in fact, a product of state and guild regulation of manufacture, not of the market and free trade.
5 Marx (1970) *Capital*, London, Lawrence and Wishart, p. 178; 1858, pp. 87–88.
6 Peter Wickens (1995) *The Ascendant Organisation*, New York, St Martin's Press, Chapter 2.
7 A. Gramsci (1971) *Selections from the Prison Notebooks*, Q. Hoare, G. Nowell-Smith (eds), London, Lawrence and Wishart, pp. 8–9.
8 Cf. L. Clarke and C. Wall (1996) *Skills and the Construction Process*, Bristol, Policy Press.
9 Smith, op. cit., Volume 2, Book V, Chapter 1, p. 782
10 J. R. Shackleton (1976) 'Adam Smith and education', *Higher Education Review*, Spring 1976, pp. 80–90, p. 81.
11 Smith, op. cit. Bk. V, p. 786.
12 Ibid. p. 785.
13 It is interesting to note how measured were Smith's views of the nature and provision of education in comparison with his contemporary neo-liberal followers. See James Tooley (1998) 'The Neo-liberal Critique of State Intervention in Education: A Reply to Winch', *Journal of Philosophy of Education*, 32, 2, pp. 267–282.
14 Smith, op. cit. p. 139.
15 Smith, op. cit. pp. 139–140.
16 Public goods are here defined in terms outlined by Orchard and Stretton (1994) *Public Goods, Public Choice and Public Enterprise*, London, Macmillan, as a form of social capital even when, as in the case of training, they are consumed privately. It is their transfer-ability as well as their social benefit that are important.
17 The quotation occurs in Marshall (1890) *Principles of Economics*, eighth edition, London, Macmillan, p. 214, the account of watchmaking, pp. 213–215.

18 For evidence of this point of view, see Frederick Taylor (1911) *The Principles of Scientific Management*, New York, Norton, p. 21.

19 Smith, op. cit. p. 143. It should be noted that Smith is here making a polemical point against the apprenticeship system, arguing that manufacturing trades located in towns do not, with the system of the division of labour, require a multiplicity of skills. List, on the other hand, argued that it was only with the introduction of manufactures that the work of the agricultural labourer became complex and demanding, cf. List, op. cit.

20 Marx, op. cit. pp. 483–484.

21 For a good account of how some para-professions made the transition to degree-level entry qualifications, see L. Merriman (1998) 'Degrees of Difference', unpublished PhD thesis, University College, Northampton.

22 I am using this distinction in a similar way to that used by David Best (1992) *The Rationality of Feeling: Understanding the Arts in Education*, London, Falmer, Chapter 12 in particular.

23 Cf. Marx, op. cit. p. 178.

24 Raimond Gaita (1991) *Good and Evil*, London, Macmillan, pp. 86–87.

25 See the account of the German 'Dual System' in Chapter 15.

10 Education and labour markets

INTRODUCTION

The importance of labour markets to vocational education

The theory of labour markets does not seem an obvious concern for a book on the philosophy of vocational education. However, one cannot consider the aims of vocational education and its fundamental ethical presuppositions without a consideration of how jobs are made available and how people are allocated to them. Labour markets, broadly speaking, are the mechanism whereby people are matched to paid employment. One cannot consider vocational education in the sense that we have, as a preparation for life in work, without at the same time considering the relationship between education and allocation to work, and to do this it is impossible to avoid looking at these allocative arrangements in their wider context. It will be argued that a labour market or, if one prefers, a set of procedures for matching individuals to jobs and occupations, needs to be planned and regulated if it is to build and maintain social capital and to provide occupations that constitute part of a worthwhile life. A society also has a duty of care, to give young people the opportunity to choose occupations that they find desirable and to afford them a good chance of having those choices fulfilled. The complete case cannot be made out in this chapter alone, but will require argument in the next to complement it.

There are two aspects to the relation of an individual to the labour market. The first, and the one that will most concern us, is employment at the start of working life. The second is concerned with movement from one job or occupation to another in the course of working life.[1] It has been argued that vocational education is a preparation for working life and this definition entails that one needs to take into account its three main features. The first is general preparation for a life in work; the second is concerned with the occupation for which one is being prepared and the third with the specific role that one will play within the workplace. Each of these requires different, although related, practices. Modern societies appear to handle the transition from compulsory schooling to the workplace in three broadly different ways.

In the dual model, exemplified in Germany but found also in Switzerland and Austria, young people leave school, but enrol in apprenticeships that involve continued general and vocational education away from the job. In the schooling model, found in Belgium, Sweden, Japan and North America, vocational education is provided in schools up to age 18. And in the mixed model, exemplified by Britain, vocational education is provided for young people outside the schools in a non-formal sector. Within the schooling model, it is possible to distinguish further between the separatist approach exemplified in France, with its distinct vocational schools, and the integrated model found in Sweden, where academic and vocational education are combined within one institution (the two types are, however, separately streamed and pupils are largely confined to one or another stream).[2]

These different models of the transition from school to work suggest fundamentally different approaches to the relationship between adolescence and adult working life. In the dual model, experience of work in employment or quasi-employment is an integral part of this transition, and, in order for it to be successful, planning for the availability of jobs is part of the process of managing the transition. The schooling model presupposes the existence of academic qualifications that indicate a readiness to enter the labour market. The mixed system, while adopting some of the features of the first two, also provides a market-based, largely voluntary, set of options for the school leaver, which include direct entry on to the labour market, apprenticeship, or some form of attachment to an enterprise through which vocational qualifications are gained, or enrolment at a specialist college, after which the student enters the labour market. The labour market is, then, a critical mediator of the transition from adolescence to adult life and young people's initial experience of it is likely to colour their attitudes to work and the transition from one job to another.

LABOUR AS A COMMODITY: THE CLASSICAL ANALYSIS

Modern capitalist societies are characterised by largely private ownership of the means of production, and on the exchange of commodities in market conditions. In addition, their aims are mainly, if not always exclusively, concerned with the maximisation of the private consumption of commodities, and these aims, it is fair to say, are identified with by a very large proportion of the population. In a capitalist system *labour*, or more strictly *labour power* or the potential for work, is a commodity owned by individuals and contractually transferable to an employer.[3] Of course, individuals can and do work for themselves, but in modern societies, the largest section of the population depends for its livelihood on the sale of its labour power.[4]

It is important to realise that the employee sells labour power, theoretically at least, to be disposed of as the employer wishes; it is not the *product* of the employee's labour that is sold. The issue of managerial control over all aspects of the work-place is very important for an understanding of the place of work in societies like ours. For labour power to be treated as a commodity, there must be labour markets which, initially at least, allocate workers to jobs and define the terms under which they are pursued. It is important to understand two features of labour markets in modern societies which have contributed towards the antipathy that is often found towards vocational education. First, vocational education as a preparation for successfully bargaining on the market to sell one's labour power appears as something essentially undignified. Not only has one to engage in bargaining about something that is as personal as one's interests and abilities, but one has little choice but to do so in order to earn a living. The constrained nature of entry on to the labour market not only appears to rob us of our human dignity, it also appears to deny the liberal ideal of preparation for a life of leisure and self-cultivation. Matters are made worse by the nature of the bargain struck in the labour market, which involves the surrender of control of one's creative abilities to another who has paid for them.

Some forms of labour market do rob individuals of their dignity and a sense of control over the most important parts of their destiny, but it is misleading to think that recognition of necessity and of the requirements of others is necessarily alienating or degrading. It will be argued that such a recognition is a fundamental part of what it is to play a full part of society and thus an essential part of education. The conditions for its achievement, without loss of dignity or sense of control over a fundamental part of life, depend in large part on the way in which labour markets are organised. There are, from the point of view of human dignity and the possibility of leading a fulfilling life, some ways of doing this that are better than others.

Say's Law and the labour market

Say's Law, which states that demand always (eventually) matches supply, is a fundamental idea of modern 'supply-side' economics.[5] In an ideal world, demand should call forth supply. In practice, however, there are various institutional bottle-necks that prevent supply coming into equilibrium with demand through the operation of the market. In terms of labour, it is very often complained that combinations of employees in trades unions or craft guilds regulate the supply of labour in order to keep up its price. Adam Smith also claimed that there is something fundamentally corrupt about employee or professional or craft control over the supply of labour, as it will inevitably be concerned with the self-interest of producers rather than the needs of consumers.[6] The solution is, therefore, to 'free up' the supply side of the labour market in order to ensure that such self-serving interests do not adversely affect supply. When this has been done, Say's Law will ensure that labour that enters the market will be employed at an equilibrium price (that is, the price at which it is worthwhile for the employer to take on labour and in the interests of the potential employee to do so.[7] Say's Law applied to the market in labour, claims that demand will match supply, and since labour is a commodity, then a given supply of labour will (eventually) be met with a corresponding demand. This is a very different claim from another, namely that price adjusts itself to supply. This is a corollary of Say's Law, given a level of supply and a level of demand for labour, a price will be found at which the employer will find it worthwhile to take it on. That price will depend on the scarcity of labour. There is, of course, a possible price at which an employer may be prepared to hire labour but at which it is not worth the while of the prospective employee to supply it, for example, if the wage does not meet the needs of subsistence. We know from Marx that, historically, the demand price can fall below what is necessary for the subsistence of workers and their families. Furthermore, as Marx pointed out, it is in the interests of employers to maintain an excess of labour in the marketplace, in order to bid down its price (what he called the 'reserve army of the unemployed'). This requirement lives on in modern economists' notion of the NAIRU or 'non-accelerating inflationary rate of unemployment' or the maximum level at which employment can exist without leading to inflationary wage pressures.[8] This feature of labour markets has profound consequences for the prospects of someone who has to consider entering one. First, it appears to exclude any measures that constrain the supply of labour, such as conditions of entry. This implies a certain hostility to the dual system, since that seems to entail that the number and nature of jobs in certain occupations have to be planned in order that work placements are available. Formal work-based learning implies another kind of regulation, namely the compulsory funding of work-based education through some form of levy. This could be seen as imposing unacceptable costs and constraints upon firms operating in a free market. Schooling also poses a threat to the free operation of the labour market if it is associated with accreditation necessary for entry to some labour markets. The mixed system, with a strong degree of informality concerning entry to employment, seems to be the approach most suited to their unconstrained operation.

Within such a system, entry is based on attempts to second-guess the likely demand for certain forms of labour. Even if Say's Law held true in labour markets, it would not guarantee that someone would find employment in their chosen occupation at a rate which would recoup the costs (including opportunity costs), of prior education and training and which would provide satisfactory remuneration. In practice, individuals and their families will try to assess what the demand for their skills and knowledge is likely to be, on the basis of imperfect knowledge. Marshall describes this process in a nineteenth-century context:

> Most parents are willing to do for their children what their own parents did for them; and perhaps even to go a little beyond it if they find themselves among neighbours who happen to have a rather higher standard. But to do more than this requires, in addition to the moral qualities of unselfishness and a warmth of affection that are perhaps not rare, a certain habit of mind which is as yet not very common. It requires the habit of distinctly realizing the future, of regarding a distant event as of nearly the same importance as if it were close at hand (discounting the future at a low rate of interest); this habit is at once a chief product and a chief cause of civilization, and is seldom fully developed except among the middle and upper classes of the more developed nations.[9]

But the problems of second-guessing the market are likely to be even more problematic in the contemporary context where, we are often told, occupations are changing with exponential rapidity. There are strong reasons for thinking that giving people little or no alternative to a free market for the selling of their labour power is open to serious moral objections. Of course, in a free society, there must always be opportunities for those who wish to take their chances on an informal labour market, rather than running the risk of training for an occupation which they then find unsuitable. But this does not absolve societies from catering for the interests of those who wish to make secure and worthwhile investments in their futures. In order to prepare for worthwhile employment, individuals and their families have to make extensive commitments to preparation for life in employment. There is an inevitable 'front-loading' about vocational education in the sense that, in order to prepare for entry into the labour market for skilled occupations, it is necessary to acquire not just a basic general education, but some of the occupation-specific skills, attitudes and knowledge that are required in the chosen field. Without a job guarantee at the end of such a period of preparation, there is the risk that effort and time will have been wasted.

Without some form of planning or regulation it is very often difficult for business people who operate in the market to predict future trends in employment. It is far more difficult for individuals and their families, who do not have any specialist knowledge concerning the workings of the labour market. Essentially to buy one's way into the labour market through vocational education or training, is to take a bet on whether or not there will be relevant employment at the end of the educational process. In economic terms, one is acquiring a commodity (personal skilled labour power) which may or may not have an adequate market value in due course. At the level of skills acquisition, the labour market is often a futures market, trading in commodities whose value will only become clear at some point in the future; a kind of market to which high levels of risk and uncertainty are attached. One is, in effect, betting that a current investment will be worthwhile in two or three years time. At a practical level, it is a hugely wasteful way of preparing the labour force and imposes a low-skill logic on the labour market from the point of view of the supplier (the prospective worker), since a low-risk strategy is to bet on the greater probability of a low-skill job without the cost of training or prior education. Neo-classical economic theory suggests that information about price and quality is transparent and available to all participants in the market place.[10]

This is patently false. It is now much more widely admitted, particularly through the influence of the 'Austrian' school of economics, that markets are not completely transparent, that they filter information and depend on local and tacit knowledge of buyers and sellers for their successful operation.[11] On this model of markets, it is the relative *lack of transparency of information* that is the key to their success. The argument is that buyers and sellers in a market place cannot cope with too much information; furthermore the knowledge necessary to handle the information that is relevant to a decision to buy or sell, is often tacit and non-discursive. For example, someone who wishes to purchase a horse in a horse market has got to rely on his often non-articulated knowledge of the signs of good and bad breeding, health or disposition of the prospective purchase. He has to integrate this with his knowledge of the seller and his business, and with his own occupational and financial priorities, before he can make a rational purchasing decision. Markets allow for concentration of the right knowledge and information in the right time and place and, when they do this, they are most effective.

However, the Austrian model relies on knowledgeable and skilled buyers and sellers who have to hand the relevant information to make a purchasing or selling decision. For our purposes, the question arises as to whether or not such conditions apply in labour markets. We have already noted the future character of the market for training and vocational education, and the fact that initial entry is by novices who, by definition, lack the knowledge and skill to make effective purchasing and selling decisions. It is true that such deficiencies may be made good by professional careers advice and by community and family expertise. However, it is still highly likely that there will be insufficient information to make an informed decision when the availability of jobs depends on larger macro-economic factors that most people will not be in a good position to understand.

Even the purchaser of a horse or a second-hand car may not have the common sense, knowledge or information to make a sensible decision, even in conditions that are favourable to the operation of markets on the Austrian model. The problems are far more likely to be acute in a highly complex national labour market, and it cannot by itself provide the necessary signals as to whether or not a particular individual should train or complete their initial education. There are exceptions to this general rule: the first is through a degree of regulation of the economy and the labour market so that reliable information about future supply and demand is available to participants. The second is where a certain level of qualification is a necessary condition for gaining employment. In this case the information is clear: if one wants to enter a certain occupation, one must be educated to a certain level.

But there is a further motivational problem for people considering whether or not to achieve a certain level of education, for while it may be a *necessary* condition to be educated to a certain level, if it is not *sufficient*, then considerable disincentives to carry on are built into decision-making. For example, lack of family or community knowledge about the availability of jobs, negative peer pressure and personal immaturity may all contribute to decisions not to go on to a further level of education. When one also considers that, where there is a lack of intrinsic satisfaction in achieving a certain educational level, extrinsic motivation assumes increasing importance, then any damage to extrinsic motivation is likely to terminate any incentive towards pursuing further education. Thus, when there is the possibility that the investment in education may not be worthwhile, since less skilled work might well be available without it, then one can see easily why many young people wish to leave school without qualifications.

It is difficult to think of a good moral reason why a society should ignore the fact that labour market signals are very difficult for individuals to pick up. Young people are expected to obtain employment that will support them, but they are potentially at the mercy of a market which may have not a particular call for their skills and knowledge at a stage in life when, by definition, and according to a well-established account of how markets work, they are in a poor position to make rational decisions on the labour and training market.[12] Considerations of elementary morality suggest that relying largely on a free training and labour market at entry level is not a satisfactory way of treating young people starting on adult life.[13]

SOCIAL INVESTMENT IN SKILLS

What is the alternative, if we no longer rely on Say's Law as a way of regulating the labour market? It seems obvious that there must be means of linking: demand and supply of labour; prevocational and vocational education and work-based vocational education. Something clearer than market signals has to exist in order to provide guidance into jobs. Part of prevocational education has to be to prepare people for the labour market as well as for generic forms of workplace skill. In terms of vocation, if one wishes to move away from a pure market approach it is necessary to link vocational education with a job (see Chapter 8). The obvious answer from the educational point of view is a workplace-based placement with a job at the end of it (as much for educational as for any other reasons). But there are powerful moral reasons for providing some form of job guarantee as well. A social investment approach entails that there is some management of the supply side of the economy so that full employment is attained in accordance with societal priorities about the kinds of economic activity that should be developed. The Say's Law approach suggests that high individual skilling is a high-risk strategy that will tend to lead to a low-skill equilibrium (see next chapter).

DIFFERENT KINDS OF LABOUR MARKET

There is not just one labour market. The division of labour to be found in any society ensures that labour markets are complex and segmented. Not only are there different kinds of industry, which tend to be concentrated in particular geographic areas, but there are also numerous divisions within the processes involved in each occupation, for instance between assembly and quality control. It is useful, though, to distinguish between different kinds of labour market, bearing in mind the importance of the division of labour.

The first kind is the *general labour market* (GLM), which does not deal in any particular kind of knowledge and skill. Jobs available on GLMs do not generally require onerous entry conditions. Employers are usually looking for workers who can work effectively with a minimum of training, and to whom a long-term commitment is not generally made. They work best when the skill levels required are minimal and when market conditions entail rapid hiring and firing. It goes without saying that they are most associated with low-skill sectors of the economy. Skills are either general or the job-specific aspects are easy to acquire. It is the kind of labour market envisaged by Adam Smith when, for example, he gave his (imaginary) account of the watch-making industry (see Chapter 9).[14]

Leaving aside the accuracy of Smith's account, it can easily be seen that the sort of situation he envisages is a general labour market in the unskilled work of watch assembly, without any regulation except market forces. Such labour markets in our society cater for the unskilled and the socially excluded, who must be prepared to change their job according to demand for their services. It is the predominant kind of labour market in a low-skill equilibrium (see next chapter) and is associated with one kind of flexibility—serial polyvalence—where workers are fitted, successively but not simultaneously, for a variety of different jobs. It follows that re-skilling in a GLM needs to be of the low-skill variety; there is little need for the employer to train except for the immediate needs of the job in hand. The general labour markets are not conducive to the initial acquisition of education, nor to the incremental development of occupation-specific skills and are therefore unlikely to be the driving force in a social capital model of the economy.

The second kind of labour market is the *occupational labour market* (OLM). Different industries, and different occupations within those industries, have their own distinct labour markets in which individuals with occupation and industry-specific skills offer their labour-power. For employers, the key market signal is relevant skill and knowledge indicated through recognised training, qualifications or experience. The occupational labour markets require more regulation than GLMs, as they rely on clear signals concerning the skill level of job applicants (and applicants need to know that their skills are relevant). Furthermore, OLMs require that there is a supply of skill and this entails that the education and training system is organised to provide it. This can take the form of the dual or of the schooling system, or a less formal arrangement whereby employers are given an incentive to train employees. The key problem is that OLMs operate across enterprises and no employer wishes to lose an investment in training to another firm. Some form of training levy which prevents free-rider activity amongst firms wishing to reap the benefits and avoid the costs of training employees is usually necessary to ensure supply.

There are distinct advantages to well-established OLMs: they provide the necessary information to both employers and employees about their mutual requirements and they provide the possibility of job movement within occupations, but in different enterprises. This allows both employers the opportunity to dispose of labour in the knowledge that there will continue to be a market for skilled workers, and employees the freedom to change jobs within their chosen occupation. Properly regulated and functioning, OLMs ensure a steady supply of relevant knowledge and skill. A system of graduated qualifications allows for individual progression within the labour market as more knowledge, skill and experience is acquired. The existence of OLMs allows enterprises to develop goods and services that have a high specification, through the availability of a skilled workforce. They offer potential employees the possibility of a secure return and a career for their investment in general education and occupation-specific skills. They do, however, require regulation and a degree of industrial and macro-economic stability in order to provide the environment in which they can provide the relevant information to employers and employees.

Occupational labour markets may be objected to by free-market theorists: they tend to lead to professional closure and artificial control of supply to the labour market, thus introducing rigidities. From the point of view of a young person considering entry into an occupation, they pose a risk of lack of return for invest-ment if the job market collapses, and also the risk of finding themselves in an uncongenial occupation. However, they provide one model of the preconditions for a high-skill/high-specification equilibrium (see Chapter 11), one which is, furthermore, compatible with relative freedom of movement for both employers and employees

Finally, there are *internal labour markets* (ILMs). These recruit from within a particular firm. They are, arguably, not genuine labour markets in the sense that job allocation takes place on a management rather than a market model.[15] Firms also need to initially recruit from outside, so the ILM needs to be supplemented with an OLM or a GLM. Internal labour markets are most suitable when there is a commitment to permanency of employment within the firm. When employers have to treat the workforce as a fixed asset, they have an incentive to use them to the best effect to give the firm a competitive advantage. The logic of this situation is to train the workforce to high levels of skill in order to develop high specification products. There is a further incentive, on the part of employees, to develop internal flexibility and to capitalise on firm-specific knowledge.

Thus, incentives can be provided in an ILM for workers to develop the range of skills to become *simultaneously polyvalent* or to be able to carry out a range of activities in short order. It encourages firms to develop team work, whereby comparative advantage is gained through the collectively held knowledge of an experienced workforce (incidentally, teams provide a basis for an educational role within the firm); it encourages employee initiative to engage in incremental improvements to both process and product and also to develop redundant skills that might be turned to advantage at a future date, and to develop an under-standing of basic principles underlying processes, which might be useful in product innovation.[16] Internal labour markets provide stability and an incentive to self-improvement for employers; they discourage movement between firms and, arguably, because of the within-firm job guarantee, encourage employers to develop a penumbra of unskilled casual workers around the core of skilled permanent employees.[17]

TWO KINDS OF FLEXIBILITY

It is common nowadays for politicians to praise 'labour market flexibility', by which they mean the absence of impediments on the supply side that are usually associated with GLMs. Yet, as we have seen, this flexibility is bought at both a human and an economic cost. Flexible GLMs have built into them a predisposition towards relatively low levels of skill among the workforce, and they often imply low pay and low levels of security. There are, of course, many people who value the opportunity to move from one job to another without a strong sense of lifetime commitment to a particular occupation, and there are many occupations that require such a workforce, so there will always be a place for GLMs in a healthy society and, indeed, in a sophisticated economy. It is quite another matter, however, to suggest that they are the ideal to which all our notions of entering and changing paid employment should aspire. It is not desirable that the economies of developed societies should be run on a low-skill basis, nor that large sections of the population should involuntarily have to endure low levels of pay and security and, in many cases, low levels of job satisfaction.

The proponents of labour market flexibility also tend to overlook the rigidity within an enterprise that GLMs tend to bring about. A low-skill, relatively uncommitted workforce is unable to provide a high level of adaptability within an organisation and so limits the room for manoeuvre that an enterprise has in organising its affairs, particularly in relation to flexible and high specification production and services. It is true that, particularly in the UK, OLMs have been historically associated with great inflexibility within enterprises: the policies of trade unions, particularly of the older craft unions, were often opposed to the innovative organisation of tasks within the workplace, but reforms to trade union law, mergers among unions and changing patterns of skill requirement and forms of production, have all contributed to a much greater recognition of both the necessity and the benefits of polyvalence within the workplace.

However, the very ability of GLMs to respond to short-term changes in supply and demand preclude them from a strong role in skill formation. High levels of skill formation, whether they take place in schools, colleges, a *practicum* or in the workplace, are a prerequisite of adaptability and polyvalence within the workplace, but successful skill-formation is a long-term process that does not happen solely through the operation of supply and demand. A modern economy needs, for reasons of material self-interest, to consider means of reducing the role of GLMs in the supply of labour. There are, as we have seen, also good moral reasons for seeking to limit their use.

CONCLUSION

General labour markets represent the purest form of labour-as-commodity and work best when they are unregulated. They have considerable disadvantages from the social capital point of view, as they do little to develop the productive powers of an economy over the long term, by their relative inability to form and sustain a skilled workforce. Their current popularity, particularly in the UK and the US, is due, in part, to a view of the dynamic of capitalism found in Smith and accepted by Marx and Braverman and, implicitly, by neo-liberal theory, namely that it will increasingly require an unskilled workforce, together with a relatively small cadre of inventors, managers and professionals to run enterprises.

Marx thought that the human element in capital would progressively diminish through the imperative of capitalist production, to create efficiencies through investment in machinery.[18] It is only relatively recently that this orthodoxy has come under a sustained and influential challenge with the increasing recognition of the importance that knowledge and skill play in economic success, although, as we shall see in later chapters, the implications of such a recognition have by no means been fully assimilated. The international division of labour into relatively high- and low-skill economies and internal tendencies within capitalism reflect this. Various commentators have pointed out that the labour element of capital has come to be of growing importance in modern economies.[19] It is increasingly the case that the skills and knowledge embodied within the workforce are a developed economy's most potent asset and that conscious efforts need to be made to sustain it. If one pillar of our conception of a worthwhile life is the possibility of developing and exercising one's abilities within a reasonably secure and well-paid environment, then economic and moral rationality look set fair to work hand-in-hand with each other.

The two other forms of labour market (internal and occupational) considered are more suited to employment that requires relatively high levels of skill and knowledge. They need regulation and commitment in order to work. For young people, they are much fairer and more considerate of the time given to preparing for work, in the sense that they are better able to provide indicators of the kind of occupations and the numbers of jobs that will be available in the future and the kinds of preparation that are necessary to enter an occupation. The most radical implication of regulated labour markets, however, is that they require not just government regulation of their internal workings, but also a development of economic activity that requires skill in the broad sense. Regulation is required to ensure that competition between employers does not impede vocational education, that professional qualifications are properly administered, and to ensure that the linkage of training places with jobs is maintained.

This latter is especially important as it appears to require some view of the kinds of jobs that are desirable if the labour market is going to work in the way envisaged. The implication is that the organisation of labour markets cannot be separated from broader questions about the structuring of the economy. Finally, there are implications that arise from economic transition and the need for large-scale re-skilling of an adult workforce in conditions of rapid economic change, which is a process that can either be left to the workings of markets or can, to some extent, be planned.[20]

These are very large questions, just to raise which will arouse a great deal of resistance among those who place a great deal of faith in a *laissez-faire* approach to economic management. The idea that educational, moral and economic ideals are linked, both conceptually and causally, suggests profoundly different approaches from those currently fashionable. Even the advocates of traditional socialist planning tended not to take seriously the role of education as a preparation for working life, let alone follow through the implications of that idea. In the next chapter these implications will be further explored through an examination of the links between education, labour markets and skill-formation.

Notes

1 In line with previous usage, *occupation* is taken to mean the *kind* of employment under-taken, while *job* refers to the specific range of tasks for which one is employed or employs oneself.

2 David Ashton and Francis Green (1996) *Education, Training and the Global Economy*, Cheltenham, Edward Elgar, p. 13

3 This account of what it is that is sold by an employee to an employer is, of course, most associated with Marx, but can also be found in earlier German writers [see Richard Biernacki (1995) *The Fabrication of Labour: Germany and Britain, 1640–1914*, San Francisco, CA, University of California Press].

  Acceptance of this account of what lies at the heart of the contractual relationship between employer and employee in a capitalist society does not, of course, imply acceptance of the labour theory of value, whereby the exchange value of a commodity is an expression of the cost of the labour embodied in it. A major problem with Marx's account is that the worker also sells knowledge and skill, which are embodied within labour power, but which are not alienated through the work process. This feature of the labour contract give an advantage to workers in a labour market which requires significant levels of skill (see Chapter 11). Marx's emphasis on unskilled labour tends to obscure this fact [see G. Hodgson (1999) *Economics and Utopia: Why the Learning Society is Not the End of History*, London, Routledge, Chapter 7].

4 Hodgson, op. cit. p. 163. Hodgson puts the figure at around 80% in many industrial economies.

5 For a definition see J. Pen (1980) *Modern Economics*, London, Penguin, p. 43.

6 See Smith's passionate statement of this view in, for example (1981), *The Wealth of Nations*, Indianapolis, IN, Liberty Fund, Book I, Chapter X, Part II.

7 A. Marshall (1890) *Principles of Economics*, eighth edition, London, Macmillan, p. 287.

8 For Marxists, the existence of a reserve army of the unemployed is a refutation of the contention of Marx that the price of labour power is fixed by the cost of its social reproduction. The tendency of this army, through ensuring excess *supply* of labour power, is to keep wages below that rate.

9 Marshall, op. cit. p. 180.

10 Paul Ormerod (1994) *The Death of Economics*, London, Penguin.

11 See J. O'Neill (1998) *The Market: Ethics, Knowledge and Politics*, London, Routledge, and John Gray (1993) *Beyond the New Right*, London, Routledge, respectively for unsym-pathetic and sympathetic accounts of the moral justification for the market.

12 By 'training market', I mean the range of options available for training as a preliminary to entry on to the labour market.

13 Much the same considerations can be applied to mature workers on the labour market who may well, like the communities and families of the young people considered earlier, also be in a very poor position to second-guess the market, particularly where disinterested specialist advice is lacking.

14 Smith, op. cit. Book I, Chapter X, Part II, pp. 139–140.

15 See Hodgson, op. cit. pp. 85–88.

16 See W. Streeck (1992) *Social Institutions and Economic Performance*, London, Sage, esp. Chapter 1.

17 See, for example, M. Kumazawa, J. Yamada (1989) 'Jobs and Skills under the Lifelong Nenko Employment Practice', Chapter 5 in S. Wood (ed.) *The Transformation of Work*,

Unwin Hyman, pp. 102–122, for an account of the operation of the Japanese system of lifetime employment.

18 K. Marx (1970) *Capital*, London, Lawrence and Wishart, Volume I, part vii; for a modern interpretation of this thesis see H. Braverman (1974) *Labour and Monopoly Capital: The Degradation of Work in the Twentieth Century*, New York, Monthly Review Press.

19 See Streeck, op. cit.; Ashton and Green, op. cit.; Hodgson, op. cit., for recent examples.

20 See Ashton and Green, op. cit. Chapter 7; F. Fukuyama (1995) *Trust*, London, Penguin.

11 Education, well-being and economic growth

INTRODUCTION

The previous chapter drew attention to the advantages, due to stability, of extensive reliance on OLMs and ILMs, and pointed out that they were grounded in relatively high-skill employment. The aim of this chapter is to look more closely at what is meant by a 'high-skill economy' and, more particularly, what is meant by a 'high-skill equilibrium'. The economic and then the moral advantages of such an equilibrium will be considered. Finally, the educational, economic and moral implications of aiming for a high-skill equilibrium will be considered.

SKILL, KNOWLEDGE AND SKILLED EMPLOYMENT

Before addressing these questions it is important to get reasonably clear about what is meant by 'skill' in the term 'skilled employment'. This is not completely straightforward, since 'skill' is nowadays used in an extremely broad and often unhelpful way.[1] The use of the word with which we are most readily familiar, is in connection with a range of activities that require manual ability, such as using a chisel or kicking a ball. Using the term in this way does not, of course, imply that chiselling or kicking do not involve any mental effort or intellectual ability, but it does seem to imply that the term has a use that fits most comfortably with physical abilities.

But, of course, the term has a wider meaning that includes what most people would call mental or intellectual activities, such as calculating or writing stories, where we are more reluctant to say that the physical side of the activity is predominant, since calculation can be performed 'in one's head' and stories can be composed in the same way and then dictated. The term is also increasingly applied to people's ability to deal with other people as in 'listening skills' and 'social skills'. This use of the term for people's social competences suggests a degree of artifice, so that one can, for example, become a skilled listener or gossip through careful application of the rules for listening or gossiping. There is, in this usage, more than a hint that there is something manipulative or something suggestive of treating people as *means* rather than *ends* in such ways of speaking, and, a connected point, a suggestion that the moral dimension of our dealing with other people can be reduced to a kind of knack. It was precisely this kind of move in our dealings with others that Socrates and Plato found so disreputable in the work of some of the sophists.[2] Finally, there is a tendency among some writers to use 'skill' as a convenient portfolio term to indicate the whole complex of physical and mental abilities, knowledge and character traits that make up one's competence in an occupation.[3]

In this discussion I shall take it that 'skill' in ordinary usage refers primarily to physical abilities and secondarily, but legitimately, to those activities that require abilities that are not primarily motor but, in some sense, intellectual, but illegitimately to social competences, moral characteristics and qualities of character. One important reason for this is that, although we often wish to say that certain skills exhibit characteristics that, in many contexts, we find morally admirable, such as persistence and painstaking care, the skills themselves are, to a considerable extent, morally neutral, they can be exercised for good or ill. Even persistence and painstaking care can be used for evil rather than good, when they are components of a skill that is being misused. Moral characteristics and those aspects of character that we call 'virtues' are not morally neutral, although there may be disputes about the extent to which a certain set of moral characteristics may be thought to contribute to a morally admirable life. There will be sincere debate, for example, about the extent to which respect for rules on the one hand and physical courage on the other, are to be prized. But it is important to keep clear the distinction between abilities and characteristics that are largely prized in themselves and those which are, to a degree, neutral.

However, it must be borne in mind that current usage among economists and labour market theorists, tends to run all these together under the term 'skill'. But it also needs to be remembered, as should be fairly obvious from the discussion in Chapter 8 on workplace learning, that many occupations require not only the deployment of physical and intellectual skills, but also abilities to work with other people and certain characteristics which can be formed, such as loyalty, trustworthiness, persistence and co-operativeness. If it is understood that the phrase 'skill' in relation to employment usually refers to a combination, in varying degrees of these personal attributes, then confusion should be avoided, provided that the earlier distinction is kept in mind. What we have in economic thinking is a term of art that has become so pervasive that it is impossible to avoid its use without causing even greater confusion.

There are also difficulties with identifying any particular job or occupation as requiring more or less skill. In practice, this is very often done through formal characteristics such as qualifications, or through classification through negotiation between employers and trade unions, and can bear little relationship to the attributes actually required to successfully perform. Adam Smith, for example, draws attention to the complexity of the work of a farm labourer in the era before farm mechanisation, when there was no question of there being formal qualifications for such a position.[4] Often, the classification of a post as skilled has been determined by the success of the holders of such posts in getting themselves so classified, and such classifications can bear little relation to the rank-ordering of occupations in terms of difficulty or ability required to carry them out.

The point, however, that the attributes required at work are very often complex and interrelated is a very important one, as it gives a better idea of the difficulty, organisation and sustained effort involved in successful performance in many occupations, whatever the difficulties of classifying any particular job, task or occupation. I take it that it is not going to be too controversial to talk in terms of occupations, jobs and tasks as being more or less skilled in content. This does not imply that there is a foolproof scale on which all of them can be uniquely ordered, or that the precise mix of different attributes can always be specified with precision, but rather that a viable system of classification is available in most cases, making use of the analytical distinctions between manual and intellectual abilities, social competences, moral integrity and individual characteristics.[5] Given that one can make these distinctions with reasonable confidence, it should be possible to classify tasks, jobs, occupations and even whole sectors of economic activity according to their relatively high or low level of 'skill' in this broad sense.[6]

One can then consider the extent to which there are advantages, economic or otherwise, involved in running an economy at a certain level of skill. It is important to the argument of this chapter that it is not taken for granted that there is only one legitimate aim of economic activity, namely the production and consumption of 'vendible commodities', but that there are also other important aims to do with personal fulfilment. Nevertheless, debates about the desirability or otherwise of running an economy at certain levels of skill do tend to take this aim, and the related one of enterprise profitability, for granted.[7] However, if the aims of personal fulfilment and social cohesion are also to be considered as legitimate, alongside consumption, then the role that a high-skill economy can play in achieving such objectives needs to be taken very seriously.

HIGH- AND LOW-SKILL EQUILIBRIA EXPLAINED

There are two broad alternative ways of running a modern industrial or post-industrial economy. Although these are presented as ideal types, they are, for the purposes of the comparisons that are to be made here, to be seen as differences along a graduated continuum from high to low skill. The term 'skill equilibrium' refers to the balance between supply and demand that results from running the economy at a certain level of skill.[8] Since skill takes time to acquire, there is usually a correlation between the amount and degree of skill and the time required. Generally speaking, the greater the degree of knowledge required, the longer the education and training period needed. A high-skill economy, which depended on highly skilled workers would, then, require long average periods of training for each worker, it would not be feasible for an individual to train for many high-skill occupations during a working lifetime. We may assume then, that high-skill economies require new workers to spend a relatively long period in initial vocational education and training and for their effort and personal cost to be compensated for through relatively high wage levels.

The cost of these high wage levels is then recouped through the greater *per capita* turnover that a high-skill employing firm manages to generate. Typically, but not necessarily, this is done through the creation of goods and services that are expensive because of the individuality and quality with which they are made.[9] Since this strategy is only possible on a large scale if there is a strong domestic market, it is also necessary that there is a wealthy and discerning class of consumers who are able to afford such products. These are the highly skilled, highly paid workers in their guise as consumers.

On the other hand, a low-skill economy requires workers whose vocational education and training period is relatively short. They do not need a great deal of theoretical or practical knowledge to carry out their work and are difficult to employ, because of their relative lack of skill, in the creation of goods and services that command a high price because of their desirability and quality, not to mention the labour (including time spent on training) that has gone into them. Since they are poorly remunerated, they can only, as consumers, purchase cheap products produced by other low-skilled workers.

Each of these situations is, in game–theoretic terms, an *equilibrium*, that is, the outcome is one which agents (in this case, firms and consumers) have good reason to follow.[10] The situation may, however, benefit one party rather more than the other, even though the equilibrium is the best that could be obtained for the second party given the choices available to the first. Thus a firm operating a low-skill strategy may be highly profitable and choose to opt for this rather than a high-skill strategy. The worker as consumer has little choice but to buy low value-added products because these are all that is available for the kind of wage levels he is able to command in a low-skill economy.

A similar situation exists when we consider the worker, not as consumer, but as potential employee. Given a low-skill orientation, the best response of the individual will be to accept a low-skill, low-wage job. The alternative is worse, namely a high risk of unemployment. This situation assumes a relatively short time-frame, in which the longer term benefits of following a high-skill strategy do not show, and a lack of choice for individual workers between high and low-skill-oriented employers.

On the other hand, a firm which considered it in its medium- to long-term interests to adopt a high-skill strategy, if, for example, it was given incentives to do so or if competitors were doing so, would employ highly skilled, highly paid workers who would also, if they existed in sufficient critical mass, constitute a reliable market for highly priced, high-value-added goods. The situation for workers as prospective employees would also be changed, as there would be an increase in the incentives for individuals to adopt a high-skill strategy in the job market.

As Ashton and Green point out, it is perfectly possible to run a successful, low-skill, profitable economy.[11] While a viable low-skill economy can be run, even in a sophisticated and developed society like the UK, the change from a low-skill to high-skill economy is not easy to make without some form of central direction. The reason for this is to be found in the interlocking sets of interests that occur in any particular skill equilibrium, which make it difficult to effect change merely by reordering one element of the relevant factors. Naturally, the model presented above is a simple one, which assumes two parties: employees/consumers and employers, a relatively homogeneous economy, a limited role for export markets and a short-term economic perspective. Change any of these variables and the preconditions for a particular skill equilibrium will change. For example, the existence of a strong export market may make it possible, provided other relevant factors are in place, for a particular firm in a low-skill environment to orient itself to a high-skill strategy in relation to that market.

However, the domestic environment sets limits to such a policy. If only one firm decides to train, then others may reap the benefits through 'poaching' their workers and inexpensively realising the benefits of a high-skill strategy without incurring the heavy 'front-end' training costs. The situation is, as Finegold points out, a prisoner's dilemma, where the dominant strategy for an employer is not to train.[12] No matter what other employers do, it is in the interest of any particular employer not to train. If others do, he reaps the benefit by poaching. If the others do not, then he does not incur the cost of training and then having his workforce 'poached'. This situation suggests that more stakeholders have to be involved in the economy if there is to be a move from a low-skill to a high-skill equilibrium, for the incentives for individual firms and employees to do so are weak. The alternative is to build up voluntarist structures of training co-operation among the employers such that default from agreements has undesirable ramifications for the business. It is doubtful, however, whether these can exist without some kind of enabling structure established by government.

Empirical research into the different skill strategies pursued by different states in different sectors of their economies is now well-established. The findings suggest that the successful pursuit of a high-skill strategy can be achieved with careful co-ordination by a central authority and that the education and training system plays a critical role in overcoming short-term obstacles to planned skill-formation.[13] Societies with a well-developed civil society, through which a sense of common purpose for both local and national projects can be mobilised, are also well-placed to pursue a high-skill strategy. Two broad routes to high-skill economic strategies can thus be found. First, one that relies heavily on institutional structures in civil society, such as has been pursued by Germany and Japan; second, one that relies more heavily on explicit direction by the state. France, Korea and Singapore are all arguably, examples of this route.[14]

A key characteristic of high-skill strategies is competition on the *quality* rather than just price of goods. 'Quality' is used here in two senses: first in terms of specification of the product and second in terms of its integrity and durability.[15] The approach typically adopted is known as 'diversified quality production' (DQP) whereby firms strive to make products tailored to segments of the market concerned with high specification, where specification is likely to be subject to rapid change.[16] Firms engaged in DQP try to develop a significant advantage through the innovation of higher specification, higher cost variations of a basic product which can be generated and discontinued quickly, according to the play of market forces, through the employment of a highly skilled and adaptable workforce. Streeck uses the example of the car manufacturer Volkswagen's ability to produce expensive 'up-market' versions of its basic saloon the Golf, during the 1970s and 1980s as a successful example of DQP.

Two provisos about high-skill routes need to be made. The first is that although it is a strategy particularly suited to manufacture in its broadest sense, it is also applicable to service industries. Second, it is not necessarily associated with DQP. As Prais, Jarvis and Wagner pointed out in relation to the hotel industry, a multi-skilled workforce can also sometimes compete effectively on cost.[17]

THE MORAL CASE FOR HIGH-SKILL EQUILIBRIA

We can now turn to the desirability of a high-skill equilibrium. There is an important distinction between the economic and moral advantages of such equilibria, but these are not entirely distinct from each other. A society that pays no attention to the relationships that people have with each other, or to the fact that great economic inequality confers disproportionate amounts of power, can be criticised for asymmetries in its power structures or the way in which it socially excludes vulnerable sections of the population. Some of the more ruthless neo-liberal theorists deny that distributions have anything to do with justice, provided that they satisfy a minimal criterion of rights constraints on acquiring property, and also deny that fairness should be a significant element in economic and social policy.[18] For such writers, the pursuit of material prosperity as the sole economic aim, provided of course that rights constraints are not violated, or that minimal prudential environmental considerations are not ignored, is unproblematic. Most societies, however, and particularly those that have adopted high-skill strategies, do not adopt consumptionism as a sole economic aim.[19]

More generally, the aims of economic policy represent a compromise among the most influential groups within a society as to their conception of the good. Since the societies under consideration consist of different groups with, at the very least, different emphases on what is good, it is not surprising that economic aims have been framed more broadly than just consumption.

The pursuit of economic success can, then, be pursued in conjunction with different aims. Even the definition of economic success in consumptionist terms is susceptible to different emphases: profitability is one, high *per capita* incomes is another, extensive market share a third. These different conceptions correspond, roughly, to the interests of employers, employees and governments respectively and while it is evident that they can come into conflict (the first two, perhaps, most obviously), it is also clear that, in certain circumstances, they can to a considerable degree be reconciled. The existence of successful high-skill routes to economic prosperity is itself an indication of this, since they can lead to high *per capita* incomes and 'shareholder value'.[20] A reconciliation takes place most readily when there is a degree of common purpose and co-ordination behind the actions of these 'social partners'.

SOCIAL JUSTICE AND THE HIGH-SKILL ECONOMY

This could be seen as a further non-economic advantage of the pursuit of a high-skill strategy. A society whose main interest groups arrange affairs so that the interests of all are to an extent co-ordinated, and which seeks to ensure that the interests of the less powerful, as well of those of the most powerful in the society, are given due consideration, has gone further towards providing for fairness than one which has not. Even on the narrow definition of distributive justice favoured by neo-liberalism, it is arguable that the corporate pursuit of harmonising aims where possible is a better instrument than the unconstrained operation of the market. One good reason for this is that distributive justice theories based on entitlement, such as that of Nozick, have major internal problems, which threaten their ability to be secured solely through the operation of market forces. The problems relate, in the first instance, to *restitution*, namely the rectification of historical rights violations, which, as Brown points out, threaten to become an enormously complicated and intractable issue for any society that takes them seriously.[21]

The second problem arises from one of the so-called 'Lockean provisos', that the acquisition of rights by individuals should not affect the interests, previously enjoyed, of others.[22] As J. L. Mackie pointed out, ensuring that the Lockean proviso is respected involves great complexities that threaten the current institutions of private property just as much as do the problems with restitution.[23] Even the strict liberal theory of rights, then, suggests that social issues and taking account of the interests of the less powerful need to be considered very seriously indeed. The co-ordination required by a high-skill strategy, even in the context of property relationships conceived of on liberal grounds, is one way of redressing inequalities of power and wealth and thus reconciling the entitlement with the restitutive and preservatory requirements of liberal theory.

On the one hand, this involves *compensation* for rights violated, through the usurpation, for example, of property at some historical period and *preservation* of those satisfactions enjoyed before capitalist forms of economic life undermined them. A high-skill strategy can go some way towards satisfying these requirements through providing increased income and work satisfaction as a partial restitution for ancestral entitlement violations and also as a preservation of enjoyments lost through property acquisition.[24] Communal and intrinsically satisfying ways of working can also be partly restored through modern high-skill forms of work. At a more basic level, high incomes are partially restorative of losses suffered through rights violations during the process of industrialisation. It can thus be argued that the pursuit of a high-skill strategy confers significant social benefits on society, and is one way of addressing a problem inherent in the liberal theory of property.

Another course is to provide direct compensation for entitlement and enjoy-ment violations through the provision of a basic income. This alternative proposal will be carefully considered in Chapter 13, where it will be argued that, from the more Aristotelian position developed here, it is a less satisfactory solution to the problem identified within liberal theorising. Although liberal theory can give rise to concerns about restitution, there are other good grounds for attending to the needs and interests of those whose livelihood depends primarily on work, and these will be the main concern of the rest of this chapter, since although the argument of the book as a whole is, of course, addressed to the concerns of liberal theorists, it is not itself derived from modern liberal or neo-liberal premises.

THE HIGH-SKILL ECONOMY AND INDIVIDUAL FULFILMENT

Important as these possible social benefits of a high-skill equilibrium are, the connected individual benefits are also very considerable. These can be classified in two complementary ways. The first are those benefits of working in a high-skill economy that lead to extrinsic non-work gain. These include, most obviously, a high degree of remuneration and relative job security and, when high-skill work leads to high productivity (itself a plausible assumption given comparative data), a greater degree of leisure and disposable time outside work. These benefits are by no means to be despised, as they allow wage-earners some of the benefits that have been traditionally valued as part of the life of the 'leisured classes', namely disposable income, the security within which to make long-term plans for the future and increased leisure in which to enjoy increased income.

At least as important, however, are the *intrinsic* benefits that accompany high-skill work. The foremost of these is greater job-satisfaction arising from the greater degree of knowledge and skill required from high-skill employment, not to mention the greater degree of autonomy, variety of task and trust that are conferred on workers.[25] In addition to these very considerable elements of intrinsic value in work can be added the increased opportunity for the exercise of workers' powers of innovation through various forms of improvement to products and processes and through the opportunities to solve problems and overcome difficulties. Since work in a high-skill environment typically involves polyvalence and team-working, these satisfactions can also be gained through working with other people and sharing difficulties and triumphs with them. High-skill work, then, often gives those who wish for it the social opportunity to work with other people and to be part of an interdependent group whose welfare depends on the concern that each member has for the others. If we consider the point made in the previous chapter, that societies have a moral duty not to waste the lives of their citizens, the provision of intrinsic value at work assumes considerable importance.[26]

It might be objected that the notion of intrinsic satisfaction is spurious and that one should only consider the extrinsic benefits of employment and, doing this, the maximisation of personal income would be the key criterion by which one should evaluate the desirability of running an economy on a high-skill basis. However, when one asks what the benefit of a large income is, then the answer can only be that it gives one the opportunity to satisfy certain of one's desires. At some point one has to admit that some desires have an intrinsic nature and we pursue them only for the satisfaction that they give us. This, however, is not as decisive a point as it at first seems, since one could argue that the intrinsic satisfaction that is to be derived, for example, from eating, comes from the removal of feelings of hunger, so that one's intrinsic satisfactions arise from the removal of discomfort. One does not necesssarily need to work in a high-skill environment to experience the removal of discomfort.[27]

There are, however, certain other important aspects to intrinsic satisfaction. As Dent has pointed out, even sensual pleasure is not just absorbent, that is the experience of removing a lack or a discomfort. It is also part of human natural history that we experience sensual pleasure through the release of our active powers. So it is also through the enjoyment of our senses, including kinaesthetic sensations, that we experience pleasure. We can, for example, enjoy the sensations of eating, running or looking at a landscape whether or not, in doing so, we are actually satisfying an appetite. 'It is clear, therefore, that hunger and a desire for gustatory pleasure are quite different kinds of desire.'[28]

Now these satisfactions are available in many forms of work, including those that might be classified as 'unskilled'. But an important dimension to intrinsic enjoyment is not dealt with in Dent's account. He distinguishes between sense-desire and passional desire, the latter being connected to ends and hence good-dependent. We desire certain things, like the achievement of a happy family life, because we have made this an end in life as it seems to us to be a key component of a worthwhile human life (I am not suggesting that this is the case for everyone). This is an example of what Dent calls a passional desire. Such a desire can be satisfied absorbatively, through passive enjoyment, but enjoyment can also occur through the release of our active powers in the achievement of it. There are two aspects to this; first the satisfaction of talking to one's spouse or playing with one's children may arise from one's experience of something that one takes to be intrinsically good (it does not involve the removal of discomfort as does the satisfaction of a particular appetite); second, through the enjoyment of activities that lead to intrinsic enjoyment, as, for example, building a swing in the garden or earning enough money to take the family on holiday. There is, then, the possibility of pleasure that arises from activities directed towards the satisfaction of passional desires, that is, not just sense pleasure, but an experience that derives from regarding the activity that one is carrying out as either contributing to a good or as good in itself.

If, then, work does give opportunities for the release of one's active powers: sensual, social and productive, then it can also provide opportunities for intrinsic satisfaction through the release of those powers and, in particular, satisfaction through releasing them through the exercise of one's abilities in attempts to do things well. To the extent that work which requires extensive deployment of knowledge, skill and exercise of character, in co-ordination with other people and, moreover, does so in an environment that provides for a degree of autonomy and trust, then it is hardly controversial to say that highly skilled work provides extensive opportunities for intrinsic work-satisfaction or *Arbeitsfreude*. Human life does not only involve intrinsic pleasure that is more than passive, through the satisfaction of sensual appetites, but also active pleasure, involving the extensive release of our powers, both those that we have naturally, and those that we acquire through education and experience.

Another important line of objection to the position developed above arises through the Marxist view of the irreconcilability of the interests of labour and capital. In the generally capitalist kind of economic set-up that has been adopted as the context for this discussion, no amelioration of working conditions will ever negate the fact that employers have an interest in degrading the working conditions, security and remuneration of employees. Therefore the idea of a satisfying high-skill capitalist economy is a utopian vision, born out of a naive appreciation of the realities of capitalism.

Marx had many powerful and valid insights into the working of capitalism. Indeed, his view that labour power is a commodity in capitalist relations of production was employed, with qualifications, in the previous chapter. However, Marx seriously misinterpreted certain aspects of capitalism and this has become more apparent over the hundred years since he wrote *Capital*. One of the problems arises from the way in which he took Britain as the model of capitalist economies in general. Britain was the first country to industrialise and the process was characterised by slow growth, a business cycle that led to significant recessions, a brutal form of capital accumulation that arose through the direct generation of capital through exploitation of the workforce and a dominant *laissez-faire* ideology that was hostile to all but minimal forms of intervention in the economy and, finally, a low-skill approach to industrial development.[29] None of these features dominated to the same extent in subsequent waves of industrialisation in Europe, the US and the Far East.

Marx made a mistake in assuming that conflicts of interest which exist between capital and labour, are necessarily irreconcilable. There are no doubt cases where they are, but the model of analysis of class conflict offered by Vico is a better model for conceptualising industrial relations under capitalism, even though it was developed as an account of the history of classical antiquity.[30] In this model, class conflict is not always irreconcilable, it can involve the temporary adoption of common objectives and even the existing power relationships. Marx's predictions that fixed capital would come to dominate variable capital (labour power) and that the labour process would require less and less skill as capitalism evolved has continued to be very influential.[31] Although there is no doubt that certain sectors of capitalist economies have evolved in this way (more so in some countries than in others), a striking feature of modern capitalism, particularly in its more advanced state, is its massive reliance on the human, skilled element of capital. New industries such as computing, electronics and biotechnology are all evidence for this and 'mature' industries in many countries also count a skilled workforce among their key assets.

It is precisely the possibility of *co-operation* between states, firms and workers, as well as *conflict* in the working out of interests that are often different, that allows for the adoption of solutions that, in many societies, gives room for the development of high-skill solutions to problems of the competitiveness and the viability of enterprises, as well as to the interests of their employees. The Marxist picture of necessary alienation of the workforce in an increasingly brutal and unstable capitalism is not, therefore, an accurate representation of reality in most modern capitalist societies. We must accept that capitalism has evolved in ways that have paid far more attention to the interests of employees and their dependants than did nineteenth century British capitalism. In doing so, they have altered the position and nature of work within these societies in ways that do not correspond at all to Marx's predictions.

In particular, we have seen an increasing variety of different forms of capitalist industrial development, each successive phase different from the previous one. Characteristic of the later phases has been an increasing shift into high-skill forms of economic activity, as development gets established and this rapid adaptation of the economy to new forms is very often accomplished through closely co-ordinated action by the state and corporate interests. The more developed capitalist economies tend to compete on quality rather than on price, and it is primarily highly skilled labour that allows this to happen. This usually involves the deepening and broadening of already existing skills, the deployment of staff in such ways that their skills are used to the best effect, and the involvement of staff in tactical, operational and strategic decision-making.[32] These factors allow staff to enjoy a relative degree of autonomy in the workplace, which may itself be a valuable personal goal, together with the relative job security that allows individuals to make plans for their destiny and that of their families.

It is not, of course, true that all modern industrial economies are run on a high-skill basis. There are three important qualifications to the general thesis. First of all, as Keep and Mayhew point out, it is more accurate not to talk of the contrast between high- and low-skill equilibria, but of a continuum of practices stretching from high to low skill. Second, different skill levels will be found in different sectors of national economies. Finally, there are some highly successful economies (in terms of enterprise profitability) that persist in taking a low-skill route. The UK and the US are commonly cited as examples.[33]

The conditions for developing skills

It would be quite wrong to suggest that economic activity has only recently begun to depend on high skill. Artisanal production in the Middle Ages, for example, depended on it, as did country trades such as that of the wheelwright, already discussed in Chapter 9. The development of mass manufacturing techniques and the process division of labour made it seem as if the general direction of industrialised societies was moving in a low-skill direction, and this still remains a viable option for some economies.[34] What, then, is distinctive about the high-skill economy of the contemporary era and why is education thought to be so important in developing it?

As in older forms of economic activity, practical know-how continues to be important. Indeed, as was argued in Chapter 8, theoretical knowledge is of no use unless it can be deployed practically. However, the increasing importance of applied theoretical knowledge in new technologies has meant that a degree of theoretical background has become necessary to the mastery of even simpler processes in the modern workplace. Mastery of this applied theoretical knowledge, or of the processes that arise from it, in its turn depends on significant degrees of literacy and numeracy.

More generally, the pervasiveness of literacy in various forms, as a means of communication in economically relevant contexts, has meant that literacy has become an indispensable work skill. Even service industries such as tourism and catering now depend on a considerable amount of background and specialised knowledge about other countries and cultures. The need for teamwork in the workplace and the ubiquity of transactions with the public in a wide variety of occupations has meant that increasing emphasis has been put on systematic instruction in various kinds of social competence that cannot just be picked up in informal situations. Finally, even low-skill activity increasingly requires a skilled stratum of middle and lower management to control the more complex environment in which firms operate nowadays. Furthermore, low-skill activity tends to lead to low worker autonomy and low levels of trust. These must be compensated for by extensive and robust management of the workplace, the most obvious example being the system of 'line-management' to be found on the Taylorised production line. Modern 'low-autonomy/low-trust' environments require relatively highly educated management to supervise them and this has meant that the persistence of low-skill sectors has often coincided with the rapid expansion of higher education in order to provide this personnel, as in the UK and the US. This tendency is often found in conjunction with the relative atrophying of the skilled intermediate level of technician or artisan worker, who can be relied upon to work autonomously.[35]

All these factors have drawn attention to the ability of public schooling systems to provide what is required at the post-compulsory level of education and, increasingly, perceived deficiencies in these areas have spurred reform of education systems. The gradual shift to high-skill economic activity has led to an increasing concern with the effectiveness of education systems in their broadest sense, so that their suitability for vocational preparation has increasingly become the major criterion of their success. This presents a challenge to educators to both be accountable to legitimate demands from stakeholders to provide what is needed in the workplace, and also to preserve the humane ideals that have traditionally inspired much of the work that has gone on in publicly funded schools. It has been argued already in Chapter 9 that this challenge can be met. In Chapters 14 and 15 the implications of meeting it will be considered in more detail.

Notes

1 For critical commentary, see for example, Robin Barrow (1987) 'Skill Talk', *Journal of Philosophy of Education*, 27, 2, 187–196; Richard Smith (1987) 'Skills: the Middle Way', *Journal of Philosophy of Education*, 27, 2, 197–202; Morwenna Griffiths (1987) 'The Teaching of Skills and the Skills of Teaching: A Reply to Robin Barrow', *Journal of Philosophy of Education*, 27, 2, 203–214.

2 See, for example, the concluding remark of the Stranger in Plato (1961) *The Sophist* in *Parmenides and Other Dialogues*, John Warrington (ed.), London, Dent, p. 225.

3 Cf. Streeck (1989) 'Skills and the Limits of Neo-Liberalism', British Sociological Association, *Work, Employment and Society*, 3, 1, March, pp. 92–101.

4 Smith (1981) *The Wealth of Nations*, Indianapolis, IN, Liberty Fund, pp. 143–144.

5 The distinction between characteristics in general and virtues an individual possesses is important, as it is generally acknowledged that the way one exercises the virtues is something that one can be held responsible for and which is under the influence of one's will. Some characteristics, such as the possession of a sense of humour are not so obviously one's responsibility, although, of course, they may be developed and may have a significant role to play in one's ability to carry out a job. For a discussion of some of these matters, see N. Dent (1984) *The Moral Psychology of the Virtues*, Cambridge, Cambridge University Press, Chapter 1.

6 Much depends on the configuration of tasks in a particular occupation. Someone employed in the industrial cleaning sector, for example, can find themselves involved in a multi- and high-skill occupation if, for example, they have to exercise a large amount of personal autonomy in work organisation, need to be able to handle and make use of complex information, need to operate effectively in a range of industrial environments and need to have the ability to develop new skills. S. Caulkin (1999) 'Arise Mrs Mopp. Drop the bucket and pick up a hand-held computer', *The Observer*, Business Section, p. 1, 12 June.

7 Related, because most economists would argue that there is a strong empirical connection between production and consumption on the one hand and profitability on the other, since successful sale for consumption, when goods are sold suitably above cost, will lead to enterprise profitability.

8 D. Finegold (1991) 'Institutional Incentives and Skill Creation: Preconditions for a High-Skill Equilibrium', in P. Ryan (ed.) *International Comparisons of Vocational Education and Training for Intermediate Skills*, Hove, Falmer Press, pp. 93–116. Skill is used in the broad sense in this context.

9 See W. Streeck (1992) *Social Institutions and Economic Performance*, London, Sage, Chapter 1 on diversified quality production (DQP), but see S. Prais, V. Jarvis and K. Wagner (1989) 'Productivity and Vocational Skills in Services in Britain and Germany: Hotels', *National Institute Economic Review*, November, pp. 52–74, for an example, in the hotel industry, where a high-skill route does not necessarily lead to the production of luxury goods and services.

10 Sean Hargreaves Heap and Yanis Varoufakis (1995) *An Introduction to Game Theory*, London, Routledge, p. 45.

11 D. Ashton and F. Green (1996) *Education, Training and the Global Economy*, Cheltenham, Edward Elgar, esp. Chapter 6.

12 Finegold, op. cit. p. 446.

13 See, for example, Ashton and Green, op. cit., Chapter 7, for a range of different societies. Fukuyama (1995) *Trust*, London, Penguin, also offers useful empirical evidence.

14 See Ashton and Green, op. cit.; Fukuyama, op. cit.

15 One could, of course, pursue each of these independently of the other, and it is arguable that the term 'high-skill equilibrium' refers to specification [Ewart Keep and Kenneth Mayhew (1999) 'The Assessment: Knowledge, Skills and Competitiveness',

Oxford Review of Economic Policy, 15, 1, Spring, pp. 1–15]. However, the question of product integrity has also historically been a major concern of enterprises engaged in high value added strategies and it can be argued that this concern is integral to a high-skill strategy when consistently pursued.

16 The term 'diversified quality production' appears to have originated in Streeck, op. cit., see Chapter 1.

17 Prais, Jarvis and Wagner, op. cit.

18 See Robert Nozick (1974) *Anarchy, State and Utopia*, Oxford, Blackwell; also Judith Jarvis Thomson (1971) 'A Defence of Abortion', *Philosophy and Public Affairs*, 1, 1 for an account of the fairness/justice distinction.

19 Cf. J. Fallows (1994) *Looking at the Sun*, New York, Pantheon.

20 Streeck, op. cit. Chapter 5.

21 Alan Brown (1985) *Modern Political Theory*, London, Penguin.

22 The issue of the Lockean proviso provides an interesting example of conflicts between will and interest accounts of the origins of rights, both of which are to be found in Locke's *Second Treatise of Government*, Cambridge, Cambridge University Press (ed 1 1690) (ed 3 1988). The will account yields a justification for property, through the exercise of labour, while the interest account grounds Locke's attempts to attach a conditional value to paternal authority, through accounting for the rights of children through proper attention to their interests (see Chapter 6).

23 J. L. Mackie (1980) *Ethics: Inventing Right and Wrong*, London, Penguin, Chapter 8. I don't, however, wish to endorse Mackie's general approach to ethical issues. Problems with the liberal theory of property have lain behind the interest of some liberal thinkers, notably starting with Tom Paine in restituting through the provision of a basic income [A. Little (1999) 'The Politics of Compensation: Tom Paine's *Agrarian Justice* and liberal egalitarianism, *Contemporary Politics*, 5, 1, pp. 63–73]. This proposal will be of consider-able importance in our discussion of the 'end-of-work' thesis in Chapter 13.

24 It is not difficult to see, for example, that the loss of clean air, water and access to the countryside as a result of economic development could, to some extent, be reinstated through such policies.

25 There is plenty of evidence for this from the studies that have been carried out into various high-skill configured occupations. Linda Clarke and Christine Wall (1996) *Skills and the Construction Process*, Bristol, Policy Press on the building industry; Geoff Mason, Bart Van Ark, Karin Wagner (1997) 'Workforce Skills, Product Quality and Economic Performance' in A. Booth, D. Snower (eds) *Acquiring Skills: Market Failures, Their Symptoms and Policy Responses*, pp. 177–197 on biscuit-making; Prais *et al.*, op. cit. on the Hotel Industry; Thompson *et al.* (1995) 'It Ain't What You Do, It's the Way that You Do It: Production Organisation and Skill Utilisation in Commercial Vehicles', *Work, Employment and Society*, 9, 4, pp. 719–742, on motor vehicle manufacturing.

26 Something of a sense of this can be found in the work of John Dewey, who refers to the desirability of personal growth and the development of social contacts, which, it seems can best be achieved in a high rather than a low-skill working environment. Dewey's account, however, seems to lack a normative framework in which these goals can be evaluated. Obviously not all forms of personal growth are good, neither are all forms of social contact. The weak autonomy framework developed in Chapter 3 does provide for such evaluation.

27 Particularly if one adopts the 'inertial' conception of disposition to action that is pervasive in neoclassical economics [M. Verdon (1996) *Keynes and the Classics*, London, Routledge].

28 Dent, op. cit. p. 49.

29 See Ashton and Green, op. cit. on comparative growth rates; Will Hutton (1995) *The State We're In*, London, Penguin, Chapter 5 on capital accumulation during the Indus-trial Revolution; A. Green (1990) *Education and State Formation*, London, Macmillan, on the dominance of *laissez-faire* and K. Marx (1970) *Capital*, London, Lawrence and

Wishart, on the degree of skill needed during British industrialisation during the eighteenth and nineteenth centuries.

30 G. Vico (1968) *The New Science*, Ithaca, Cornell University Press.

31 See, for example, H. Braverman (1974) *Labour and Monopoly Capital: The Degradation of Work in the Twentieth Century*, New York, Monthly Review Press.

32 This is a particular feature of the German economy through the institutionalised system of *Mitbestimmung* or 'co-determination' and, is arguably, one of the factors behind Germany's economic success. See Streeck (1992) op. cit.; *Die Zeit* (1998) 'Modell mit Zukunft', 22, 20 May, p. 1; Streeck (1998) *Mitbestimmung und neue Unternehmenskultur*, Hans Böckler Stiftung.

33 Ashton and Green, op. cit. quite rightly point out that this characterisation of the US does not encompass all sectors. It is evident that some of the most successful sectors of the US economy have a strong grounding in high skills. E. Keep and K. Mayhew (1999) 'The Assessment: Knowledge, Skills and Competitiveness', *Oxford Review of Economic Policy*, 15, 1, Spring, pp. 1–15, conclude that the UK situation is still based on relatively low skills, but concede that the evidence is patchy.

34 See G. Hodgson (1999) *Economics and Utopia: Why the Learning Society is Not the End of History*, London, Routledge, p. 214, for example.

35 The contemporary UK building industry is an example of this.

12 The social value of work

INTRODUCTION

One of the key assumptions behind the argument in this book concerns the significance of the *intrinsic* value of work. Since this assumption is likely to be widely challenged, it is necessary that it be defended. Up until now, a series of arguments have been deployed which aim to show the potential richness, variety and value of certain kinds of work (see, in particular, Chapter 2). Even if they have been successful, however, they will not have demonstrated that work is necessarily a universal, let alone desirable, aspect of human experience. Failure to demonstrate this in turn threatens the moral arguments in favour of taking vocational education seriously. For if work is nothing but a tiresome necessity, then preparation for work is hardly likely to be one of the more valuable aspects of education. Furthermore, it would be quite right for educators to concentrate their efforts on preparing young people for the more valuable parts of their adult lives. This is just what liberal educators have claimed is the principal role of education, with vocational preparation, quite properly, delegated to a subordinate role.[1] Unfortunately the task of arguing for the intrinsic worth of work is made more difficult by the record of mistaken attempts to do so. The area suffers from further confusion concerning exactly what the nature of work is and how it is to be distinguished from play and leisure.

WORK AS A DEFINING HUMAN CHARACTERISTIC

The most immediately tempting way of arguing for the proposition that work is an invaluable part of human life is to claim that the ability to work is, in some way, an *essential* part of our humanity. An alternative is to claim that work is ordained by God as a way of achieving, or as a sign of, virtue. Many believe one or other of these claims and both underlie some of our contemporary attitudes to work. Part of my approach will be to point out that the fact that people attach value to work gives one at least a *prima facie* reason for supposing that it is somehow central to the human condition. But, of course, people may suffer from mass delusions and many of a non-religious disposition would be inclined to say that religiously inclined work enthusiasts are indeed suffering from such delusions. This claim, though, can itself be undermined if there are independent philosophical reasons for wishing to attach importance to work as an indispensable part of a worthwhile life. However, it is my belief that attempts to show that work is somehow part of the essence of what it is to be a human being are mistaken. They make a claim that is simply too strong to be sustainable. To approach the question we need to reconsider what is meant by 'work'.

The essence of work and the essence of humanity

Non-religious attempts to argue for the importance of work appear to derive from Enlightenment and post-Enlightenment thinking. Rousseau, for example, although he did not argue that work is somehow essential to fulfilment of human nature, did maintain that working is an important way of maintaining human dignity. Emile, in the eponymous treatise, is to be taught a trade so as to be able to independently earn a living and thus to sustain a healthy *amour propre*.[2] But the best-known, and most influential, attempt to ground human essence in work is undoubtedly that of Karl Marx, which has itself had many influential followers. Marx identifies human fulfilment with the exercise of creative powers to produce something from the raw material provided by nature. It is evident that he means more than just brute physical production, however, as it is essential to his case that what is produced is originated and consciously carried out by the same person. In a famous passage in *Capital* he writes that:

> Labour is, in the first place, a process in which both man and Nature partici-
> pate, and in which man of his own accord starts, regulates, and controls the
> material relations between himself and Nature. He opposes himself to Nature
> as one of her own forces, setting in motion arms and legs, head and hands, the
> natural forces of his body, in order to appropriate Nature's productions in a
> form adapted to his own wants. By thus acting on the external world and
> changing it, he at the same time changes his own nature. He develops his
> slumbering powers and compels them to act in obedience to his sway. We are
> not now dealing with those primitive instinctive forms of labour that remind
> us of the mere animal. An immeasurable interval of time separates the state
> of things in which a man brings his labour-power to market for sale as a
> commodity, from that state in which human labour was still in its first
> instinctive stage. We pre-suppose labour in a form that stamps it as exclusively
> human. A spider conducts operations that resemble those of a weaver, and a
> bee puts to shame many an architect in the construction of her cells. But what
> distinguishes the worst architect from the best of bees is this, that the architect
> raises his structure in imagination before he erects it in reality.[3]

Thus for Marx it is characteristic of work that it is directed towards altering nature for a human purpose and that it is preceded by an act of planning.[4] Just as important is the fact someone puts into effect the plan that they have made. The general outline of Marx's philosophy also suggests that the whole process typically takes place in a social context, often with the co-operative efforts of other human beings and is thus, in an important sense, bound up with the capacity to use language. Marx appears to rely on a notion of work that is widely accepted. Its key characteristics seem to be as follows: it involves planning and·effort, it is not necessarily the same thing as wage labour, since it can be remunerated in other ways, and it has as a goal the production of something beyond itself. The last point is important, as various attempts to distinguish work from play or leisure have recognised (see Chapter 2).

WORK AND EMPLOYMENT

The common meaning of 'employment' in contemporary society is bound up with the selling of one's labour power to an employer or the selling of the product of one's labour. In defining 'labour power', Marx had in mind the strength that one brought to a task, together with the skill with which that strength was employed. As was observed in Chapter 10, while this broadly characterises labour power adequately, there are some problems with the definition that suggest that our economic system may not have the purity of capitalist characteristics that both Marx and other classical economists supposed. It was noted in the previous chapter that knowledge, often collectively held, is a vital constituent of what a worker brings to the task in hand. Marx's idea of labour power was of an intangible quality that was transferred from a worker to the product. There is thus a strong analogy between the employment contract and other forms of commodity exchange, in that a mutual transfer occurs between two parties.

As pointed out in the previous chapter, however, the role that knowledge plays in work complicates this picture. First, although one's effort is expended on a product or service, knowledge or skill is not transferred from the employee to something that is now owned by the employer. Given that the knowledge or skill is a key component of the potential for labour that is offered to the employer, there is an important inalienable element in it.[5] The alienation is only complete when nothing more than the use of physical strength is sold. The employer cannot control the employment of skill, only the external environment in which it is employed and, to an extent, the use of the employee's time available. To a considerable extent, employers rely on the good will and judgement of the employee, which is difficult to specify within the labour contract, but which forms a background to the successful operation of labour markets. If he receives the utmost efforts of the employee, then the employee has been *supererogatory* in relation to the labour contract.

Furthermore, when the skills required are collective, only useful when employed by a team of workers, an employer is effectively dependent, not only on each individual within the team, but on their willing co-operation with each other, as well as with him. The effect of this situation, particularly prevalent in high-skill work environments, is to partially shift control of the work process to the employees.[6] These considerations suggest that, in assessing the role that paid employment plays in our society, it is not just enough to consider that work is valuable because we 'earn a living' through it, but because it affords us opportunities to exercise our creative powers with others in the context of a well-understood aspect of necessity (that of 'earning our living').

Nevertheless, if we are to understand the moral and social importance attached to paid employment in our society, it is a good idea to start with the notion of 'earning one's living'.[7] The fact that, as Marx and others pointed out, ordinary working people have, historically, had little choice about how they earned their upkeep does not diminish the perceived moral importance of doing so. The reason is that the recognition of necessity in the form of the need to reproduce the means of subsistence of oneself and one's family, is seen as a fundamental part of life, not peculiar to capitalism.[8] In this sense, there is a strong element of mutual obligation in the efforts and time that we expend in gaining the necessities of life. Either we do so, or someone else does it for us. This is usually perfectly acceptable when, for example, one makes an essential contribution to this reproduction through unpaid domestic or communal labour.[9]

This was historically taken account of through the institution of the male 'living wage', which was intended for the reproduction of the family as well as the individual. Our views of those who have sufficient resources not to need to be employed or self-employed, are more ambivalent. When their position is self-evidently the result of their own legitimate efforts, there is usually not too much controversy. However, when wealth is inherited, we are more inclined to falter in our approval. On the one hand, we may accept the entitlement to inherited wealth through something like an entitlement account of the transfer of property rights.[10] On the other, we may regard the enjoyment of even legitimately gained wealth with disapproval. We think, for example, of the deleterious moral effects of being a member of the 'idle rich', precisely because of the evacuation of necessity from their lives or, like Mill, we might connect this thought with the ramifying effects of inherited wealth in a society and the unedifying spectacle that it gives of power and prestige without effort. Mill proposed a very severe inheritance tax to deal with this situation and it could be argued that a true meritocracy of the kind he advocated, would enforce something like this.[11]

A key component of the perceived necessity of paid employment is, then, a feeling that it is required by our mutual obligations. In fending for ourselves we signal to society that we are playing a part in its survival, and at the same time, not unduly burdening others. This can take on a harsh and unlovely aspect when any failure is regarded as a fall from grace, even when it occurs through no fault of one's own, as a result of accident or illness, for example. On the other hand, it has more of the character of mutuality when it is understood that those who cannot provide for themselves through no fault of their own are, nevertheless, entitled to a degree of comfort and dignity as citizens.

This seems to be a universal background concern that we have with the moral desirability of work-as-necessity. It does not rest on any particular definition of work or even on the need, at all times, to make a physical, social or mental effort, but on the perceived desirability of some degree of independence (which could fall well short of autonomy) and on willingness to contribute to a common good.[12]

However, the symbolism of work is much more potent than that, because it is also caught up in various, currently influential, normative accounts of the worthwhile life. In modern Protestant and post-Protestant societies, this bears some relationship to the Calvinist 'work ethic', especially in those economies which are based on the Anglo-Saxon (neo-liberal) model. There are three very influential normative strands running through our attitudes to work, which in certain respects reinforce and in other respects contradict each other. The significance of these normative 'strands' (to call them theories would be to suggest a systematisation that is simply not there), will be examined in relation to contemporary approaches to work and their implications for education will be examined.

THE CALVINIST 'WORK ETHIC'

According to Weber, the secular exaltation of work has its roots in Christian and Judaic doctrine. The second commandment, 'thou shalt not make unto thee a graven image' was taken to mean, in part, in the Jewish tradition, that sensuous enjoyment was to be avoided and a rational approach to life developed.[13] While it might promote a rational and somewhat ascetic attitude to life, and hence a predisposition towards 'earning a living', it would not, of itself, promote the positive attitude to manufacturing, business and associated activities characteristic of the 'Protestant work ethic'. The Calvinist doctrine of predestination precluded any personal knowledge of one's own or anyone else's grace as a member of the elect, but it was, nevertheless, considered an absolute duty to consider oneself a member of the elect and a sign of this would be self-confidence. 'On the other hand, in order to attain that self-confidence intense worldly activity is recommended as the most suitable means. It and it alone disperses religious doubts and gives the certainty of grace.'[14] This could best be achieved through the kind of rational, methodical activity exemplified in capitalist enterprise. The Calvinist attitude to work then spread through the other variants of Protestantism.

Weber's account allows an important insight into certain aspects of the contemporary attitude to work in the 'Anglo-Saxon' economies, namely its apparent connection with moral worth through being in some sense, touched by grace. Paid employment, and to a considerable extent, commercial self-employment, provided the systematic methodical activity and requirement for intense effort that was considered by Protestantism to be a sign of grace. It is not merely work, but work that is prolonged, intense and systematic that is of specific value. It is also notable that it is the nature of *the work itself* that is of primary significance on this account; the accumulation of riches is a by-product, or at best, a secondary sign of grace. In this Protestant attitude can be found the source of a number of features of the contemporary obsession with work.

There is a particular emphasis on the idea that work is an intrinsic good. It is sign of holiness, not because it is enjoyable or because it expresses one's connection with society, but simply because it is intense, prolonged, rational and orderly. To the extent that there can never be sufficient sign that one has been 'chosen', one cannot perform enough work in this sense, hence the familiar pathology of work as shown in the phenomena of the 'workaholic' and of 'presenteeism', with which we are now plagued.[15] In the contemporary case, the religious idea of grace has been replaced by a secular idea of status or worthiness, a sign of which is constant 'busy-ness', preferably allied with fatigue or 'stress'.

The methodical habits and discipline imposed through paid employment by its contractual nature and the command that the employer has over the employee's labour power, are themselves thought to be desirable, partly as an example to the young, who may 'fall' if not presented at the earliest possible age with exemplars of virtue. The emphasis on work as such, provided it has the qualities mentioned above, is also significant, as it suggests that the release of a person's active, productive or creative powers is not important. Indeed, the potential sensuality of such an engagement with work could prove harmful, if it results in 'passional' or even merely 'sensuous' enjoyment of work or in the construction of 'graven images' or their secular equivalent, the beautiful but unsaleable product.

One must be careful not to present too deterministic an account of the 'Protestant attitude to work' and suggest that there is, in Protestant thinking about the world, nothing more than an ascetic refusal to engage with the sensuous or passional side of nature. The work of painters in the Protestant tradition should be enough to dispel such a view.[16] Nevertheless, the features of the attitude to work that were identified by Weber seem to be so influential, even in a secular post-Protestant society, that one must ask seriously whether they do not have a much greater cultural significance to us than their supposed efficacy in capitalist production. There is good reason to see in these attitudes, particularly when carried to extremes, an attitude to life that is profoundly unbalanced and spiritually unhealthy.

MARXISM AND THE DIGNITY OF LABOUR

The second normative account that influences our culture is one derived from the philosophy and economics of Marx, which we have already had occasion to discuss and criticise. There are features of the Marxist account of work, just as there are of the Calvinist one, which although they now form part of our normative beliefs about work, also serve to obscure the overall importance that it has in our lives.

The first of these is the emphasis in Marx's work on *manual* labour, albeit manual labour informed by intelligent planning and social co-operation. The Marxist account of labour-power as a quasi-substance, transmitted to inanimate objects and thus becoming 'congealed' through physical effort, presents us with a picture of the primacy of manual labour. The effort that men put into production becomes alienated from them in what they produce, just as the physical effort that we put into the making or doing of something is no longer part of us. Even teaching is the imparting through labour or effort of one quasi-substance to another person. This conception underlies the presentation of labour-as-commodity that lies behind his account of labour markets.

Yet not all that is sold need, strictly speaking, be alienated. The knowledge and skill that contribute to a task remain with the worker, who is the primary authority on how they should be deployed. This, in one sense, tends to be ignored in Marx's analysis, but it can only be in the case with completely alienated labour, where *all* that the worker contributes is muscle-power. But the other side of Marx's account is, of course, that the worker is capable of forming a plan and putting it into effect, and of employing special skills in doing so. Nevertheless, even unalienated labour is largely of a physical kind, humans interacting with the raw material provided by Nature.[17] There seem, thus, to be two aspects of Marx's account of work, each in tension with one another. The idea that work is physical labour on the one hand, and the idea that the 'essence' of human labour is an integrated process of plan-making and putting the plan into effect. The tension is apparently resolved through the concept of alienation, whereby the ideal form of physical labour, involving plan-making and social interaction, becomes debased into the solitary employment of unskilled physical effort in the apotheosis of capitalist production, the Taylorised production line.

One final point about Marx's account is worthy of note. He took a view that the development of capitalism is inexorable, a view shared by neo-liberal thinkers.[18] It has a pure form (outlined in *Capital*) and economic laws ensure that all pre-capitalist impure forms will disappear. Thus alienated paid labour will become the universal form taken by all work in fully developed capitalism. The account of work inherited from Marx contains, then, the following features: an emphasis on the physical aspect of work (even unalienated work); the ideal of autonomy; the inevitability of the degeneration of work under capitalism. In some ways, the Marxist heritage that can be found in contemporary attitudes to work contradicts the Calvinist heritage. Work is not good *per se*, but only in an unalienated form and especially when it involves, in a significant way, physical labour.[19] Under capitalism it is likely to become more and more worthless, while at the same time encompassing more and more of life. In some respects, then, Marxism contributes to attitudes that are profoundly opposed to the 'work ethic'. On the other hand, the celebration of autonomy gives the basis for a moral justification for individual entrepreneurship (an unintended consequence of this way of thinking), by the fact that it, to a striking degree, exhibits the qualities of unalienated autonomous labour.

The celebration of autonomy in capitalist societies is thus largely a sham, valid only if work allows for the pursuit of other, self-determined aims. Self-determined work, such as found in entrepreneurship or self-employment has an intrinsic value, as it is at the same time an exemplification of autonomous labour. If one takes the economic determinism of Marxism seriously, then we should all work (literally) for the overthrow of capitalism. Take away the determinism, we are left with a set of attitudes that glorify physical, artisanal labour, suggest that certain kinds of work are bad and provide a justification for the individual entrepreneur. These attitudes, like the Calvinist ones, when emphasised to a very strong degree, tend to undermine the background attitudes to work discussed earlier, and make it more difficult to present young people with a coherent idea of the role of work and how it might connect with other aspects of their lives.

PRODUCTIVE LABOUR AND THE PROFESSIONS

We saw in Chapter 2 how Adam Smith introduced a highly dubious idea of 'productive labour' into our thinking about work and how, to a certain extent, this notion was taken on by Marx. Broadly speaking, the distinction made in both the minds of economists and non-economists is between work that is worthwhile and work that is not. Broadly speaking, the concern has been to distinguish between worthwhile and non-worthwhile occupations. Thus, in Smithian terms, it is natural to distinguish between labour that contributes to the production of 'vendible commodities' and, by implication, to the profitability of enterprises, and that which does not.[20] Marxists have made the distinction in a different way, or in more than one way. They have tended to look askance at some types of 'non-productive' labour in Smith's sense, particularly those which apparently contribute directly to the maintenance of the institutions of capitalist society, such as law enforcement and military activity, and particularly the functions of management and direction of enterprises, which are usually regarded as parasitic on direct production work.[21] They have also tended to deprecate alienated labour (which Smith saw as an economic necessity), while at the same time recognising that it is the fate of workers in capitalism to submit to it, although they can, through resistance, impart a dignity to their work which would otherwise be lacking. Even those sorts of work which contribute to the welfare of the proletariat, such as nursing, are not thought to be on quite the same high plane of approbation as the archetypal industrial worker, preferably exploited by a capitalist.

Whether or not work is classified as 'productive' depends to a large extent on one's view of the aims of economic activity, and hence on one's general ethical stance. In accordance with this principle, one can then classify 'good' 'productive' labour as that which contributes to ends which one approves of, and 'bad' 'unproductive' labour as that which fails to do so. An obvious problem here is that a dominant conception of 'productive' may well exclude less dominant conceptions and consign them to an ethical limbo. Very often, the quite legitimate question of whether this kind of employment would suit an individual, gets mixed up with the question of which kinds of occupation should be developed, or even tolerated, within our society.

These distinctions can be made in different places according to one's predispositions. Someone like Carr, for example, wants to distinguish *professions* (see Chapter 9) as especially worthy of approval, in contradistinction to activities that Marxists and neo-liberals might particularly approve of. Carr's concern is to show that certain kinds of occupation have a particular ethical value and are, hence, particularly suited to a certain kind of preparation, namely a liberal one concerned with the development of an ethics of the profession and this feature distinguishes them from other occupations.[22]

The argument is that certain occupations have a peculiarly important role in promoting human flourishing; no society can flourish without some form of health care, education and legal procedure.[23] Furthermore, it is a characteristic of the occupations concerned with these matters that their ends are *contested*. It is a matter of legitimate and continuing debate as to what kind of education, health care or legal services most contribute to the promotion of human welfare. A further component of Carr's argument is that ethical considerations are built into our ideas of what it is to be a good professional, to an extent which is not true of other occupations.[24] On this view, these occupations occupy a particularly important role in the hierarchy of paid employment that give them the deserved title of *profession*. Carr, then, constructs a philosophical argument for attaching greater ethical importance to one sort of occupation than to others. In this respect he is doing something, albeit in a more systematic way, that I have accused Smith and Marx of doing.

Carr acknowledges, of course, that other occupations such as farming and plumbing not only contribute to human well-being, but fulfil necessities of life-and-death importance, but argues that, in some way, the professions do so in a way that other occupations do not. Many occupations contribute marginally to well-being and fewer still to life-and-death necessity. On the one hand, plumbers and farmers, for example, by ensuring that we are fed or that we drink clean water, may be doing just that. So, incidentally, may those medical personnel, not recognised as full professionals, such as nurses. On the other hand, one would be hard put to it to make out a case for saying that a divorce lawyer, a lecturer in Finnish philology or a cosmetic surgeon were making contributions to society, however, valuable, that make a difference between life and death. So on this criterion, Carr's argument is not decisive, or even suggestive, of the conclusion that he wishes to draw.

The next criterion for being a profession is that ethical considerations are some-how bound up with the qualification for being a practitioner. It is oxymoronic to try to characterise someone as a good doctor and, at the same time, as someone who abuses the trust of his patients. On the other hand, one can be a highly rated builder and short-change one's customers.[25] It is obvious that this criterion will not work. There are many 'technically' good lawyers, doctors and teachers, who nevertheless fail to fulfil the ethical requirements of their profession. They may, for example, overcharge, carry out unnecessary operations or indoctrinate children in their own pet theories, and yet perform the technical side of their functions with great skill. These misdemeanours may even be enough to get them excluded from the roll of members of their profession. But they hardly suffice to deny them the epithet 'good doctor', 'good lawyer' or 'good teacher' in the relevant sense. To be sure, we may not wish to employ such people for legitimate purposes, but this is equally true of dishonest builders, farmers or plumbers. It is not easy to see exactly what Carr's confusion is here, but it may be to do with the fact that occupations require 'internal' as well as 'external' virtues and that he has confused the two.

To be a good doctor in the internal sense, one needs diligence, patience and self-discipline. One may misuse these virtues in various ways, through not attending properly to the constraints on acceptable practice, or through perversion of the ends of medicine. On the other hand, one also needs 'external' virtues in order to practice in a way that is socially acceptable (see Chapter 6). Thus honesty and trustworthiness in one's dealings with clients and the public are required in order to meet this criterion. The fact that professions require internal virtues in order to be successfully practised may have led Carr to think that the external virtues are in some way bound up with successful practice, by wrongly identifying the internal with the external virtues. But many other occupations are no different in this respect. As was argued in Chapters 6 and 9, virtually all occupations that lay demands on our abilities, require certain internal virtues, such as diligence and perseverance to practice them successfully in the technical sense and many also require, at least to some extent, more other-regarding virtues and characteristics such as consideration for others, sociability and loyalty, if they are to be done well in the technical sense. In this instance, as with the first criterion, Carr seems to have exaggerated what is required for his favoured occupations and deprecated what is required for the less favoured.

Finally, we are asked to accept that while the ends of the professions may be contested, this is not true of other occupations. But we have already seen, in distinguishing between the technical and civic aspects of occupations, that this can be a problem for other occupations, just as much as it is for the professions. On the other hand, a profession may well arrive at a settled view of its ends for many decades. While non-professional occupations may not, in current circumstances, give sufficient consideration to the ends for which they are employed, this may be a function of inadequate occupational organisation or inadequate formation, rather than anything intrinsic to the occupation itself. Once we accept that an occupation can contribute, however, obliquely to human well- or ill-being, the question as to the ends to which the occupation is directed becomes one that is capable of being asked.

A farmer, for example, might wonder whether it was legitimate to treat animals in a certain way or to care about the consequences for future generations of using genetically modified crops. A plumber could worry about whether the trade was sufficiently engaged in providing equity in access to water supplies, or in promoting public sanitation and a car-worker might have serious questions about the extent to which the kinds of vehicles that he is involved in making are detrimental to the environment.[26] Once again, it is only by concentrating on certain aspects of favoured occupations and ignoring them in less-favoured ones that one can hope to make such hard-and-fast distinctions. It might be said, of course, that plumbers and car-workers do not sufficiently attend to these aspects of their work (what one might call the 'civic ends' of their occupations), but one of my contentions (see Chapter 6) is that the serious consideration of such aspects is not just a legitimate, but an essential part of occupational formation in the context of a concern for the development of productive powers.

It seems, then, that there are serious difficulties in trying to construct a systematic normative hierarchy of occupations based on personal preferences or even one's personal set of values. This is true whether one adopts a consumptionist approach (Smith), a Marxist approach, or one based on the perceived ethical significance of certain occupations in terms of human flourishing. The mistake here is sometimes, as already remarked, in confusing personal taste or ethical predisposition with the value of an occupation, not just in one's own eyes, but in those of the public and those who practice the occupation. But there is a more subtle error in this approach, which is to identify one's individual preferences *vis-à-vis* legitimate occupations with those that society should prefer.

This is a very understandable error, because normally one would expect what one approves of and, therefore, what one sees as a possible occupation, to determine what one thinks should happen. However, we have seen that, in the political sphere, we are dealing with *competing conceptions of the good*, which need to be accorded their space if the interests of other sections of society are not to be ignored. Since the recognition that we may be fallible entails that it is possible that others have a legitimate point of view (even if we can't quite see it), there are potential dangers in suppressing too much of what we disapprove of, rather than allowing competing conceptions of the good to find a place within the society. It is a necessary and inevitable fact of life in a polity which accommodates different outlooks (as any complex one must) that a citizen recognises that the existence of competing conceptions of the good, and their associated occupations, need to receive their own due recognition if they are to make a contribution to the society. Our ability to tolerate that of which we do not approve gives our society a resilience and adaptability that can benefit it in unforeseen ways. A more pragmatic, but related, reason, given by Hodgson, is that an economic system like capitalism depends on 'impurities' that give it the wider resources to adapt and survive. Therefore, for a supporter of capitalism or socialism to seek to denigrate, or even to squeeze out of existence, any kind of employment that is associated with the system of which he disapproves may well be courting disaster in the longer term.[27]

CONCLUSION

In Chapter 2, it was argued that all societies have a background concern with independence and mutual dependence, which informs their attitudes to the business of 'gaining one's living'. This concern arises from the pervasiveness of necessity, from the need of humans to produce what they need for life and from a recognition of mutual dependence. Beyond these background concerns, however, matters become more complex. We considered how Marx's attempt to provide a differentiating criterion of human activity failed both to completely characterise it and to ground a definitionally satisfactory account of 'work'. Marx did, however, draw attention to certain aspects of human activity which, if not universal are nevertheless so important and pervasive that any philosophical account of this area which ignores them is seriously incomplete. These include the idea that *making*, in a social context, is an important aspect of our lives and one, further-more, from whose engagement we gain considerable intrinsic satisfaction. Marx also emphasised the importance of human interaction with natural raw material as a condition for our continued individual and social existence and thus drew attention to the social role of work in ensuring both individual independence (not being a burden on others) and interdependence (through contributing to projects that are expressive of a common good).[28] All these considerations suggest that, while it is wrong to try to construct an *a priori* philosophical argument for the universal importance of work in human life, it is possible to assemble reminders from our natural history that indicate its enormous significance, albeit subject to considerable cultural variation.

Finally, it is possible to see how particular conceptions of work and related concepts may arise within specific cultural traditions, such as that of the Protestant west and Marxism, and may radically alter even deep-seated traditional concep-tions of work and necessity. It is important to realise that these conceptions are not absolute, in the sense that they supersede all previous traditions of thought on these matters, but can themselves be subjected to an 'internal critique' based on other conceptions of the value of life, in this case, implicitly through an Aristotelian account of the need for a balance in the exercise of the virtues, which translates itself into a sense of balance and proportion in the ordering of human life.

The obsession with paid work found in both the Calvinist and the Marxist inheritance, threatens to crowd out other aspects of life, such as leisure, domestic and voluntary activity, to the general impoverishment of life generally. It is not, then, surprising that there is now a powerful intellectual current that proclaims the coming end of work, representing at least a partial reaction to the dominance of these views. Nor is it surprising that many philosophers of education have had a strong antipathy towards the idea that education should, in any sense, be a preparation for work.

For vocational education, it is important to maintain a very broad vision of 'preparation for work' which not only encompasses the different forms of paid employment, but also domestic and voluntary labour. It also follows, from the reluctance that I have argued one should have towards unduly elevating the value of some occupations and denigrating others according to personal taste and preference, that a society that wishes to continue to develop various currents not just of skill, but of value and outlook on life, needs to take a generous attitude to the provision of vocational education, so as to allow for the proper development of a wide variety of occupations. Consideration of Carr's arguments also prompts the thought that careful consideration of the ends to which an occupation may be employed ought to be an important component of occupational formation, in line with the liberal conception of vocational education developed in Chapter 9.

Notes

1 See for example, Robin Barrow (1981) *The Philosophy of Schooling*, Brighton, Harvester.

2 J.-J. Rousseau (1966) *Emile ou l'Education*, Paris, Editions Flammarion, Bk. 4; J. Darling (1993) 'Rousseau as Progressive Instrumentalist', *Journal of Philosophy of Education*, 27, 1, 27–38.

3 K. Marx (1970) *Capital*, London, Lawrence and Wishart, p. 178.

4 A. Gramsci (1971) *Selections from the Prison Notebooks*, London, Lawrence and Wishart, however, saw that it is possible for the purpose of an activity to be immanent in the activity itself (pp. 364–365).

5 G. Hodgson (1999) *Economics and Utopia: Why the Learning Society is Not the End of History*, London, Routledge, Chapter 7.

6 See the scenarios set out by Hodgson, op. cit. p. 214.

7 There is no necessary reason why this should be through paid employment in the capitalist sense. But given the pervasiveness of the wage-relation in our kind of society, I will take it that this is the primary sense 'earning a living'.

8 It is important not to get confused over the issue of 'subsistence'. There is a level of subsistence in all societies that has implicitly some notion of minimal participation within the society, that is, a 'socially acceptable' rather than biologically adequate level. It is important that 'subsistence' is recognised in both senses and here it is meant to encompass the social sense. This is an important issue for the discussion in the next chapter.

9 It is arguable, though, that this perception is growing much less powerful as a result of feminist arguments about the 'oppressive' nature of domestic labour and a growing belief that paid employment is the only valid form of work, as evidenced in the UK 1997 Labour government's anxiety to make childcare a paid, rather than a domestic, activity.

10 R. Nozick (1974) *Anarchy, State and Utopia*, Oxford, Blackwell.

11 See J. S. Mill (1994) *Principles of Political Economy* (first published 1848) edited with an introduction by Jonathan Riley, Oxford, Oxford University Press, Book II for an extended discussion.

12 Indeed, we are sometimes inclined to denigrate employment that requires no effort whatsoever, even though it is paid, as somehow degrading to the person who undertakes it.

13 M. Weber (1958) *The Protestant Ethic and the Spirit of Capitalism*, New York, Scribner, pp. 270–271.

14 Ibid. p. 112.

15 I do not, of course, mean to suggest that these phenomena cannot be found in cultures with a different form of 'work ethic'. Identification with the group and its purposes, as in Japan, may produce a similar effect. For obvious reasons, many employers are only too eager to cultivate these attitudes to work.

16 For example, David Teniers the Younger's *Kermis* is, arguably, an example of an awareness of the sanctity of the individual moment, this time in the spontaneous enjoyment of a dance.

17 Marx, op. cit. quoted earlier.

18 Pointed out by Hodgson, op. cit., Chapters 5, 6.

19 Purely 'cerebral' work shows signs of alienation of the plan-making from the putting into effect of parts of the process.

20 See Chapter 2.

21 One of the points on which the labour theory of value in its Marxist form insists, is that there is really no such thing as managerial or entrepreneurial labour, the fruits of which the manager or the entrepreneur is, in some way, entitled to. This is one of the main criticisms of Marxist theory made by Marshall [(1890) *Principles of Economics*, eighth edition, London, Macmillan] in discussing the remuneration of management (e.g. p. 487). Quite apart from Marx's distaste for recognising the 'productive' role of the entrepreneur, his conceptualisation of labour power makes it difficult to account for

labour power which is largely composed of knowledge, social skill and temperament, rather than physical effort.

22 D. Carr (1999) 'Professional Education and Professional Ethics', *Journal of Applied Philosophy*, 16, 1, pp. 33–46.

23 Ibid. p. 37. Curiously, Carr does not mention the police as a profession, although this and the following two criteria seem to apply to them just as much as to lawyers.

24 Ibid. p. 36.

25 Ibid. p. 36.

26 Indeed, the practice of codetermination and other forms of industrial democracy may oblige employees to come to terms with these kinds of question about their work (see Chapter 14).

27 This is not to say, of course, that a society needs to approve of any kind of employment, such as prostitution or criminal activity of various kinds; the existence of recognised competing conceptions of the good does not entail that any occupation can enter the competition. Even on 'strong autonomous' Millian grounds, those activities that do harm to others without their consent would not gain a foothold in the legitimate occupations within the society.

28 In conditions of absolute plenty, this aspect of Marxist thinking, which is one of the bases of historical materialism, would no longer apply. Consideration of the concept of *effort* along the lines that I have suggested, by contrast, suggests that although necessity would be greatly changed by absolute plenty, it would by no means disappear.

13 Education and the end-of-work thesis

INTRODUCTION

The argument of the previous chapter suggested that individual effort in a social context is important in any society. In some societies, much will take place through paid employment. This remains true despite the validity of arguments that it is not part of our 'essence' to work. However, specific cultural influences have an effect on our conception of work, and can give it an importance that undermines the balance between different aspects of life, while at the same time narrowing views of legitimate forms of work. The role that paid employment has come to play in our culture, and the effect that its preponderant role has had on other spheres of activity is, arguably, a case of this. These cultural influences may themselves promote a reaction against the idea of paid employment and even against work in general. These complications make the relationship between education and work a peculiarly fraught one and it is simpler and certainly tempting to attempt to deny the relationship altogether.

One of the most influential reactions to the apparent domination of paid work in contemporary industrial societies has been to prepare for the time when, allegedly, paid work will cease to be a necessity. Put crudely, the supposed reason is that developments in what Marx called the 'means of production' (labour-saving artefacts) render human effort unnecessary in securing even our more sophisticated requirements. It is a practical possibility that the production of necessities through the paid employment of large numbers of people will become unnecessary and in this way 'work' as we know it will cease to be important, to be replaced with opportunities for freely chosen activities.[1]

THE AUTOMATION THESIS

The idea that machinery can replace labour is hardly new. Ricardo analysed the possible overall effects on employment of the replacement of labour by machinery and found that it was not as straightforward as might be supposed.[2] Since Ricardo's time, the use of machinery and automated processes has increased enormously and shows no signs of decreasing. Industries have disappeared, been radically transformed and have had their labour requirements vastly reduced as a result of the introduction of machinery, agriculture being, perhaps, the most striking example.

If labour is replaced by machinery, then there will apparently be a smaller net requirement for it. But we know that this is not yet the case, despite machinery's onward march for over two hundred years. Not only has the population in the countries that were industrialised in Ricardo's time vastly increased, but many more countries have become industrialised, and have themselves greatly increased their populations. Not only has unemployment remained relatively low during this period, but labour markets have vastly changed, with the entry of growing numbers of women.

Initial thoughts about the consequences of machinery are not necessarily a good guide to its effect on employment, for two reasons. The first is, in a sense, technical (although of strong philosophical interest), the other is bound up with the aims of economic activity discussed in Chapter 4. When one form of activity is displaced, another may take its place. It does not follow, for example, that when agricultural workers are displaced from agricultural activities that there will be nothing left for them to do. The Industrial Revolution in Britain testifies to the way in which a displaced agricultural workforce became available for new forms of industrially based economic activity. It is not merely the fact that people move from one activity to another, but that new forms of industry and occupation come into existence as a result of social and technological change. This is particularly evident at the present time: new industries connected with computing, communication and biotechnology have all recently appeared. Leisure itself provides opportunities for economic growth; witness the popularity of eating out and holidaying, for example.

It might be argued that eventually the process of automation will catch up with all forms of industry, and lead to a final displacement from paid employment for the majority of the workforce. But there is no evidence that this is happening. One (misleading) way of putting this is to say, like Adam Smith, that human desires do not have a natural limit.[3] Economic activity exists to satisfy demands to consume various kinds of goods. There is no natural limit to the types of demands that an individual will make according to economics, although there are limits to the amount of any good that can be consumed during any fixed period of time.

So, for example, there are limits to the amount of beer that the brewing industry can produce because there is a limit to the amount individuals wish to drink in a fixed period of time. The more beer one pays for and consumes, the less satisfaction one gains from each successive pint, until the point comes when expenditure of the same amount of money that is available for beer will produce marginally more satisfaction if spent on something else (a curry, for example). This is known as the principle of 'diminishing marginal utility' and expresses the idea that each choice made yields a margin of satisfaction over the next most desirable possibility. Eventually the margin disappears altogether and the satisfaction of eating curry is greater than that of consuming another pint of beer.[4] There are thus natural limits to the amount of beer that can be drunk in a given time, but these need not affect other desires and may even stimulate them (e.g. beer arouses an appetite for curry). As Marshall argues, want-satisfaction leads to the generation of new activities, satisfying new wants.[5]

One important qualification to the law of diminishing marginal utility is that certain products become *obsolescent* and manufacturers can enhance obsolescence. This applies most readily to goods that, unlike beer, can be used repeatedly. Thus, the satisfaction produced by a car or a dress will diminish partly because of wear and tear, but partly also because the item becomes less desirable over time in comparison with newer varieties. Older cars without power steering become less desirable than new ones with it, because they require more effort to steer. Changes in fashion can make a dress socially impossible to wear. So the law of diminishing marginal utility only places restrictions on how much of certain kinds of things can be consumed at one time, it does not impose an upper limit on human desire. It is not possible, therefore, to add up the aggregate demand for goods at any one time and to extrapolate a fixed limit for demand in the future and hence the future demand for employment.

While there is something important in this, it is, nevertheless, not quite satisfactory. The problem resides in the portrayal of human beings as consumers and, in particular, as consumers of commodities. The limits on our desire to consume may be very elastic, but this does not mean that they are unlimited. Individuals, in even the most consumption-oriented societies, find that there are costs attached. One comes in the form of what economists call *externalities*, that is, costs (or benefits) imposed through economic activity which are not reflected in the purchase price. The most obvious of these is environmental degradation, through the extensive use, for example, of cars. Externalities like environmental cost may eventually undermine an individual's wish to consume.

The second arises from another central idea of economics, that of the *opportunity cost*. Resources expended on any one item at any time cannot simultaneously be expended on something else. The opportunity foregone is a cost in terms of satisfaction to the purchaser. So long as they are still gaining marginal utility, these costs will be borne. Once, however, the margin disappears, they will not. This idea applies obviously to the consumption of commodities, but it has a wider application, for satisfaction can be foregone by the very act of consuming *per se*.

This has traditionally been difficult for economists to grasp because, as Verdon has pointed out, the 'Copernican' view of human nature held in classical and neo-classical economics, has assumed that people are 'at rest' unless they are actively pursuing utility, either through consumption or through work carried out in order that consumption be possible.[6] However, if people are active producers and not just consumers, then there is an opportunity cost involved in consumption itself, namely foregoing of the satisfaction involved in producing or carrying out some other activity. There may well come a point where people are simply satiated with consumption and the idea of it, and may wish to turn to other sorts of activity. So there is something not entirely satisfactory about the idea that there is no natural limit to our desires, particularly when this is expressed in terms of the consumption of commodities. Although our desires to consume may be very great, they are not limitless, and hence the work that can be generated to satisfy them is not limitless either. Nevertheless, consumption as a generator of paid employment certainly has a great deal going for it, as we shall see below, and this consideration alone severely compromises the arguments of those who claim that we should prepare for the 'end of work'.

One of the assumptions of 'common sense' that Smith and his successors were concerned to attack was the idea that any society has fixed quantity of work that needs to be 'done', sometimes called the 'lump of labour fallacy'. The argument from wants is important in refuting this, but not decisive and, in an important way, misses the point about the role of work in our lives. This brings me to the second point of criticism of the end-of-work thesis. One of the difficulties with the consumptionist approach is that it begins and ends with individual consumers, and, as we have seen, the desires of consumers, however great, are not limitless. Furthermore, the 'Copernican' assumption of economics suggests that once desires are satisfied, the individual will revert to an inert state, in which no significant activity is carried out, least of all work, as effort involves disutility.[7]

There are then, two main problems with the classical approach to the finitude of work. First, its emphasis on individuals and their wants and, second, its assumption of inertness unless there is motivation to satisfy individual desires. To some extent, Keynes, in his treatment of full employment, moved beyond at least one of these assumptions.[8] He did not think that the supply and demand of labour would tend towards balance, as Say's Law states, and hence that full employment would result.[9] It is sometimes necessary to provide demand for labour through action by the state, in those circumstances, which are particularly associated with high rates of interest, when investment is likely to be low.[10] This action has, according to Keynes, a multiplier effect, whereby the stimulatory activity generates demand and hence further employment.[11]

According to Keynes, then, capitalism will not guarantee full employment, because it is unable at all times to provide mechanisms that match the demand for labour with its supply. Given a society's wish to eliminate unemployment, however, the slack in the demand for labour can be taken up by deliberate state expenditure. Keynes was at pains to point out that its aim was not necessarily productive investment (building pyramids or filling old mines with banknotes, concreting them over and then having them dug up would meet the purpose very well), but the stimulation of demand by providing potential consumers with the financial resources to make purchases.[12] Full employment can be guaranteed if it becomes a sufficient priority for the society and thus an urgent political priority.

The decision to accept a certain level of unemployment is, ultimately, not a technical one, largely determined by market forces, but social and political, based on a view about the relative desirability of full employment compared with other economic objectives. There is no set limit to the amount of work that a society needs to get done; this depends on both what society believes is desirable and on the extent to which it is prepared to ensure that it is done. Although household analogies can be misleading, the following one illuminates this issue. Consider a household that recognises a range of tasks that need to be carried out: apart from day-to-day housekeeping, there are jobs like the repainting of walls and refurbishing the kitchen. When these are completed it is natural to suppose that the amount of work available in the household reduces, as needs have been fulfilled, hence some members of the household will have more leisure.

But this is misleading. Further improvements might be looked for: the building of a conservatory, for example, or the depreciation of assets (such as paintwork) can be dealt with more frequently (once every two years instead of every five). In these cases, a commitment is made to increase the amount of labour required, based on a new view of the amount of labour that is considered to be socially necessary or desirable. These are policy decisions, not the result of supply and demand in the market. In other words, societies can create work: they may do so on Keynsian principles, to give a stimulus to consumer demand; they may decide to upgrade the level of public goods (environment, transport, public housing, health, education); or they may decide to develop the productive powers of the economy through the stimulation of private and public investment (in which case some of the policies followed would correspond to the second case described). They may also (and frequently do) adopt policies of steering economic activity, either through direct interventions or through fiscal or corporate means, to create new industries. When these industries have particular skill requirements, the vocational education and training systems of the polity are affected.

The 'high-skill equilibrium' discussed in Chapter 11 need not come about as a result of state intervention, but in practice, this is how it frequently happens.[13] There is no obvious limitation to the demands that a society might wish to make of its members; it is very much a question of broader considerations concerning the pursuit of the good and the role that full employment is thought to play in its achievement. We can conclude then, that if there is a long-term decline in the amount of work available in a developed society, this is, in large part, the result of political rather than market decisions.

THE EMPIRICAL EVIDENCE CONCERNING EMPLOYMENT

The popularity of the thesis that automation is bringing about the end of work is, in many ways, surprising. No doubt the high rates of unemployment in Europe that came to be the norm after the 'oil shocks' of the 1970s, and the inflation that followed the Vietnam War, coming as they did in sharp contrast to the low levels of unemployment that existed in the first two and a half decades after the Second World War, had something to do with this perception, but they do not constitute anything like convincing evidence for the idea that paid work is about to go into terminal decline. For this reason, it is worth briefly surveying current trends in employment, particularly in the developed and developing industrial countries.[14] First, the *number* of paid jobs is not only not declining, it is increasing at an extra-ordinarily rapid rate. In percentage terms, the US for example, has increased the number of jobs between 1975 and 1995 by 45.57%. Even the EU managed a growth rate of 4.12% in the number of jobs during this period.[15] Industrial employment in the world rose by 31.12% between 1980 and 1994, while in China during the same period it rose by 81.99%, which Rojas comments, is probably an underestimate.[16]

It might be thought that there has been a particular effect due to the very rapid development of computing since about 1980, showing that, whatever happened during the immediate postwar period, we are now in an era of job loss. Thus Viviane Forrester, writing about the effects of cybernetics on employment, says:

> Instead of paving the way for a reduction or even a welcome, universally desired, abolition of the compulsion to work, it is reducing and will soon have abolished the demand for work without either the duty to work or the chain of relations in which work is deemed to be the central connection having been diluted or even modified to the same extent.[17]

Evidence, however, does not seem to bear this out. The two countries most affected by the IT revolution, the US and Japan, both increased their rates of job formation both before and after it occurred. In the US, the rate of increase went from 37.94% in the period 1955–75 to 45.57% in the period 1975–95. In Japan, the figures are, respectively, 27.70% and 23.63%.[18] In Germany the rate of increase in jobs rose between 1960–73 and 1980–94, while in France the rate of increase declined over this period. France presents one of the few cases of real jobless economic growth over this period.[19] Those countries that have recently been affected by higher rates of unemployment seem to have been the victims of a decline in rates of growth rather than an onset of jobless growth.[20] The overall effect of increasing IT involvement in the economy seems to have been a more job-intensive phase of growth, and this is due to the growth and creation of new forms of economic activity, mainly related to the service rather than the manufacturing sector.

This does not imply that the newly created jobs are low-skill menial jobs of no value to those who take them. Even the US, which exhibits some of the characteristics of a low-skill equilibrium, has created more jobs in the professional and managerial categories and technical, supervisory and administrative categories than it has in the low-skill labouring and service type of occupation.[21] The figures for the percentage growth of new jobs in each of these categories between 1983 and 1995, are, respectively, 48.73%, 32.82% and 18.45%.

It is natural to suppose that the 'end of work' scenario is particularly applicable to the developed industrial world, where the workforce is unable to compete on price with equally skilled, but lower paid workers in the newly industrialising countries. So, for example, jobs in some areas such as textiles have been relocated from Europe to countries such as India. Even high-skill jobs, such as software development are exported, given the high levels of education available in some Third World countries.[22] The evidence does not seem to bear this out either, for three reasons. First, the international division of labour has allowed for the successful specialisation of work in the export-sensitive sectors, so that there are plenty of market niches that high-skill high-wage industries can occupy (see the remarks on DQP in Chapter 11). Second, the sheer growth of trade on world markets has ensured that there is enough growth to allow for job creation both in the developed and in the newly industrialising world. Finally, most jobs are in sectors such as services, which cannot be affected by foreign competition. So far from the industrialised countries (the EU, Japan, Canada, Australia, US, Switzerland, Norway and New Zealand) being net importers, they in fact increased their share of world commodity exports from around 65% in 1980 to around 70% in 1994. The EU has a very strong balance of trade with the rest of the world, including rapidly growing areas such as South East Asia.[23]

It is hard to maintain the 'end-of-work' thesis on empirical grounds. If anything, paid employment seems to be assuming a greater importance than previously in the lives of many people. Some countries have succeeded in reducing the working day for many categories of people, but many others, such as the UK and the US have increased the length of the working week as well as the number of jobs available. What is true, of course, is that certain kinds of employment may be getting scarcer. The traditional kind of unskilled manual labour through which young men without any qualifications have traditionally entered the labour market is disappearing rapidly. This poses particular difficulties for certain sections of the population. More generally, it seems to be the case that the growth in employment is greater in those sectors that demand some degree of skill, than in those which do not.

It is also possible that there is a tendency, identified by Ashton and Green for some countries (particularly those dependent on low-skill equilibria in many sectors of economic activity), for a divide to open up between graduate level managerial jobs and unskilled manual work. These trends pose specific difficulties for different sectors of the economies of some countries, the UK being one, but they cannot be used as evidence, either of a general demise of paid employment or of the demise of skilled work. If anything, the problem in some countries appears to be one of keeping the increasing role that paid employment has in our society, at bay. But the prevalence of ideas about the supposed virtue of working at any cost, particularly for lengthy periods of time, that are so prevalent in some countries, should not make this so surprising.

EDUCATION FOR LEISURE

Those, like White, who advocate education for leisure on the basis of an assumption that paid work has gone into an irrevocable decline, are wrong in their empirical assumptions about future trends. Given that this is so, then the future of vocational education does not seem threatened. The main business of education, on this account, is to prepare young people for high-skill employment. Nevertheless, there are good reasons for thinking that the end-of-work thesis and its alleged educational implications should not just be ignored.

While for many people hours of work are getting longer, and leisure time and time for family life are coming under growing pressure, this is not something that should be particularly welcomed. The background reasons for having a job outlined in the previous chapter do not suggest that there is any merit whatsoever in engaging in paid work to the extent that it 'crowds out' other activities. One's connection with society through paid employment should not obliterate the particular social connections represented by family, friends and civil associations. It is therefore a perfectly legitimate aim of those who recognise the continuing importance of work to seek to redress the balance between paid work, voluntary or civic activity, domesticity and leisure, which are all important to well-being. It is to be hoped that more people will have the opportunity to rebalance their commitments in the future, so that paid employment assumes less of a central role, particularly during that period when they are raising children. At the same time, many older people who wish to go on working are denied the opportunity because of the growing pressure associated with their work or because their business does not wish to employ older workers. There may be, in other words, an imbalance between age and work commitment which could be resolved to the mutual satisfaction of older and younger workers.

It is usually assumed that because liberal education was designed for a leisured class, that education for increased amounts of leisure will be traditionally liberal. This is not at all obvious. There are good reasons for thinking that there is a great diversity of propensity and talent in any population which very often manifests itself in areas such as the arts, sport, agriculture, practical and technical activities of many different kinds, and music.[24] While many people who pursue such activities to make a living, many do so for their own personal satisfaction. In some cases, leisure and employment may be interchangeable, for example for a professional musician who plays for his own enjoyment during leisure periods.

There are activities which, although they may interest people intensely, do not necessarily have an outlet in paid employment for everyone, but may, nevertheless, prove to be of enormous benefit, and may, at periods in someone's life, lead to paid employment. While these are often best followed in adulthood through adult education classes, it is a great mistake to discount the value of giving young people, while they are still at school, the opportunity to develop their interests in ways that may not necessarily be their main source of employment in adulthood. Modern liberal, like liberal vocational education, can take practical forms. There is an impact, particularly on the 14–16 curriculum, of allowing young people to follow interests that are not necessarily academic in the strict sense, but which may issue in employment through their practical applicability.[25]

EDUCATION FOR NON-PAID WORK

The literature on the consequences of the decline or 'end' of paid employment is often connected to policy recommendations. The main thrust of these is a basic income.[26] The idea is that individual *autonomy*, thought to be a desirable characteristic of both capitalist and socialist society, can be ensured in an era where paid employment is scarce, through guaranteeing all citizens an adequate basic income, irrespective of whether or not they are employed. When employed, the basic income is 'topped up' with a wage. The moral case for the basic income can be derived both from liberal and from socialist theory. The liberal can argue, following Tom Paine, on generally restitutive lines.[27] The basic income is an entitlement that can arise either from presumed ancestral rights violations or from the Lockean proviso that attaches rights to enjoyments held from previously public goods that have been appropriated through the acquisition of private property (see Chapter 11) or both. The socialist, on the other hand, can justify basic income on the reciprocal needs/obligations principle of 'from each according to his ability, to each according to his needs' which, in a work-scarce era, implies that needs may have to be met without a corresponding contribution.[28]

The arguments for a basic income are by no means to be despised, but they do contain, in their universalist form, serious objections. The first is the empirical one dealt with in the section above; there does not seem to be any evidence that we are moving into an era where paid employment is becoming scarcer; if anything, the contrary is the case. The liberal case for the basic income as a form of restitutive justice depends on the force of the entitlement theory of distributive justice, which, for reasons beyond the scope of this essay, is difficult to sustain.[29] Even if the liberal case proves to be intellectually convincing to liberals themselves, however, it is unlikely to be implemented in a capitalist society imbued with neo-liberal principles. Thoroughgoing adoption of the basic income principle would entail a massive redistribution of resources through taxation from the richer to the poorer sections of the population, which would, given neo-liberal hostility to taxation, be very difficult to implement except in a situation of great crisis. A more likely outcome in a crisis of work shortage would be the provision of various forms of compulsory paid employment or 'workfare' as a kind of outdoor relief of the poor, thus allaying qualms about the idea that the workless might be parasitic on the employed.

The socialist case is contingent on the truth of the proposition that work is scarce. However, the matter is not purely empirical, because, as was argued in the previous section, the amount of paid employment available in a society is essentially a social and political decision. This is clearly the case where a liberal society decides to deal with high unemployment through low-grade 'outdoor relief' types of employment, just as much as it is in a more socialist scenario, where there is a political decision to develop certain kinds of high-skill economic activity. There is no single answer that can be given, even from a broadly socialist point of view, since different socialist societies may come to very different views about the amount of paid employment that it is proper for the society to maintain. Hence there is no single socialist case for a basic income.

Given that paid employment is taking up more and more of our lives and threatening the balance between domestic, leisure, voluntary and paid activities, it is far more plausible to suggest that a basic income could be introduced in a more limited way. The problem with the scheme as it is usually conceived, is that it seems to be based, at least implicitly, on an assumption that individuals should enjoy *strong*

autonomy, that is, that individuals choose their conception of the good life independently of the conceptions of the rest of society.[30] Ultimately, strong autonomy
requires a commitment to emotivist ethics and is not acceptable to the conception
of morality that attaches significant importance to the development of character
that has been argued for throughout this book.[31] In addition, the background
'work ethic' would remain, even if society were to grow out of its post-Calvinist
obsession with the redeeming character of paid employment. The view that paid
employment constitutes one very important way in which individuals are
connected with society is unlikely to follow the demise of that obsession. On the
other hand, the background conception recognises that paid employment is by no
means the *only* way in which this connection need be expressed.

The idea that the expenditure of effort or any attempt to connect with society
or contribute to its welfare should be allowed to atrophy does not, of course,
follow from the demise of paid employment. A society which provided a basic
income could expect from its citizens various kinds of contribution, either through
personal development of knowledge and skills, or through participation in the
voluntary, civic or political life of the society or through child-rearing. It was
argued in Chapter 2 that effort is a background condition of most forms of human
life and is fundamental to our moral realisation of ourselves as members of a
community. It is thus rare in most cultures that complete idleness is viewed as an
acceptable option. This in turn suggests that societies with moralities based on
weak autonomy would attach various conditions to a basic income, only those
based on strong autonomy would not. It certainly does not follow from the truth
of the end-of-paid-employment thesis either that a society has put an end to work
in the broader sense, or that it accepts that some people no longer need to make
any significant efforts in their lives.[32]

If the promotion of strong autonomy is not an acceptable aim of providing a
basic income, however, it is possible to look at the desirability of *some* form of basic
income as a way of satisfying the pluralist requirement that there be a number
of different ways of realising the good life, which may vary from individual to
individual and from one stage of life to another. This becomes particularly
important if there are good reasons to suppose that life is becoming unbalanced
by the demands of paid employment. If a society felt sufficiently strongly that
there was a need to encourage people rebalance their lives towards raising children
or supporting the civil structures of society, then a good case could be made out
for providing a basic income for, say, parents who wished to devote themselves to
child-rearing. With the demise of a rigid sexual division of labour and the
concomitant 'living wage' paid to the husband, it has become increasingly difficult
for families to support themselves comfortably on a single income and this, as
much as the increasing desire of women for independence, has been a decisive
factor in making the two-income household so prevalent.

The 'living wage' at least recognised the social role of the parent whose main
task was child-rearing, and there was thus no sense that such a person was
stigmatised. Its demise not only financially undermines families who wish to
make such a choice, it goes some way towards depriving those who make the

child-rearing choice, both of their self-respect and of the respect of the rest of society. A basic income for at least one parent would give a welcome opportunity to those who felt that their role as parents was being hindered by the need to work, would make it less easy for those who still wished to work to be excluded from the labour market and, due to the tightening of the labour market that it would entail, would place pressure on employers to use their staff more carefully, through upgrading the skill levels of their activities.

The level of employment that is settled on is, to a large degree, a matter of choice by a society: it depends on the priorities attached to paid employment in the overall economic objectives of the society. The conventional economic teaching that most capitalist societies accept, entails that an economy needs to be run at a certain level of unemployment (the NAIRU—see Chapter 10) in order to maintain inflation at an acceptable level. There is, then, a measure of hypocrisy, both in advocating full employment on the one hand and in stigmatising unemployment and cleaving to the NAIRU doctrine on the other. Once we accept, for whatever reason, that full employment is not a desirable objective, then some form of basic income has to be taken seriously.

EDUCATIONAL SCENARIOS WHERE PAID EMPLOYMENT IS NOT THE UNIVERSAL DESTINY OF ALL CITIZENS

If the arguments of this chaper are well-founded, education should not prepare for anything remotely resembling an 'end of work' scenario. This in turn means that, since paid employment is still going to constitute the principal arena of life in which people's identity is formed and in which their capacity to act and interact with other people is exercised, education as a preparation for life must include, as one of its aims, that of preparing young people for a life where paid employment constitutes a major part of their adult lives. Therefore, vocational aims will remain for the foreseeable future and, if anything, will require more attention as the degree of skill and complexity in paid employment continues to increase.

However, it has also been argued that education is a preparation for life *as a whole* and must include aims concerned with personal fulfilment, citizenship and parenthood. If it is true that we currently place too much emphasis on paid employment, then much thought needs to go into the way education is planned so as to enable people to achieve an appropriate balance in their lives. Consideration of this problem naturally raises questions about the curriculum which is, after all, no more than the normative structure within which educational aims are articulated and set out in a practical form.[33]

Different aims can be pursued through similar or identical educational programmes, and identical aims can be pursued through different programmes. So the achievement of autonomy and of employability can be realised, both through practical forms of education and through more academic programmes. What has to be recognised however, is that this cannot be done by assuming that everyone will follow exactly the same programme at every stage in their lives; some people will achieve these aims through a more practical, others through a more academic, route. Likewise, the aim of personal fulfilment may be achieved through a largely practical route for some and through a more academic route for others.

Multiple aims can thus be achieved by different, but interlocking and interdependent curricula. Within these aims, due weight needs to be given to the needs of those who, for example, wish to withdraw from the labour market for a significant period of time, for example, to raise children. They, of course, will continue to have vocational as well as liberal educational needs, since it is unlikely that they will wish to permanently withdraw from the labour market. Even should they do so, it is likely that they would wish to follow some programmes designed principally, if not exclusively, with vocational aims in mind, for example, if their personal interests were of a strong practical bent.

It is important, however, that if people are to continue to feel a sense of worth when they leave the labour market, and if the rest of society is to value them, then there need to be *educational* means through which they remain connected, and which give them the opportunity to contribute again in the future through paid employment. In other words, if withdrawal from the labour market is taken seriously as a perfectly legitimate way in which one can both fulfil oneself and make a contribution to social well-being, various forms of adult educational provision need to be made available to those currently outside paid employment. People who take time out of work for whatever reason, need to have their educational needs looked after; hence the importance of providing educational opportunities for those on basic income, or who are not currently part of the workforce.

That these are genuine educational issues, and not optional 'quality of life' extras follows from the characterisation of the concept of education as a *preparation for life*. While it is inevitably principally concerned with preparation for *adult life* in the general sense, it is also a preparation for *different phases* of adult life. Nor does this concept of education make things difficult for those who hold that *autonomy* should be the principal educational aim. It only becomes a problem if one defines autonomy as *the ability to formulate a plan for life*.[34] But autonomy is concerned with the achievement of *means* as well as *ends*, and, furthermore, it is unreasonable to suppose that one's life-plan may not undergo modification over the years. A fully comprehensive form of education has to recognise this and provide for it.

Notes

1 This is 'scenario 2' as set out in J. White (1997) *Education and the End of Work*, London, Kogan Page.
2 D. Ricardo, *Appendix on Machinery* in J. R. Hicks (1969) *A Theory of Economic History*, Oxford, The Clarendon Press; Ricardo (1951) *On the Principles of Political Economy and Taxation*, Cambridge, Cambridge University Press, Chapter XXXI. First published 1817.
3 A. Smith (1981) *The Wealth of Nations*, Indianapolis, IN, Liberty Fund, Chapter VII.
4 A. Marshall (1890) *Principles of Economics*, eighth edition, London, Macmillan, pp. 78–79.

5 Marshall, op. cit. p. 79.
6 M. Verdon (1996) *Keynes and the Classics*, London, Routledge; Marshall, op. cit. p. 54, 117.
7 Ibid. p. 117.
8 Keynes' denial of the Copernican, in favour of a Newtonian assumption of motion can be seen in his discussion of the propensity to consume [J. M. Keynes (1973) *The General Theory of Employment, Money and Interest*, second edition, London, Macmillan, p. 91] and stock market behaviour (p. 161). A propensity to activity is, however, an important part of the critique of the finitude of work.
9 Keynes, op. cit. pp. 19–20.
10 Ibid. p. 112.
11 Ibid. Chapter 10.
12 See Keynes, op. cit. p. 129 for his discussion of 'make work' projects.
13 F. Fukuyama (1995) *Trust*, London, Penguin; D. Ashton and F. Green (1996) *Education, Training and the Global Economy*, Cheltenham, Edward Elgar.
14 This section gives data which can mainly be found in M. Rojas (1999) *Millennium Doom: Fallacies about the End of Work*, London, Social Market Foundation.
15 Rojas, op. cit. p. 5.
16 Ibid. p. 11.
17 Viviane Forrester (1996) *L'Horreur economique*, Paris, Fayard, cited in Rojas, op. cit. p. 18.
18 Rojas, op. cit. p. 20.
19 Ibid. pp. 21–25.
20 ILO (1996) *World Employment 1996/7—National Policies in a Global Context*, International Labour Office, p. xv, cited in Rojas, op. cit. p. 25.
21 On the complicated nature of the levels of skill available in the US economy see Ashton and Green, op. cit. pp. 126–135. On growth of different categories of employment in the US, see Rojas, op. cit. p. 33. Evidence of state coordination of training in the US can be found in 'Twenty First Century Skills for Twenty First Century Jobs', US Department of Commerce Paper, January 1999.
22 See Rojas, op. cit. pp. 45–46.
23 Ibid. p. 47.
24 See, for example, H. Entwistle (1970) *Education, Work and Leisure*, London, Routledge; M. Sanderson (1994) *The Missing Stratum: Technical Education in England 1900–1990*, London, Athlone Press; M. Howe (1990) *The Origin of Exceptional Abilities*, Oxford, Blackwell; C. Winch (1990) *Language, Ability and Educational Achievement*, London, Routledge.
25 Using Matthew Arnold's definition of high culture as the 'best that has been thought and said' and adding 'and done', one can easily see that a curriculum concerned with high culture could, and arguably should, have at least a wide range of practical options. See J. Gingell and E. Brandon (2000) *In Defence of High Culture*, Oxford, Blackwell.
26 A. Little (1998) *Post-Industrial Socialism*, London, Routledge, esp. Chapter 5.
27 A. Little (1999) 'The Politics of Compensation: Tom Paine's *Agrarian Justice* and Liberal Egalitarianism', *Contemporary Politics*, 5, 1, pp. 63–73.
28 K. Marx (1875) (1970) *Marginal Notes to the Programme of the German Workers' Party*, Karl Marx, Friedrich Engels *Selected Works*, London, Lawrence and Wishart.
29 For a detailed criticism of entitlement theory concerning rectification see A. Brown (1985) *Modern Political Theory*, London, Penguin, Chapter 4, for a criticism of Locke's proviso, see Mackie (1980) *Ethics: Inventing Right and Wrong*, London, Penguin, Chapter 8.
30 Cf. Little (1998) op. cit. Chapter 4.
31 Chapter 1; see also J. O'Neill (1998) *The Market: Ethics, Knowledge and Politics*, London, Routledge.

32 One of the problems with White's book is that he goes on to assume that the end of paid employment leads naturally to the end of work as such, which is an assumption which I hope that I have shown is quite misleading.

33 See C. Winch (1996), *Quality and Education*, Oxford, Blackwell, Chapter 5.

34 J. White (1982) *The Aims of Education Restated*. London, Routledge. Strict adherence to this definition led White to deny that higher education had, properly speaking, any specifically *educational* aims.

14 Education and work in a social capital perspective

INTRODUCTION

The aim of this chapter is to draw together the various ethical, political, economic and educational threads that have run through this book and to present an overview of vocational education that allows both for an understanding of its importance and of its relationship with liberal and civic aims of education. The nature and importance of what is now called 'lifelong learning' will also be considered.

PRODUCTIVE POWERS

In Chapter 5, the Listian concept of *productive powers* of an economy was adopted as a suitable model for considering the role of vocational education. To recapitulate, productive powers are an economy's *potential* to fulfil its aims. In many societies these are the maximisation of individual consumption. But they need not be solely this. Germany and Japan adopted the development of national strength as economic aims and, as argued throughout this book, human well-being in a broad sense is a legitimate but neglected aim. When the primary aim of economic activity is conceived of as the development of human well-being in a broad sense, then the productive powers of the economy will constitute its potential for achieving it.

It is not, of course, being claimed that the development of productive powers should be the *only* aspect of economic activity that deserves attention. Maintenance of the capacity for consumption is extremely important as, quite apart from satisfying a host of needs, it maintains demand and hence a healthy level of paid employment.[1] But consumption can be of public as well as private goods, and there may be strong arguments for maintaining high levels of expenditure on, for example, health, education, the public environment, transport and non-paid employment.[2] But these themselves, although they embody capital goods to a large extent, also promote consumption. In creating, using and maintaining them, employment is created and demand for consumable commodities generated. These goods stimulate the development of various kinds of industry: publishing in the case of education, medical and biomedical technology in the case of health, energy-saving devices in the case of the public environment, and rail and aviation technology in the case of transport, to give single examples from each area. There is, therefore, no reason to suppose that the building up and maintaining of productive powers in their aspect of *physical assets* is in any way inimical to the generation of a healthy level of consumer demand.[3]

Important as they are, physical assets are only an aspect of productive powers. For example, education needs such things as buildings, books, computers, but teachers and pupils who are able and willing to learn are absolutely vital to the enterprise. Thus the human aspect of productive powers is of the greatest importance. Education is inconvenienced by the absence of buildings and books; it is fatally compromised by incompetent and unwilling teachers and pupils or hostile parents.[4] It is therefore vital to consider social capital as an aspect of productive powers.

SOCIAL CAPITAL

It was argued in Chapters 1 and 5 that modern conceptions of social capital show a tendency to ignore its cognitive element. They also fail to take into account its *civil* element. It is considered, by Coleman, for example, that the density of social networks and concomitant levels of non-commercial relationships between the participants, principally those characterised by trust, is its prime constituent. But social networks of themselves may or may not contribute to productive powers. A prejudiced, backward-looking community, hostile to any kind of formal education, may impede, rather than enhance productive powers.[5] Trust may exercise a powerful normative influence within a community, but may exist only negatively in relation to outgroups, making the society as a whole 'low trust'.[6] Like physical capital, social capital has to be *available* to fulfil some economic purpose. Not all forms of social relationship, even 'dense' ones are available for such purposes, or for purposes that are considered legitimate (for example, non-criminal forms of economic activity). Social networks do not, of themselves, constitute social capital, although they may, in certain circumstances, contribute to its composition.

It is also a mistake to concentrate on social networks without taking due account of *social institutions*. This is, to some extent, done implicitly by social capital theorists when they describe the social relationships that hold within a family or church for example.[7] But this misses two aspects of institutions: first, they very often themselves have aims, however implicit these may be, which partially define the nature of the social relationships to be found within them. This was enormously important, as we saw in Chapter 6, in the formation of occupational identity. Second, institutions themselves exist in a political context. As constituents of social capital, they are dependent to a considerable extent on the state. It is, of course, important to recognise that they have a spontaneous element, which is at the root of the formation of trades unions, churches and charitable organisations, for example. But the political context in which they operate also has an extremely powerful influence and can hinder, as well as help, their development. This can be done by altering the legal and economic framework in which they operate, or by policies that change public attitudes towards them. For example, the decline in influence of trade unionism in the UK after 1979 is partly due to the influence of all three of these factors.

As well as more or less formal institutions, social capital exists in customs and practices such as that of cuisine, music-making or sport.[8] Again, it is difficult to describe these simply in terms of social networks and accompanying norms, because they are also characterised by purposes, patterns of activity and a sense of identity, which cannot be grasped simply through a description of their constitutive social networks.

Both the institutional and the customary sides of association bring with them more than social networks and norms of trust, important though these are. They are also training and educational institutions and practices in the secondary sense that participation in them requires skill (in the broad sense described in Chapter 11) and practice in the primary context in order to become consolidated. They are repositories of skill and serve to perpetuate and develop it. When skill is available for conceptions of the good that are recognised within the society, it is a constituent of social capital existing in customs, practices and institutions. These informal elements constitute an important part of the educational resources available within a society.

Productive labour

Adam Smith's definition of productive labour, as we saw in Chapter 2, confined it exclusively to labour directed towards the production of vendible commodities.[9] Even suitably modified to cover saleable services, it proposes an extremely narrow conception of what is worthwhile.[10] The same activity can be either productive or non-productive depending on the context. A driver on a privatised railway charging fares is productive, while one who works for a public service railway funded from taxation is non-productive. A teacher in a private school is productive, one in a state school is not. Many, if not most, of the activities that contribute to the maintenance and development of productive powers in List's sense are non-productive on this account.

We can, however, retain the normative implications of 'productive' in 'productive labour' if we consider that productive powers are those assets that potentially contribute to fulfilling the economic aims of the society, whatever they may be. To define 'productive labour' as that which contributes to economic aims, including the development of productive powers, is to capture both the narrower group in Smith's definition, together with those who indirectly contribute to the production of commodities through providing, for example, health care for workers engaged in the production of commodities, but also those, not necessarily engaged in either the direct or the indirect production of commodities, who engage in reproduction, either physical or spiritual, of the workforce, for example, child-carers, musicians, priests, etc.[11]

On this conception, vocational education is properly concerned with the development of productive labour. At the individual level, it is concerned with the development of the ability to contribute economically, either through producing saleable goods, through indirectly contributing to the production of saleable goods or through contributing to the development of productive powers in the broadest sense.

We can see why vocational education need by no means be confined to preparation for producing commodities, or even necessarily for paid employment. Social capital is the sum of knowledge, skill, attitudes and attributes of character that are embodied in customs, practices and social institutions, that is available for a society's economic aims, including consumption and the further development of productive powers. Productive labour, then, contributes either to production for consumption or to the development of productive powers, and if social capital is an essential component of productive powers, then those forms of education that contribute to the formation and maintenance of social capital are themselves productive. These considerations give us further reason for being cautious about circumscribing too narrowly what should count as 'vocational', 'liberal' or 'civic' education, since it is evident that developing the culture of individuals and a sense of civic responsibility all contribute to the formation and maintenance of social capital in this sense.

These reflections on social capital should make us aware of one extremely important aspect of vocational education, even when it is conceived of in a fairly narrow sense, as a preparation for paid employment or for commodity production. Employees are individuals with their own needs and interests, with family and other relationships, as well as being citizens. As List noted, unhappy individuals are less likely to be productive workers, even in Smith's narrower sense. Disaffected or poorly educated citizens are unlikely to value the wider contribution to society that their work may make, and are less likely to take seriously the social role and obligations that their employment implies.

One possible objection to this line of thought is that one is building a high level of redundancy into preparation for work. The cost of preparing young people for work on this model is unacceptable and also wastes their own time, if their main focus is to gain employment. The fact is, however, that any commitment to a high-skill economy is bound to involve redundancy, because vocational education in a high-skill context, as opposed to training for specific tasks, is preparation for an occupation in a certain kind of environment. Since both the environment and the occupation are likely to be subject to high levels of change, it is unavoidable that much of the preparation will involve coping with change. In one sense this is often directly vocational, where, for example, employees acquire work-specific skills in the workplace or a *practicum* (see Chapter 8) which are not immediately applicable.[12]

It may involve the development of 'deep' skills in or outside the workplace, which allow workers the capacity to adapt, through a deeper understanding of the applied theoretical knowledge that informs their work.[13] But it should also involve a greater awareness of the ethical, social and political context in which the occupation is situated, in order to promote a greater understanding of the wider effects of the industry concerned. This is important as part of what is known as 'quality assurance', which crucially involves worker commitment to the integrity of what is produced. But it is also important in making it easier for individuals to understand and accept the need for change and to ensure that their occupations are conducted in a socially responsible way.

It was pointed out in Chapters 10 and 11 that knowledge in high-skill processes tends to be collective. An individual's own skills are only fully useful when employed in conjunction with those of fellow-workers. But it follows that if there has to be a change in the mix of skills employed, that has to be understood and accepted by the team, not just by the management, or some individuals in the team. Change is usually more acceptable if there are intelligible reasons for it. These are likely to arise from changes in the techniques involved in production, or in the economic, political, social and environmental context in which the product is made and used. In the kind of economic environment in which, for example, diversified quality production (DQP) is carried on, there is a particular need for rapid adaptation to the requirements of the market. This in turn requires rapid and consensual decision-making procedures within the enterprise. When the collective knowledge of workers gives them a high degree of autonomy over the work process, then collective assent by production teams is vital to successful adaptation.[14]

This is likely to become not just an issue concerning successful management, but one concerning corporate governance and the nature of control over the enterprise. If workers already have substantial control over the work process, and if their willing assent, and even anticipation, of change is necessary to economic success, then it makes good sense to involve them more in the direction and management of their enterprises. There is a need to do so at the level of plant and team for obvious reasons, but also at the level of the strategic direction of the company. This implies changes in corporate governance both at the 'works' and at the board of directors level and, possibly within the managerial structure of companies. Such a change in employees' relationships with the organisations in which they work is going to have implications for their vocational education in the broad sense that has been described above.

How practical is this suggestion? We have long been familiar with universities, 'knowledge industries' *par excellence*, instituted centuries ago, whose self-governing aspects have been retained with adaptations, as an appropriate form of managing such a kind of enterprise. Readers in the English-speaking world are by now familiar with the more consensual and less hierarchical management practices of Japanese companies, but relatively few are likely to be aware of the forms of corporate governance known as *Mitbestimmung* or *co-determination* practised in Germany for the last 50 years.[15] Co-determination in its full form involves works councils that have statutory rights to information and consultation and that elect representatives to the supervisory board of the enterprise, giving employees a very substantial say in the running of company affairs.

The historical and contemporary evidence for the success of co-determination appears to suggest a small competitive advantage (expressed in shareholder value), especially in the older established areas of co-determination.[16] This can be attributed to a number of factors: increased ability to adapt to changing market conditions; increased firm-specific pay flexibility; a growth in trust between management and workforce without a loss of management competence; the development of structures which aid rapid consensus-reaching and decision-making. Streeck *et al.* also point out that co-determination can be seen as part of a wider development towards greater autonomy within the society; that it can further increase competitiveness through co-operative decision-making; that innovation can be increased through the development of organisational flexibility based on co-determination.[17] Co-determination is but one way of adapting to the requirements of a high-skill economy, the self-governing aspects of the *Handwerk* or artisanal sector of the German economy is another model, as are worker co-operatives along the lines practised, for example, in Spain.[18] As Streeck also argues, the adoption of such structures also obliges employers to move towards higher skill forms of activity. Co-determination makes it difficult to sack workers and obliges employers to treat their employees largely as a fixed asset that needs to be developed in order to ensure the best return for the company.[19]

Co-determination is not a form of direct democracy, it involves the election of representatives of employees to responsible positions. But, in order for it to work, employees have to be committed to their enterprise and be informed about the general conditions in which it works, just as citizens in a democracy need to have some basic understanding of political, social and economic issues if they are to vote in an informed way. The success of such forms of employee participation and, *a fortiori*, of more direct forms, implies the broader form of vocational education described above, with the inclusion of significant aspects of civic education. In the development described above, the formation and maintenance of social capital and the development of broader vocational education can be accomplished in close concert. Both involve education in forming and maintaining effective social relationships, knowledge of the implications of one's actions in a broad social context, and a good working knowledge of the way in which one's society operates.

Education for productive labour

The social environment is universally acknowledged to be an extremely important factor in educational achievement, at least at the beginning of the twenty-first century. The idea that the efforts of pupils and teachers are decisive seems to have been more prevalent in the nineteenth century, and also amongst newer immigrant groups in the UK and the US. For many years it was thought that schooling had a negligible effect on educational success, the decisive factor being the social background of pupils. It is only with the rise in influence of school effectiveness research that this widely held assumption has been challenged.[20] It is, of course, absurd to think that schools do not educate.

Even the children of educated parents will learn little of value if they are not systematically taught. What proponents of the 'no difference' thesis meant is that one school is as good as another, and that differences in achievement are due to social class differences. One complication, of course, is that the social class differences are, very often, differences in attitude to the importance of education, and reflect differences in knowledge as to the best ways of achieving it. The notion of social capital is sometimes used to explain these social class differences in achievement.[21] As remarked earlier, however, a conception of social capital that ignores its cognitive features and the fact that capital implies availability for a given purpose, is not likely to provide a fully illuminating account of the way in which social background factors affect educational achievement.

It is evident then, that social relations, customs and institutions do not, of themselves, constitute social capital. If they are not available for investment in productive powers, either because of social indifference or antagonism, or because they embody inappropriate cognitive abilities, then they are not capital, any more than natural resources which are unexploitable or inappropriate to economic activity are. However, social relationships can constitute social capital in the right circumstances, just as physical resources can constitute physical capital. Social relationships constitute a 'raw' form of social capital when they are deployed to serve educational ends, which in turn form a set of new relationships and cognitive dispositions more directly at the disposal of productive powers. Minimally, these social relationships need to embody an identification with and commitment to at least some of the aims of education. Sometimes there are cognitive barriers to the exploitation of educational opportunities, although it is important that these are not exaggerated. It is far more likely, for example, that these barriers will be of a specific rather than of a general nature, consisting of, for example, a lack of engagement with the written rather than the spoken word, instead of a generalised lack of linguistic ability or even general cognitive disadvantage.[22] A closely connected issue relates to educational aims. It was argued in Chapter 3 that the educational aims adopted by a polity involve a negotiated outcome between different *conceptions* of education held by different groups embodying different points of view. In political practice, however, it is often the case that a dominant or hegemonic group succeeds in making its own conception dominant to such an extent that it effectively excludes alternative conceptions from any prospect of serious implementation.[23]

When this happens, there is usually a partial disengagement from the aims of the system by those who are least inclined to identify with them. In such circumstances, one is likely to find significant levels of low educational achievement. Successful engagement with education involves identification with, and hence knowledge of, and commitment to, at least some of its aims on the part of parents and communities. It would be very easy to blame them for a lack of vision in failing to encourage children to get the most out of education. However we should, perhaps, pause when considering what children and parents actually want from education, that is, what *their* aims are. The evidence in the UK is that aims are overwhelmingly vocational, yet the system is run by people whose aims are largely liberal. The report of the National Commission on Education makes it very clear that education is viewed vocationally, while the current UK national curriculum now incorporates a statement of aims which makes tangential references to work in the context of liberal and civic aims.[24] Such a situation is a recipe for an economy dominated to a considerable degree, by low-skill general labour markets (see Chapter 10).

Despite protestations from the two main political parties in England and Wales, that they see education as a crucial factor in the development of the economy, there remains a strange reluctance to align the system, at least partly, with vocational aims. This is not just a matter of academic interest; the aims of education are the benchmark against which the appropriateness of the curriculum is to be judged. It becomes difficult, if not impossible, to alter the curriculum in a vocational direction if this cannot be justified according to the aims. One may conclude that there is still a great reluctance to admit a genuine pluralism about aims and hence curricular diversity into the British system, and this in turn reflects a cross-party consensus on the aims of education which, as was seen in Chapter 3, can be traced back to the gentry education of the seventeenth and eighteenth centuries. It is hardly surprising that there is a persistent problem with educational disaffection in the UK, associated with high levels of exit by young people with few or no academic qualifications at the end of the compulsory period.

Confusingly, much of the rhetoric associated with the political push to raise levels of achievement emphasises the benefits in terms of employability. The dissonance between aims and rhetoric might not be too much of a problem in the short term, since most parents and children are extremely unlikely to read government legislation or curriculum documents. The effects of the dissonance are more likely to be felt at the political level in the longer term, as any substantial change in the curriculum in a vocational direction requires a change in aims. There is, however, a much more pressing problem with the drive to raise educational standards when other changes are not made. It was noted in Chapter 11 that much of the UK economy is run as a low-skill equilibrium and therefore does not require a majority of the workforce to have high levels of either academic or vocational qualifications. Furthermore, there appears to be a strong bipartisan political consensus that the interventionist steps necessary to move economic sectors towards a high-skill equilibrium are unacceptable.

A predominantly liberal academic curriculum has a certain vocational value: it serves as a gateway to higher education; it, together with a higher education, leads to vocational opportunities in the professions and management, where literary and numerical aptitudes are required, together with a modicum of 'cultural literacy'.[25] However, it is redundant for entry into low-skill occupations and is only of value at school-leaving age if it provides a gateway into intermediate level apprenticeships and artisanal and technical training. And, as we have seen, it is at this level that a high-skill equilibrium draws a very significant part of its strength. We can conclude that, in the absence of a substantial number of occupational opportunities in this category, there are limited incentives, from a vocational point of view, for many young people to even complete their school-leaving qualifications. These are the ones who do not have a desire or aptitude to continue further academic study, who wish to be involved in some practical engagement with life, such as in a workplace, but who, nevertheless, wish to pursue an interesting and demanding, as well as a remunerative occupation.

Lifelong learning

The phrase 'lifelong learning' could almost have been coined to suit the varied and changing purposes of professional politicians. It has three key properties that give it political appeal: (1) it has normatively positive connotations; (2) it suggests contemporaneity and relevance; (3) it is ambiguous and almost protean in the meanings that it can adopt. Taking the first, it is hard to be against lifelong learning—who could be in favour (publicly at least) of lifelong ignorance? As for the second, it connects with preoccupations about rapid socio-economic change, globalisation and competitiveness which are hard to ignore and to which it promises to offer a solution. The third property of the phrase is the most significant. It is in its ambiguity that its real genius is to be found. By the word 'learning' rather than 'education' or 'training', learner autonomy is suggested. Similarly, 'lifelong' suggests a rich variety of possibilities which range from immediate post-school professional formation, through mid-career reskilling, to a third-age liberal enrichment. 'Lifelong learning' promises to have something to suit everyone. Unfortunately, at some point choices have to be made as to what the main focus is going to be, and these choices depend not only on budgetary constraints but also on political priorities and the general direction in economic development. The phrase itself masks these choices and suggests a fool's paradise where all realisations are possible.

If this sounds excessively cynical then further reflection in terms of the themes already covered in this book might persuade the reader to see it instead as realistic. The first step is to ask oneself the question: 'Why should someone be committed to a lifetime of learning?' On the liberal conception of education the question does not present much difficulty: if one's aim is personal cultivation, this is a process that has no obvious stopping point and can be incorporated into someone's leisure activities. When vocational education is considered, however, the question becomes more difficult to answer, for the clear implication is that individuals will never cease to need to upgrade their work-related knowledge. This is hardly difficult to envisage in a professional or high-skill environment, where the main aspect of many jobs is response to rapidly changing circumstances and market conditions. But the use of the phrase in this context merely expresses a banality, that some occupations, particularly complex ones, require constant employee adaptation. Furthermore, it is in the interest of the employer to make this adaptation as easy as possible, so that old products can be upgraded and new ones developed. When 'lifelong learning' is within the enterprise, or organised by the enterprise then there is little need to make it a political initiative, although politicians can make it easier for enterprises to provide in-house training, through controlling the financial environment and ensuring a robust and credible system of accreditation in occupational labour markets.

A process of elimination, therefore, leads to a consideration of the relevance of lifelong learning to the lives of the unskilled. We have already noted that not only do unskilled jobs require little training (this is almost a tautology), but they are increasingly characterised by impermanence. The pace of economic change means that such jobs come and go according to market conditions. There is little incentive for employers to train workers in this category, since they do not require much skill to do the job and the employer is under no obligation to be concerned about the employee's future prospects. It is no surprise, therefore, to be told that this kind of learning is the individual's responsibility.[26]

While individuals working in high-skill occupations might reasonably expect to continually adapt and improve their skills if, for example, they wish to gain promotion within an internal labour market or to work for a different enterprise, possibly at a different level, in an occupational labour market, they are essentially building on and developing both their general education and their occupational formation. It is misleading to call this 'lifelong learning'; it goes with the job and with the career structures available in high-skill occupations, and those who enter such occupations expect it and have prepared for it through general education and initial formation. There was a time when the need to adapt and upgrade skills was less pressing, but nowadays the challenge is increasingly to adapt occupation-specific general abilities and knowledge of the fundamental principles that govern one's occupation, to highly specific and possibly impermanent contexts.

There are also practical reasons why occupational learning in high-skill occupations is incremental. There is a long period of post-compulsory education during which one is involved in formation, either through alternance or apprenticeship, or through a full-time college-based vocational course. During this period, individuals are not fully effective workers and their low remuneration is justified by the employer because of their low effectiveness and the cost of their formation. Subsequent learning, as it builds on what has been acquired during formation, is incremental and does not require time out of the workplace to anything like the same extent. If it did, very serious consequences would result. Skilled workers who had to completely renew their skills up to half a dozen times within a lifetime could expect to spend approximately 18 years of a maximum 49 years of working life in non-remunerated occupational formation.

Not only would the personal and financial cost of such enforced learning be very heavy, but it would become subject to diminishing returns, both emotionally and financially, as retirement drew nearer. Nor is it clear who would have an incentive, apart from the individual concerned, to finance it. But that individual on their own would be incapable of doing so. Furthermore, the loss of 18 years of pension contributions would provide another very powerful disincentive for anyone who wished to follow such a path, or for the government that had to pick up the bill for retirement. We can safely conclude that non-incremental lifelong learning in a high-skill working environment is not a practical option.[27]

On the other hand, workers in low-skill occupations do not require the same kind of skill base on which to build their work-specific abilities or, if they do, then these are relatively limited and can be accounted for by a limited amount of general education. It is possible for them to change occupations half a dozen times during the course of their working lives, precisely because the limited amount of training required to do each successive job competently need not be disruptive of their earning a living. But if 'lifelong learning' in the sense of constant retraining for new jobs is most associated with low-skill work, it is not, nor should it be, an attractive prospect for most of the population. At its worst, therefore, the phrase 'lifelong learning' is an exortation to low-skilled workers to keep on their toes or be out of a job. When coupled with a refusal to take the steps necessary to create a high-skill economy, its promotion becomes hypocrisy.

Renewing social capital

The 'reproduction' of the workforce obviously depends on the maintenance of workers and their families at a socially acceptable level of subsistence. But if the arguments advanced in this book have any validity, this is only the beginning of maintaining social capital. High-skill production requires dedication and enthusiasm and a sense on the part of workers that they are doing something intrinsically, as well as extrinsically, worthwhile. For that to be the case, para-doxically enough, it is necessary that paid employment takes its proper place in their lives alongside domestic, leisure and voluntary activities. Reproduction, as List recognised, involves spiritual renewal in the sense that workers need to be able to dedicate themselves to their work and their workmates.[28] Civil society, as well as the family, has a critical role to play; in the past workers have built up their own institutions of churches and chapels, libraries, choirs, bands and sports clubs in order to provide for their spiritual as well as their practical needs, and, in so doing, have developed various cognitive abilities as well. Unfortunately, the very success of working people in gaining education and sufficient disposal income to be able to afford more private leisure activities has, to some extent, led to the atrophying of some of these institutions, through their provision by the state and commercial organisations.

There are good reasons for not wishing to see the community level of civil society atrophy completely. The range of interests and abilities that can be collectively catered for is far greater than can be provided for in a single household, offering far more resources for spiritual renewal. The cognitive abilities that are developed in such networks are a valuable resource, both economic and non-economic; habits of sociability, the prevalence of trust and mutual concern that arise from civil association are valuable in themselves, but in economists' terms, reduce 'transaction costs' that arise from having to deal contractually with interactions that would otherwise take place spontaneously and without sanction. When they are provided on a commercial or a welfare basis, less involvement is required of the recipients. In this area, it is increasingly apparent that liberal and citizenship aspects of education are closely related.

People often wish to develop skills which they can use in their leisure and within their communities, not just at work. They want opportunities to develop their abilities to work with other people and to manage the affairs of collective projects, as well as of their workplace. Many of these skills are learned informally by participation, but formal education has a role to play in giving young people experience of planning and running their own affairs through participation in community activities, by organising and facilitating a controlled engagement with them. This suggests a fairly 'thick' notion of citizenship education which goes beyond education for participation in the formal institutions of representative democracy, to include the strengthening of civil society.

CONCLUSION

The argument of this chapter derives naturally from the account of educational aims offered in Chapter 3, which should be relatively uncontroversial. In non-normative second-order terms, education involves preparation for self-fulfilment, for employment and for citizenship. Depending on the balance of cultural, economic and political forces within any particular society, the particular dominant conception of education that is developed will adopt liberal, vocational and civic education in various different configurations. As far as particular conceptions of education go, an outlook that considers the development of productive powers and social capital will not issue in particular prescriptions, since such an outlook will have very different manifestations in different societies. However, a society that sees the development of individuals, of economic strength and of civil institutions as closely connected, would find it natural to attempt to achieve a balance in combining liberal, vocational and civic education.

A further question arises concerning the role of *schools*, and other institutions where learning takes place, in promoting such a mix of aims. This is more likely to be a question of determining the role of schools in concert with other institutions, rather than a question of replacing schools, and has to be related to different historical and cultural traditions of education.[29] But, to the extent that some knowledge, skill and understanding can only be acquired, or at least consolidated, in the primary contexts in which it is exercised, then the role of organisations whose *primary* role is non-educational need to be carefully evaluated. This complex relationship will be one of the main themes of Chapter 15.

Notes

1 Cf. Mark Lutz (1999) *Economics for the Common Good*, London, Routledge, 1999, esp. Chapter 4.
2 Meaning by this last, employment which is not remunerated through a commercial labour contract but which has attached to it, for example, a basic income.
3 The neo-liberal view that public investment 'crowds out' private consumer-oriented investment ignores the fact that public investment requires the participation of the private sector to bring projects to fruition.
4 Anyone who doubts this should examine the educational achievements of some of the less wealthy countries in the eastern Carribean, for example, in comparison to what is

often achieved in certain educational sectors of the developed world [cf. C. Winch and J. Gingell (1994) 'Dialect Interference and Difficulties with Writing: An Investigation in St. Lucian Primary Schools', *Language and Education*, 8, 3, pp. 157–182].

5 J. Field (1999) 'Investigating Community Based Learning: Social Capital, Capacity Building and Regeneration'. Unpublished paper in the ESRC Seminar Series, *Working to Learn*, 24 June.

6 Cf. F. Fukuyama (1995) *Trust*, London, Penguin, Part 2.

7 J. Coleman (1988) 'Social Capital in the Creation of Human Capital', *American Journal of Sociology*, 94, Supplement S, pp. 95–120.

8 See Chapter 1.

9 Note, however, that as remarked in Chapter 2, he 'wobbles' over this definition, defining it at one point as that which adds value to a good.

10 The term is not used neutrally, as Smith's examples of non-productives makes clear (e.g. servants and lackeys). The clear implication is that non-productives are 'parasites'.

11 Friedrick List (1991) *The National System of Political Economy*, NJ, Augustus Kelley.

12 See W. Streeck (1992) *Social Institutions and Economic Performance*, London, Sage, Chapter 1.

13 See D. Ashton and J. Sung (1997) 'Education, Skill Formation and Economic Development: The Singaporean Approach' in Centre For Labour Market Studies, MSc in Training, *Module 3*, Units 1, 2, pp. 351–372.

14 See G. Hodgson (1999) *Economics and Utopia: Why the Learning Society is Not the End of History*, London, Routledge, pp. 211–227.

15 A very detailed account of its evolution is, however, to be found in Streeck, op. cit. Chapter 5. The nearest that the UK has come to adopting some form of co-determination was with the publication of the Bullock Report (1977) *Report of the Commission on Industrial Democracy*, London, HMSO, which recommended a similar system to that of Germany. It was, however, rapidly scotched by political opposition from a wide range of political quarters.

16 W. Streeck *et al.* 'Mitbestimmung und neue Unternehmenskulturen' (1998) Hans Böckler Stiftung. See also Streeck (1992) op. cit. for further information on shareholder remuneration in co-determined companies.

17 Streeck (1998) op. cit. For a brief report, see *Die Zeit* (1998) 'Modell mit Zukunft', 22, 20 May, p. 1.

18 Hodgson, op. cit. pp. 215, 218; Lutz, op. cit. Chapter 8.

19 Streeck (1992) op. cit. Chapter 5.

20 For nineteenth-century attitudes, see J. C. B. Gordon (1981) *Verbal Deficit*, London, Croom Helm; on school effectiveness research see John Gray, Brian Wilcox (1995) *Good School, Bad School*, Buckingham, Open University Press. For a philosophical survey of the school effectiveness literature, see Winch (1996) *Quality and Education*, Oxford, Blackwell, Chapter 7.

21 See, for example, Coleman, op. cit.

22 There is an extensive literature on this topic. For a survey and critique see C. Winch (1990) *Language, Ability and Educational Achievement*, London, Routledge; for evidence of literacy-specific dissonances between social groups and educational requirements see C. G. Wells (1981) 'Some Antecedents of Early Educational Attainment', *British Journal of Sociology of Education*, 2, 2, 1981.

23 Cf. A. Green (1990) *Education and State Formation*, London, Macmillan, on the evolution of the UK education system, for example.

24 National Commission for Education (1993) *Learning to Succeed*, London, Heinemann, p. 151; DfEE (1999) *The National Curriculum: Handbook for Secondary Teachers in England*, pp. 10–12, London, HMSO.

25 E. D. Hirsch (1987) *Cultural Literacy: What Every American Should Know*, Boston, Houghton Mifflin.

26 DfEE (1999) *Learning to Succeed*, London, HMSO.

27 Organisations like the Open University in the UK do not constitute a counter-example to this case, since they do not, in the main, provide workplace formation, but higher liberal or vocational education preparatory to formation for employment.

28 List, op. cit. p. 144.

29 That these can be highly specific and resistant to change even in countries that have close political ties can be seen in A. Green, A. Wolf and T. Leney (1999) *Convergence and Divergence in European Education and Training Systems*, London, Institute of Education.

15 Policy issues

Schooling, qualifications and the transition to work

INTRODUCTION

Models of the transition from school to work

Fifty years ago, a few percent of the population went to university, some went into apprenticeships and the great majority entered work. In some countries this progression was more complex, for example, in Germany a system of training in the workplace, coupled with compulsory part-time vocational education had already been established before the Second World War.[1] However, in the last 20 years or so, the transition from school to work has become increasingly long and complex. This is due in large part to the increasing skill demands of modern work, but also to an increase in wealth, and to the ever-growing role of credentials as a positional good.

Although these broad trends apply across practically all the industrially developed nations, there remain, nevertheless, very significant and enduring differences between the practices of different countries, which are rooted in the historical evolution of patterns of induction into work and the original development of their education systems. These historically persistent differences should remind us how difficult it can be to bring about significant breaks with tradition through political and educational reform, when certain customs and practices are embedded in the life of the society. The institution of apprenticeship, for example, is difficult to 'graft on' to economies and industries where it does not have deep historical roots.[2] The experience of the UK in carrying out a far-reaching reform of compulsory education is another case in point. Although in some respects great changes were made, particularly in the instituting of a national curriculum and system of assessment, in other respects matters remained surprisingly the same. For example, the whole vexed issue of debate on the aims of the national education system was studiously avoided, and the detail of the curriculum proved to be extraordinarily difficult to take from the control of teacher-based subject interest groups. Politically speaking, educational reform is highly difficult business, requiring time and the detailed attention of politicians. Given the fundamental importance to the life of a society of the way it prepares its young people for adulthood, this should hardly be surprising. The fact should, however, provide educational reformers with a salutary reminder of the patience, preparedness to compromise, attention to detail and hard work that they should be prepared to expend if they are to effect lasting changes in a country's education system.

These considerations, fortunately, need not prevent philosophers from arguing for the direction that they think educational change should take. Their arguments, if sound, will at least provide a good foundation for commencing the process of reform. Although this chapter is not specifically concerned with the UK, its proposals are, perhaps, particularly relevant to that country, for a number of reasons. First, it has always been uneasy about debating educational aims, and thus stirring up controversy that might expose the social divisions within the society. Second, its status as a relatively low-skill economy makes it a prime candidate for reforms tending to move it towards higher skill economic activity. Third, its economic thinking is dominated by a tradition (deriving from Adam Smith) that attaches little importance to, and is indeed contemptuous of, systematic vocational education. Finally, its repeated attempts to upgrade its vocational education have been dogged by a reluctance to take a fundamental look at what it wants and how vocational education relates to the more traditional liberal conception of education which is the dominant paradigm.

AIMS AND CURRICULUM

The question of the aims of education has been settled in terms of the dominant liberal tradition, with some attention paid to civic aims. Vocational aims are largely ignored. Naturally enough, the newly revised curriculum reflects these priorities, with the liberal theme dominant, while a civic harmony can be detected alongside. There is thus a common compulsory curriculum for children from the ages of 5–16. For 14–16-year-olds, there is some remission of these requirements in relation to certain subjects, which become optional after 14. However, the gaps are to be filled by schools as they see fit; there are no branching curricula which take account of different conceptions of education for this age group.[3] One may safely say, then, that apart from some experimentation with specialist technology, language and sports schools, which offer an enhanced curriculum or wider curriculum choice in certain areas, a unitary liberal/civic curriculum, offered through a largely comprehensive state schooling system is what is offered to most children in the UK.[4] Even the older tradition of technical education, which existed from the beginning of the century died shortly after the end of the Second World War.[5]

There are, in modern circumstances, very good reasons for maintaining a common curriculum into the lower secondary years of schooling, even in societies that have well-defined vocational aims. Quite apart from the need to promote a common level of competence in numeracy and literacy, together with the common knowledge necessary for common understandings, the increasing need for applied theoretical knowledge in many areas of work (see Chapter 8) makes a common curriculum for a large period of compulsory schooling a vocational necessity. On the other hand, if schooling is effective, it may be doubted that this common framework continues to be necessary beyond the age of 13 or so. Dropping certain compulsory elements of the national curriculum is an acknowledgement of this.

But the issue concerns not just whether a single curriculum is necessary beyond a certain age, but also a serious consideration of how to address the needs of those children who by that age, are beginning to think about what they would like to do in life and are, in very many cases, coming to the conclusion that they are best suited for employment. For these children, it is not sufficient to have an abatement of the common curriculum, they need new branches that allow them to pursue challenges connected to those occupational areas that interest them. These programmes should be at a level that gives pupils a rigorous introduction to the principles underlying their chosen area and should issue in qualifications that command respect in the labour market. It would be appropriate, in many cases, to incorporate a *practicum* and a workplace element (see Chapter 8).

Prevocational education

The aims of lower prevocational education (roughly for the 13–16 age group) should be to introduce young people to some of the basic principles underlying their provisional occupational choice, its place in economy and society, its traditions and history and some practical acquaintance with what it is like to work in that occupation.[6] Prevocational education is distinguished, then, from vocational education in that it does not aim to prepare for a specific occupational role. In practice, prevocational and vocational elements in a programme become harder to distinguish as one considers higher skill levels, as the mastery of these usually demand a broader view of the occupation. For this reason I will treat prevocational and vocational education at the tertiary level as largely identical. Prevocational education is characterised through being (a) school-based (b) containing an element of practical but general training in a *practicum* context and limited or no workplace experience. It is important to realise that where the balance of these elements shifts, the education becomes more vocational than prevocational. The shift of institutional context from school to college usually signals a concomitant shift towards the *practicum* and greater involvement in the workplace. However, intermediate and tertiary vocational education often have limited elements of the latter in the UK and, arguably, this constitutes one of their weaknesses. Normally, those taking a prevocational course at this level would either expect to move on to a higher prevocational course or to enter the labour market as an apprentice or in an alternance scheme (see below) or at the lower technical or artisanal level. It would certainly be expected, however, that their general level of educational achievement, together with the vocational acquaintance already received, would fit them for further study and progression within their chosen occupation.

Intermediate prevocational education (roughly for the 16–19 age group) extends general educational competence, particularly in the critical areas of literacy and numeracy, as well as further academic study relevant to the chosen occupational field (e.g. geography for the tourism industry, biological sciences for medical technology). It should involve more extended general acquaintance with the occupational field, together with the opportunity to pursue specialist options. *Practicum* and workplace experience should be more extensive at this level. In some cases, these prevocational programmes will equip graduates to take on subordinate technical or supervisory roles, in tandem with further workplace based occupation-specific training.

Prevocational education is subject to a number of objections from liberally minded educators. It is socially divisive; it is academically inferior; it is inappropriate to unskilled work; it distracts young people from having higher expectations. In relation to social divisiveness, there is nothing more damaging to someone's self-esteem to fail at an important enterprise. One is more likely to fail something to which one is not committed by interest. Such failures are not just personal, but damage young people's future career prospects. Harmful forms of social divisiveness arise when people feel that they have had a bad deal from an education system that appears not to be attuned to their aspirations. Social differentiation occurs when, among other reasons, people choose different occupational routes in life. Since this inevitably happens in any society where there is an occupational division of labour, it is scarcely a complaint to be levelled at prevocational education. On the other hand, if preoccupational differentiation leads to success, enhanced further occupational prospects and a sense of achievement and self-respect among young people who do not wish to follow an academic route, then it is difficult to argue that this is harmful.

The academic rigour of programmes raises interesting questions. A considerable body of liberal academic opinion is not in a good position to raise it, because they are opposed to formal assessment on philosophical grounds.[7] Since formal assessment is the only way of maintaining a publicly credible form of national accreditation of educational courses, those who oppose formal assessment cannot seriously argue that they are concerned with rigour. On the other hand, the issue of rigour is one that is very serious. There are two aspects to this: the first is concerned with ensuring that the standards that are appropriate to a discipline are actually aspired to and reflected in courses; the second concerns the demands of the discipline itself. The latter is a particularly thorny question in an era when new subjects are constantly appearing on the syllabus. It may, however, be reasonably doubted whether some of these disciplines, pursued as academic subjects, as opposed to practical ones, are really capable of incorporating any serious intellectual rigour at the level at which they are taught. Suspicions may be raised about such subjects as computing, business, media and cultural studies, pursued as academic subjects, particularly when, as is often the case, they are treated as introductions to the subject rather than an engagement with its basic principles. There is increasing evidence that some of the growth in academic qualifications is a result of the pursuit of these subjects. It can be argued, therefore, that the growing pressure to place everyone on a course that at least appears to be academic rather than practical places intolerable pressure on the integrity of the awards system, to the detriment of everyone who relies on it.

On the other hand, there is no reason why vocational and practical qualifications should not be rigorous. This would, of course, partly depend on the presence of robust and credible awards, but would also crucially depend on whether the demands made by the curriculum were sufficient to permit eventual successful engagement with the occupation or task for which the course prepares the students. Whether the content of the course is practical or theoretical, or a mixture of both, is dependent on whether the question above is answered in the affirmative. When assessing the rigour of awards, in other words, we should not be so concerned with how academic they are, or the extent to which they are based on profound theoretical principles, but whether or not they are 'fit for purpose', that is, whether they provide a good indication of a candidate's ability to enter the occupation at cadet level. Clearly, the more knowledge, skill and understanding are required, the more intensive the formation will be and the more demanding the assessment. Rigour and credibility of vocational qualifications are, in other words, largely a function of the degree of skill (in the broad sense) that the occupation demands. This can be seen, for example, in the fact that the EITB prefers to use City and Guilds in addition to NVQ Level Three as an exit certificate for their modern apprenticeship scheme, on the grounds that NVQ Level Three does not demand sufficient knowledge for successful engagement in the work.[8] Whether these qualifications are called 'A levels' or 'GNVQs', is secondary to their credibility. The debate about whether or not there should be an 'artificial' divide between academic and vocational qualifications is really a side-issue to the much more important question as to how rigorous and credible the awards are. As long as occupations are organised on a low-skill basis, entry qualifications are likely to occupy a low status, providing low levels of challenge and being therefore, of little interest to practically and vocationally minded young people.[9]

It can be seen then that the credibility of vocational qualifications, and hence of vocational education as a distinct route within education, is bound to be connected with the expectations and demands that occupations and the world of work make on young people. One is obliged to return once again to the point made in Chapter 11, that increasing the level of skill in occupations is contingent on having some form of economic and industrial strategy that gives a sense of direction to long- and medium-term economic aims. The point made here is that questions of raising skill levels and raising the status of vocational educational qualifications are bound up with each other. Reform is unlikely to take place if only one aspect of a complex range of issues is tackled at a time.

Acceptance by parents and children of school-based prevocational education will depend in large part as well on the schools that provide it. The historical prevocational route for 'non-academic' pupils during the first three decades after the Second World War was through attendance at a secondary modern school. It was during this period that the tradition of technical schooling in the UK that had existed since the turn of the century was also extinguished. To say that secondary moderns were unpopular with parents and children is in no way to impugn the often heroic efforts of the staff who taught in them.[10] The problems with them were systemic and can be summarised as follows. Since the only recognised aims of education were academic and liberal, the secondary modern school (which had to eschew these aims) was literally aimless. Until a late stage in their history, secondary moderns did not offer any exit qualifications, so they had no credibility on any labour market that required skill. They were not equipped, as the technical insitutions were, to provide a significant practicum element of prevocational education.

Finally, assignment to them was based on an irrevocable selection process that took place at the age of 11, based on an extremely dubious pseudo-scientific theory of innate ability. This perceived injustice was compounded by the fact that selection did not follow well-understood practices of procedural justice; girls were subject to more demanding assessment than boys, and different local authorities had different levels of provision for children so that one's chances of being branded a 'failure' at 11 varied across the country. They were an enormous sector of compulsory secondary education which no one knew what to do with, and if one were to say that their main, although unstated purpose, was to warehouse non-academic children before release on to a general labour market or into an apprenticeship or a college course, one would be unkind but not inaccurate. It was inevitable that, in the absence of any substantial constituency arguing for vocational qualifications and technical prevocational education, the reform of the secondary system that began in the 1960s should incorporate all secondary education in a form of largely liberal, academic education.

Given the changing demands of work at the turn of the century the old model of institutional differentiation, particularly at the lower secondary level (11–14 years) has become less suitable as a way of separating the academic from the vocational routes. The increasing demands that the modern workplace makes on the numeracy and literacy of employees, imposes a strong pressure on the primary sector to ensure that all children leave literate and numerate. This pressure has, in itself, a tendency to narrow the gap between the academic and the non-academic child; all are required now to become minimally academically competent. The pressure currently placed on the primary sector in England and Wales is, in large part a consequence of this realisation, brought home by international comparisons, and by the performance of European neighbours in particular. The academic demands of employment do not end with primary schooling, and continue to be met during the lower secondary stage.

In countries such as Germany, which practice institutional differentiation, common schooling continues to the age of 12 in some regions and specialisation continues to 15 and beyond, according to the track adopted.[11] The differences between the German and the British systems of secondary selection are instructive. The German system relies heavily on a consultative procedure that involves parents, children and schools, and allocations can be reviewed and changed according to progress. Thus children have a better opportunity to consider what path they would like to take in adulthood. There are three types of selective school, the *Hauptschule* (general vocational), the *Realschule* (technical vocational) and the *Gymnasium* (academic) which each have distinct missions and, usually, provide young people with exit qualifications. In addition, they are integrated with a post-compulsory system of alternance and apprenticeship which constitutes the beginning of vocational education proper. It is hardly surprising that institutional selection practised as part of a carefully worked out pattern of prevocational education, alongside a well-established and extensive system of lower and inter-mediate vocational education, commands a far greater degree of popular consent than did the British binary system.[12]

Nevertheless, trends in Germany reflect social pressures and the changing demands of the workplace. Although the former German Democratic Länder in the main abandoned the comprehensive system instituted under the communist regime and reverted to institutional specialisation, they did so, in the main, on a binary rather than a tripartite basis. In those areas where the tripartite system operates, one can see the increasing popularity of the *Gymnasia* and the *Realschulen* at the expense of the *Hauptschulen*, reflecting both a general tendency to favour academic higher education and the demands of the labour market for a more educated workforce.[13]

This tendency, which is clearly associated with the growing integration of the academic with the vocational curriculum, is also associated with an increasing 'permeability' of qualifications that allow for greater progression to higher levels of study. In some cases this is well-established, with the *Realschulen* providing a leaving certificate that permits entry into higher education. The professional baccalaureat in France has a similar function.

These movements suggest changes at the upper secondary level that would provide further opportunities for vocationally minded young people. These would include a differentiated 14+ curriculum with vocational and technical tracks leading to qualifications that could serve as credentials for entry on to good quality, post-compulsory vocational programmes, including apprenticeships. Given the equipment and specialist teaching staff necessary to operate such programmes, the current practice of designating specialist schools in the UK could usefully be extended, with substantial investment in schools providing expert prevocational tuition in certain areas. This form of institutional differentiation would imply close involvement with local enterprises who could offer elements of work-experience as part of the programmes. Taken seriously, the development of this kind of specialised upper secondary education would require heavy investment in buildings, equipment, staff and school-work liaison. However, an advantage of spending money on it is that it would go some way towards persuading the public that vocational education was not something seen as a 'second best' for stupid children, but something vital to the well-being of the society. The secondary modern school was rightly seen as a second best, since the investment in this sector, in terms of money, commitment and thought was low. Children who attended them were publicly labelled as stupid through the 11+ examination and the schools were unable to provide very much in the way of pre-vocational education, even their provision for practical educational programmes was limited and they offered no qualifications worth speaking of. Any attempt to reform the upper secondary school through institutional differentiation has a terrible legacy to overcome in the British historical memory. This means that reform requires a serious commitment of thought, political will, persuasion and resources.

VOCATIONAL EDUCATION

Lower and intermediate

Education for work has, as was argued in Chapter 9, three components: academic, *practicum* and work experience. Vocational education, therefore, consists of some or all of these components in varying mixes, according to the country concerned and the level of entry into the labour market being aimed for. When it is predominantly college-based, the dominant modes of learning tend to be academic and through the *practicum*. Work-based forms make greater use of the workplace and less of the *practicum* and academic study. The best-known, and most admired, continental model is the German dual system, which combines work or apprenticeship with compulsory attendance at a vocational college (*Berufschule*) where academic education and the theoretical aspects of the occupation are pursued for a period of up to three years. There is often a *practicum* element associated with this form of training, which takes place within the *Berufschule* or the workplace.

The UK, by contrast, operates a mixed system of lower vocational education which can involve apprenticeship, alternance or college study. Apprenticeship is a form of vocational education which involves in-company training, leads to a qualification and has a contract which defines the apprentice in relation to the *employer*, rather than the state, although the state regulates the main aspects of the employer–apprentice relationship.[14] Its historical roots go back to the guilds or occupational associations of the Middle Ages, organisations which set standards, developed and maintained occupational identity and traditions, trained new workers and controlled access to the labour market. In Britain, apprenticeship has survived in certain industries and has received a boost in recent years with the advent of the state-sponsored modern apprenticeship, which is available at the intermediate vocational level. However, much vocational education at this level takes place in vocational education colleges, which provide a theoretical and *practicum*-based occupational formation. Alternance is a form of training or formation that involves in-company training and off-the-job school or college academic learning. The trainee is not an employee and is expected to work towards a qualification. It is an important feature of both college and alternance programmes that they do not closely affect and reflect the structure of the labour market in the way that apprenticeship programmes do.[15]

Apprenticeship has a number of features that align it with the outlook on the relationship between economic life and vocational education that has been recommended in this book. Well-run, it offers scope for a broadly-based form of vocational education that includes the three elements pertinent to successful workplace-based learning described in Chapter 8. It is structured in relation to particular occupations and depends on inductees to the occupation working in association with senior practitioners in the occupational field, thus acquiring a practical acquaintance with the traditions and norms of the occupation. It is important that the status of the apprentice is one of *employee* and hence a cadet member of the occupation. Hence if offers a formation in the broad skills relevant to the occupation, not vicariously, but as part of the individual's initial participation in the occupation. It offers a structured and regulated system of qualification approved at national level, which allows for a degree of mobility in an occupational labour market. Finally, it entails some form of political manpower planning so that the number of apprenticeships is matched to the full-time employment available. In the UK, the introduction of CBET (Chapter 7) was associated with attempts to break down the apprenticeship system, to shorten training periods and to give employers more control over qualifications. The narrowness (i.e. internal labour market specificity) of the qualifications and their lack of an academic basis led to their growing unpopularity and to the introduction of the modern apprenticeship scheme.

College-based and alternance schemes do not have all these features. There is no guarantee of employment for a graduate from an alternance or college programme, particularly if places available relate to student demand, rather than the requirements of the economy. This puts the prospective student in the onerous position of second-guessing those requirements. The problem is made more difficult by the fact that colleges have a financial incentive to recruit students, but not to place them in employment. It is morally dubious to expect young people and their parents to take on such a responsibility for their futures and to develop non-transferable skills for opportunities that may not exist. College-based vocational education, even with well-developed *practicum* elements and with well-structured alternance through work experience, cannot offer students the position of cadet worker, and of the development of an occupational identity which, it was argued in Chapter 6, is a vital part of occupational formation. Alternance programmes are often associated with 'work experience' in a generalised sense and offer preparation for unskilled work; for example the schemes that the UK government has offered in different forms since the 1970s, up to, and including, the New Deal. They thus have a relatively poor image and tend to be regarded by all parties as emergency measures for getting young people into work, rather than as structured preparation for long-term, worthwhile employment.

Given the fact that qualifications tend to lose their value through a general 'qualification inflation' due to the increase in certification across all labour markets, the fact that employees might wish to upgrade their qualifications in their chosen occupation or to pursue a course at the tertiary level at a later stage, means that careful thought needs to be given to the quality of vocational qualifications, at whatever level they are pursued. It seems that they have to fulfil the apparently contradictory functions of providing a credible general qualification on the one hand, and a rigorous, specific occupational qualification on the other. How can such a circle be squared?

The answer lies in earlier remarks about the need for *rigour* in both the teaching and the assessment sides of occupational formation. Rigour is associated, not necessarily with academic difficulty, but with fitness for purpose.[16] An occupational qualification, in other words, needs to prepare students to become good workers at the level for which they are preparing. The more skill required, the greater the demands of formation, and the more rigorous the assessment, since the demands on the student will be greater. Well-regarded vocational qualifications require skilled occupations for which they are qualifications. Although this rigour is likely to be increasingly associated with academic demands, vocational qualifications can also demonstrate practical skills, engagement with workplace problems and the demands of working with others and gaining respect in the workplace, qualities which are not so readily available through conventional academic routes. The increasing demands of applied theoretical knowledge in modern industries in turn requires increasing aptitude in literacy, numeracy, information technology and scientific knowledge. Vocational programmes, to provide credible assessment, have to be academically rigorous in the testing of these fields. Primary and secondary education is important in ensuring this, but its role is made easier if children know that what they learn there is relevant to the kind of work that they may wish to do, as well as to academic progress.

The increasing academic content of these programmes also makes progression on to tertiary programmes more possible, particularly when these programmes continue formation within the same occupational field. Thus the options of apprentices and other trainees are left open. The raising of the status of vocational qualifications depends on ensuring higher levels of achievement in compulsory schooling, and this in turn does not just depend on pressure on schools and children to do better, although, in the UK at any rate, underperformance has been endemic, partly due to extremely low expectations of children from the lower social classes. In the longer term, however, one cannot expect a generalised and prolonged rise in standards of achievement without giving vocationally minded young people the prospect that, at the end of compulsory education, there will be something for them to aim for, in the form of a satisfying and reasonably well-paid job. In other words, educational reform and reform of the labour market and industrial practices need to go hand in hand, making the job of a government a complex and, in the UK context, a controversial one.

How does one get opinion-makers and the public to accept that rigour in education need not only be achieved through academic success? In the long term the economic success of industries based on high levels of occupational formation will be a powerful force in changing public opinion. In the shorter term, there needs to be a programme of persuasion, backed by the resources necessary to convince parents, children and employers that vocational education is being taken seriously. This would include the proposals for the revival of technical and vocational education argued for above.

Higher vocational education

Tertiary education in the UK tends to be seen, somewhat misleadingly, as primarily liberal in character. Popularisation of the arguments of Arnold and

Newman, together with increased funding from the state for non-vocational programmes, has tended to foster this idea. It is important to realise, however, that historically, the universities were set up to provide an occupational formation for clerics, lawyers and, later, doctors. They have always been closely associated with the *professions* (see Chapter 9). Only later did universities become involved in education in the natural sciences and only later still in technical education, particularly in engineering. Other countries, notably France, developed a system of institutional specialisation whereby different occupations had dedicated élite institutions for the formation of their leading cadres.[17]

A more recent development in Europe is the introduction of tertiary institutions with a more explicitly vocational mission, particularly in industries involving technical or applied scientific expertise. These provide an extended tertiary education up to and beyond first degree level for higher technical, managerial and research positions in the relevant industry. In the UK, these were Colleges of Advanced Technology and, later Polytechnics. In Germany, the equivalent institutions are the *Fachhochschulen*. In 1992, however, the UK abolished the institutional and administrative division between the polytechnics and the universities. In fact, among the EU countries, only Italy, Sweden and the UK maintain a unitary tertiary sector.[18] Increasingly the higher technical subdegree level qualifications, the HND and the HNC, are offered in the colleges offering lower and intermediate level vocational education.

There is a place both for alternance and the *practicum* in tertiary higher education. What distinguishes the sector is the relatively high level of applied theory required, together with a lesser emphasis on craft and manual skills. It is accepted that applied theoretical knowledge is a key ingredient of vocational tertiary courses, which is why there are, for example, furniture studies, but not carpentry degrees. So it is not enough to say that higher education is what higher education institutions do: there is a distinctive role for tertiary vocational education, which is to do with the increasing complexity of, and theoretical knowledge required for, senior roles.[19] It is quite possible to advocate tertiary continuity with lower level vocational study, provided that the importance of routes from lower levels of vocational study to the higher are recognised and catered for with appropriate provision for progression to higher levels of applied theoretical knowledge. Since this itself requires a good grounding in literacy, numeracy and basic science, a case can be made out for the 'permeability' of such qualifications, namely the property of being a credible sign of fitness to transfer to more traditional academic routes in areas of less direct vocational application.

Alternance is a common feature of vocational higher education programmes, providing the essential *practicum* and work-based experience which is needed for a thorough-going vocational qualification. Provided that the applied theoretical knowledge taught in the theoretical parts of such programmes is genuinely applied in the employment-based segment of the programme, there is no reason to think that its rigour as a higher level course is compromised, since it is a feature of applied theoretical knowledge that, to be useful and to be understood as a form or component of practical wisdom, it needs to be used in appropriate contexts.

Without such use, it is arguable, it is learned in a relatively superficial way. What is not appropriate in alternance programmes at the higher level is exclusive engagement in *practicum* and workplace experiences that do not systematically seek to apply the applied theoretical knowledge gained within the theoretical part of the course.

Qualifications and assessment issues

A complaint that could reasonably be levelled against the growing length and academicisation of vocational education at all levels, is what is sometimes called 'credentialism', or a seeking of academic credentials merely as a positional good, not because they have any value as tokens of competence or expertise. If it were true that the increase in demand for qualifications was only the result of academic institutions seeking to gain students through offering superfluous qualifications, that then become an indispensable positional good for those seeking employment, then one would be faced with a good example of what neo-liberals sometimes call 'producer capture', or the self-interested pursuit of their own interests by suppliers at the expense of consumers.[20]

There is a strong element of positionality in all academic qualifications, so the complaint applies to all suppliers of credentials. Attempts, therefore, to justify the growth of credentialism in terms that are not just to the advantage of educational suppliers have to show that an increase in credentials is important to the quality of the work of those who receive them and hence to the society which buys that work. The general argument of this book has been for the value to society and individuals of high-skill work, both in terms of specification and reliability. High-skill work requires extensive and complex formation.

It was argued in Chapter 7 that assessment is an intrinsic element of any educational process, and that formal assessment and public certification is the most sure way of signalling that reliable formation has taken place. If this argument is valid, then a general case for the widespread recognition of credentials in modern high-skill economic conditions can be made. This does not, of course, mean that good formation cannot take place outside the formal assessment and certification system or that every course that has a certificate attached to it is a reliable indicator of quality. Assessment and certification do, however, provide the general conditions for public faith in the worth of vocational qualifications. Problems arise when courses and assessment regimes are inappropriate to the levels and kinds of occupation that they give an entry to. The most common problem is associated with the term 'academic drift' which is discussed in the next paragraphs. It may also arise when the type of formation is simply too costly and elaborate to be 'fit for purpose'.[21]

'Academic drift' is a term used to describe the process by which the entry level qualification for any given occupation becomes progressively more demanding, when, for example, it moves from uncertificated formal training, to a journeyman certificate, to a higher technical certificate or diploma, to a degree. In particular, it is far from obvious that all the occupations that have, or now aspire to, degree level status as a certificate of competence to practice, do so because of the changing requirements of the occupation or because of its status aspirations, or the interests of the training institutions. There are two distinct issues to be considered: first, whether the level of qualification offered is appropriate to the occupation and, second, whether the academic and practical content of the course is. Clearly, the two may vary independently of each other, but one would hope that they would both be appropriate.

There is some evidence in some occupational areas in the UK that the latter, if not necessarily the former, condition is not being fulfilled. This is a particular problem for occupations offering qualifications at the subdegree level, that wish to upgrade them to degree level. A particular case in point may be some of the professions allied to medicine (PAMs), whose formation has been transferred from specialist colleges to more general institutions of higher education.[22] If anything, however, this example suggests the need for careful regulation of occupational qualifications by the government so as to ensure both that formation is appropriate and that some occupations do not lose out in the positional stampede towards degree-level qualifications.

In the relatively deregulated environment of British higher education after 1988, particularly in the old vocationally oriented polytechnic and college sector, it became possible to offer degree courses in subjects which were previously subject to regulation by the Privy Council. It was in the interest of both occupational associations (for positional reasons) and for higher education institutions (for financial ones) to offer degrees instead of diplomas in occupations such as podiatry, occupational therapy and radiology. In order, however, for a case to be made out for such courses to merit the title of degree, it became necessary to justify the level of study that was being pursued. This was achieved in two ways: first by redefining occupational knowledge so as to place greater emphasis on the *service* rather than the *technical* element and, second, by emphasising the *knowledge acquisition* and *evaluation* capacities of a qualified worker in the field. The first was achieved by introducing significant elements of the social sciences into the courses, the second by including a dissertation component in the degree (which was also used to justify its 'honours-worthiness').

The most obvious way for these occupations to have changed their formation requirements to degree status would have been to increase the medical knowledge component of the theoretical element and to have integrated that knowledge through the clinical practice element of the course (which is a form of *practicum* in these occupations). Such a course of action had three problems: first, it had a tendency to make academic demands on potential practitioners which they would have found difficult to meet; second, it was difficult to justify further applied medical theoretical knowledge to professional activity, given the current development of the professions; finally, it would have increased the length and expense of the clinical practice elements of the course. In practice, the three occupations referred to, achieved degree status for their qualifications through incorporating social science at the expense of some medical knowledge (thus giving employment at marginal cost to social scientists already working in the institution), reducing the element of clinical practice (which offset some of the cost of running a longer programme) and by incorporating a small-scale research element.

It may be doubted whether such changes have worked to the benefit of patients. However, the problems seem to have arisen, not through excessive regulation of the entry requirements of these occupations, but through deregulation and the introduction of a quasi-market in higher education. If the producers are the strongest players in a marketplace, then 'producer capture' is likely, as in this instance, to be a consequence of the *market* rather than of regulation. The moral is that governments should pay continuing and careful attention to the entry requirements of different occupations and they should be reminded that they have a particular responsibility for the positional status of occupations. Episodes such as the one described above do not invalidate credentials; they counsel us to take them seriously and to scrutinise and regulate them carefully in both the public and the occupational interest.

Social capital, diversity and social cohesion

The conclusion of this book is that social cohesion, the formation and main-tenance of social capital and social well-being and prosperity can be promoted through making a serious place for vocational education in the life of the society. It would, of course, be foolish to attempt predictions for any particular society, and, as Green, Wolf and Leney remind us, even in Europe, with a common history and culture, national diversity is likely to remain strong, even in conditions of increasing economic and political integration. Nevertheless, some important points can be made which suggest necessary conditions for achieving the goals above, over the long term.

First, there is a need for *academic integrity*, so that systematic forms of vocational formation, which take proper account of civic and liberal as well as vocational aims, are available to all who want them. Second, *social cohesion* can be enhanced through valuing the attributes of different forms of high-skill work. This can be done through raising and maintaining the status and cognitive integrity of occu-pations by paying attention to the particular forms of workplace knowledge they require and by providing the appropriate kind of vocational formation. *Social capital* needs to be maintained through the fostering of occupational identity through the institutions of civil society. This includes the encouragement of occu-pational associations, but also informal opportunities for occupational association free from over-strong commercial pressures, so that young people, in particular, may gain an insight into what is involved in different occupations. These would include links between schools, unions and enterprises, together with various kinds of voluntary activity sponsored by enterprises or by their employees. Finally, *economic well-being* needs to be maintained through the development of high-skill, high-quality, work which makes good use of the vocational aspirations of all citizens.

High-skill-oriented vocational education, with a significant workplace element, careful differentiation on the basis of a strong common core, and controlled entry into appropriate occupations is the best way to achieve this.

Notes

1 Max Planck Institute (1983) *Between Elite and Mass Education/Education in the Federal Republic of Germany*, Albany, State University of New York Press.
2 See A. Green, A. Wolf and T. Leney (1999) *Convergence and Divergence in European Education and Training Systems*, London, Institute of Education, Chapter 4.
3 There are various courses on offer, including vocational GCSEs offered by some schools and a proposed pre-GNVQ.
4 The presence of a large private sector of schooling, catering largely for the wealthier sections of the population exerts, of course, a massive distorting effect on the rest of the system by making it *de facto* selective through the financial ability of parents to buy superior personal and positional goods of education. Reform of this aspect of the British system seems to be as far away as ever. For a reforming proposal see G. Walden (1997) *We Should Know Better*, London, Fourth Estate.
5 See M. Sanderson (1994) *The Missing Stratum: Technical Education in England 1900–1990*, London, Athlone Press.
6 See also H. Entwistle (1970) *Education, Work and Leisure*, London, Routledge.
7 For example, A. Davis (1998) *The Limits of Educational Assessment*, Oxford, Blackwell; J. Tooley (1998) 'The Neo-liberal Critique of State Intervention in Education: A Reply to Winch', *Journal of Philosophy of Education*, 32, 2, 267–282; J. White (1999) 'Thinking About Assessment', *Journal of Philosophy of Education*, 32, 2, 201–211.
8 H. Gospel, A. Fuller (1998) 'The Modern Apprenticeship: New Wine in Old Bottles?' *Human Resource Management Journal*, 8, 1, 5–22.
9 This is, of course, the problem referred to with CBET in Chapter 7. The assessment procedures criticised by, for example, Prais (1991) 'Vocational Qualifications in Britain and Europe: Theory and Practice', *National Institute Economic Review* 136, May, pp. 86–89 are precisely of the kind that are poorly equipped to do justice to a high-skill occupation. In fact, NVQs are better equipped to assess limited *job*, rather than *occupational* ability (see Chapter 9). For more on these limitations, see P. Robinson (1996) 'Rhetoric and Reality: The Evolution of the New Vocational Qualifications', Centre for Economic Performance, London School of Economics.
10 Taylor provides a comprehensive and balanced account of the secondary modern schools. W. Taylor (1963) *The Secondary Modern School*, London, Faber and Faber.
11 Max Planck Institute, op. cit. p. 165.
12 It is important not to exaggerate this, however, nor to gloss over the fact that the *Hauptschulen* often have to deal with significant social problems (Max Planck Institute, op. cit. Chapter 7).
13 Green, Wolf and Leney, op. cit. p. 90.
14 Ibid. p. 180.
15 Ibid. p. 180.
16 Plato (1950) *The Republic*, J. Llewelyn Davies and D. J. Vaughan, London, Macmillan, Books IV, X for a definition of quality along these lines.
17 Green (1990) *Education and State Formation*, London, Macmillan.
18 Green, Wolf and Leney, op. cit. p. 211.
19 J. White (1997) 'Philosophy and the aims of higher education', *Studies in Higher Education*, 22, 1.
20 For an example of this argument in the German context see 'Ein mittelälterliches Sieb gegen neuzeitliche Bönhasen' by Angela Schurfeld and Markus Fredebeul-Krein in the *Franfurter Allgemeine Zeitung*, 28 August 1999, p. 15.
21 See Schurfeld and Fredebeul-Krein, op. cit.
22 The rest of this section draws on the work of L. Merriman (1998) 'Degrees of Difference', unpublished PhD. thesis, University College Northampton, which provides the case study on which this argument is based.

Bibliography

Abbs, P. (1987) 'Training Spells the Death of Education', *The Guardian*, 5 January.

Ainley, Pat and Helen Rainbird (eds) (1999) *Apprenticeship: Towards a New Paradigm of Learning*, London, Kogan Page.

Aristotle *Nichomachean Ethics*, translated by Sir David Ross, London, Dent (1925).

Aristotle *The Politics*, Stephen Everson (ed.) (1988) Cambridge, Cambridge University Press.

Arnold, Matthew (1932) *Culture and Anarchy*, John Dover Wilson (ed.) Cambridge, Cambridge University Press.

Ashton, David and Francis Green (1996) *Education, Training and the Global Economy*, Cheltenham, Edward Elgar.

Ashton, David and Johnny Sung (1997) 'Education, Skill Formation and Economic Development: The Singaporean Approach' in Centre for Labour Market Studies, MSc in Training, *Module 3*, Units 1 and 2, pp. 351–372.

Baker, G. P. and P. M. S. Hacker (1988) *Language, Sense and Nonsense*, Oxford, Blackwell.

Bantock, G. H. (1963), *Education in an Industrial Society*, London, Faber.

Barrow, R. (1987) 'Skill Talk', *Journal of Philosophy of Education*, 27, 2, 187–196.

Barrow, R. (1981) *The Philosophy of Schooling*, Brighton, Harvester.

Beardsmore, R. W. (1992) 'The Theory of Family Resemblances', *Philosophical Investigations*, 15, 2, 111–130.

Beckett, David (1998) 'Anticipative Action and its Contribution to an Emerging Epistemology of Practice', *Proceedings of the Annual Conference of the Philosophy of Education Society of Great Britain*, pp. 209–222.

Bernstein, Basil (1973) *Class Codes and Control*, Volume I, London, Paladin.

Best, David (1992) *The Rationality of Feeling: Understanding the Arts in Education*, London, Falmer.

Biernacki, Richard (1995) *The Fabrication of Labour: Germany and Britain, 1640–1914*, San Francisco, CA, University of California Press.

Bloor, David (1997) *Wittgenstein, Rules and Institutions*, London, Routledge.

Braverman, Harry (1974) *Labour and Monopoly Capital: The Degradation of Work in the Twentieth Century*, New York, Monthly Review Press.

Brittan, Samuel, quoted in John Kay (1996) 'Staking a Moral Claim', *New Statesman*, 11 October.

Brown, Alan (1985) *Modern Political Theory*, London, Penguin.

Bullock, Alan (1977) *Report of the Commission on Industrial Democracy*, London, HMSO.

Burke, Edmund (1790; 1986) *Reflections on the Revolution in France*, London, Penguin.

Callan, Eamonn (1996) 'Political Liberalism and Political Education', *Review of Politics*, 58, 1, 1–33.

Carr, David (1991) *Educating the Virtues*, London, Routledge.

Carr, David (1999) 'Professional Education and Professional Ethics', *Journal of Applied Philosophy*, 16, 1, 33–46.

Carr, David and Jan Steutel (eds) (1999) *Virtue Ethics and Moral Education*, London, Routledge.

Carr, Wilfred (1995) *For Education*, Buckingham, Open University Press.

Caulkin, Simon (1999) 'Arise Mrs Mopp. Drop the bucket and pick up a hand-held computer', *The Observer*, Business Section, 12 June, p. 1.

Chomsky, N. (1988) *Language and Problems of Knowledge*, Cambridge MA, MIT Press.

Clarke, Linda (1999) 'The Changing Structure and Significance of Apprenticeship with Special Reference to Construction' in Ainley and Rainbird, op. cit.

Clarke, Linda and Christine Wall (1996) *Skills and the Construction Process*, Bristol, Policy Press.

Coleman, James S. (1988) 'Social Capital in the Creation of Human Capital', *American Journal of Sociology*, 94, Supplement S, 95–120.

Cooper, David (1980) *Illusions of Equality*, London, Routledge.

Culpepper, Pepper D. (1999) 'The Future of the High-Skill Equilibrium in Germany', *Oxford Review of Economic Policy*, 15, 1, 43–59.

Darling, John (1993) 'Rousseau as Progressive Instrumentalist', *Journal of Philosophy of Education*, 27, 1, 27–38.

Davis, Andrew (1998) *The Limits of Educational Assessment*, Oxford, Blackwell.

Davis, Andrew (1999) *Educational Assessment: A Critique of Current Policy*, London, Philosophy of Education Society.

Dearden, R. F. (1968) *The Philosophy of Primary Education*, London, Routledge.

Dearden, R. F. (1979) 'The Assessment of Learning', *British Journal of Educational Studies*, 27, 2, 111–124.

Dearden, R. F. (ed.) (1984) *Theory and Practice in Education*, London, Routledge.

Dearden, R. F. (ed.) (1984) 'Education and Training', *Westminster Studies in Education*, 7, pp. 57–66.

Dent, Nicholas (1984) *The Moral Psychology of the Virtues*, Cambridge, Cambridge University Press.

Dewey, John (1916) *Democracy and Education*, New York, Macmillan.

DfEE (1999a) *Learning to Succeed*, London, HMSO.

DfEE (1999b) *The National Curriculum: Handbook for Secondary Teachers in England*, London, HMSO.

Entwistle, Harold (1970) *Education, Work and Leisure*, London, Routledge.

Fallows, J. (1994) *Looking at the Sun*, New York, Pantheon Press.

Field, John (1999) 'Investigating Community Based Learning: Social Capital, Capacity Building and Regeneration'. Unpublished paper in the ESRC Seminar Deries, *Working to Learn*, 24 June.

Finegold, David (1991) 'Institutional Incentives and Skill Creation: Preconditions for a High-Skill Equilibrium', in P. Ryan (ed.) *International Comparisons of Vocational Education and Training for Intermediate Skills*, Hove, Falmer Press, pp. 93–116.

Flew, Anthony (1976) *Sociology, Equality and Education*, London, Macmillan.

Forrester, Viviane (1996) *L'Horreur Economique*, Paris, Fayard.

Fukuyama, Francis (1995) *Trust*, London, Penguin.

Gaita, Raimond (1991) *Good and Evil*, London, Macmillan.

Gide, Charles and Charles Rist (1948) *A History of Economic Doctrines*, translated by R. Richards and E. F. Row, Harrap.

Gingell, John and Edwin Brandon (2000) *In Defence of High Culture*, Oxford, Blackwell.

Gordon, J. C. B. (1981) *Verbal Deficit*, London, Croom Helm.

Gospel, Howard and Alison Fuller (1998) 'The Modern Apprenticeship: New Wine in Old Bottles?' *Human Resource Management Journal*, 8, 1, 5–22.

Gramsci, Antonio (1971) *Selections from the Prison Notebooks*, Q. Hoare and G. Nowell-Smith (eds) London, Lawrence and Wishart.

(1993) *Beyond the New Right*, London, Routledge.

Gray, John (1995) *Enlightenment's Wake*, London, Routledge.

Gray, John and Brian Wilcox (1995) *Good School, Bad School*, Buckingham, Open University Press.

Green, Andy (1990) *Education and State Formation*, London, Macmillan.

Green, Andy (1996) 'Education and the Development State in Asia' in Centre for Labour Market Studies, MSc in Training, *Module 3*, Units 1 and 2, pp. 251–270.

Green, Andy, Alison Wolf and Tom Leney (1999) *Convergence and Divergence in European Education and Training Systems*, London, Institute of Education.

Griffiths, Morwenna (1987) 'The Teaching of Skills and the Skills of Teaching: A Reply to Robin Barrow', *Journal of Philosophy of Education*, 27, 2, 203–214.

Gutmann, Amy (1987) *Democratic Education*, Princeton, NJ, Princeton University Press.

Hager, Paul (1999) 'Know-How and Workplace Practical Judgment', *Proceedings of the Annual Conference of the Philosophy of Education Society of Great Britain*, pp. 21–34.

Hall, Nigel (1988) *The Emergence of Literacy*, London, Hodder.

Hamm, C. (1989) *Philosophical Issues in Education*, Brighton, Falmer.

Hargreaves Heap, Sean and Yanis Varoufakis (1995) *An Introduction to Game Theory*, London, Routledge.

Hicks, J. R. (1969) *A Theory of Economic History*, Oxford, The Clarendon Press.

Hirsch, E. D. (1987) *Cultural Literacy: What Every American Should Know*, Boston, Houghton Mifflin.

Hirst, Paul (1974) *Knowledge and the Curriculum*, London, Routledge.

Hobbes, Thomas (1968) *Leviathan*, edited and introduced by C. B. MacPherson, London, Penguin. First published 1652.

Hodgson, Geoffrey (1999) *Economics and Utopia: Why the Learning Society is Not the End of History*, London, Routledge.

Howe, Michael (1990) *The Origin of Exceptional Abilities*, Oxford, Blackwell.

Hume, David (1948) *A Treatise of Human Nature*, Henry D. Aitken (ed.) (1948) *Hume: Moral and Political Philosophy*, New York, Hafner.

Hutton, Will (1995) *The State We're In*, London, Penguin.

Hyland, Terry (1993) 'Competence, Knowledge and Education', *Journal of Philosophy of Education*, 27, 1, 57–68.

Illich, I. (1971) *Deschooling Society*, London, Penguin.

ILO (1996) *World Employment 1996/7—National Policies in a Global Context*, International Labour Office.

Kant, Immanuel (1959) *Fundamental Principles of the Metaphysic of Ethics*, London, Longmans.

Kay, John (1996) 'Staking a Moral Claim', *New Statesman*, 11 October.

Keep, Ewart and Kenneth Mayhew (1999) 'The Assessment: Knowledge, Skills and Competitiveness', *Oxford Review of Economic Policy*, 15, 1, Spring, 1–15.

Keynes, J. M. (1936) (1973) *The General Theory of Employment, Money and Interest*, second edition, London, Macmillan.

Kumazawa, M. and J. Yamada (1989) 'Jobs and Skills under the Lifelong Nenko Employment Practice' Chapter 5 in S. Wood (ed.) *The Transformation of Work?* London, Unwin Hyman, pp. 102–122.

Lawrence, D. H., *The Rainbow*, London, Penguin.

Letwin, Oliver (1988) *Education: The Importance of Grounding*, London, Centre for Policy Studies.

Levi-Faur, David (1997) 'Economic Nationalism: From Friedrich List to Robert Reich', *Review of International Studies*, 23, 3, 359–370.

Lieberman, David (1990) *Learning*, CA, Wadsworth.

List, Friedrich (1837) (1983) *The Natural System of Political Economy*, London, Frank Cass.

List, Friedrich (1841) (1991) *The National System of Political Economy*, NJ, Augustus Kelley.

Little, Adrian (1998) *Post-Industrial Socialism*, London, Routledge.

Little, Adrian (1999) 'The Politics of Compensation: Tom Paine's *Agrarian Justice* and Liberal Egalitarianism', *Contemporary Politics*, 5, 1, 63–73.

Locke, J. (1690) (1988) *Two Treatises of Government*, P. Laslett (ed.) Cambridge, Cambridge University Press.

Longfellow, Henry Wadsworth (1919) *The Poetical Works of Henry Wadsworth Longfellow*, London, Humphrey Milford.

Lutz, Mark (1999) *Economics for the Common Good*, London, Routledge.

Mackie, J. L. (1980) *Ethics: Inventing Right and Wrong*, London, Penguin.

Macmillan, Carol A. (1982) *Women, Reason and Nature*, London, Macmillan.

Malcolm, Norman (1982) 'Language and the Instinctive Basis of Human Behaviour', Swansea, University College of Swansea.

Marshall, Alfred (1890) *Principles of Economics*, eighth edition, London, Macmillan.

Marx, Karl (1887) (1970a) *Capital*, London, Lawrence and Wishart.

Marx, Karl (1970b) *Economic and Philosophic Manuscripts of 1844*, edited with an introduction by Dirk Struik and translated by Martin Milligan, London, Lawrence and Wishart.

Marx, Karl (1875) (1970c) *Marginal Notes to the Programme of the German Workers' Party*, Karl Marx, Friedrich Engels *Selected Works*, London, Lawrence and Wishart,

Mason, Geoff, Bart Van Ark and Karin Wagner (1997) 'Workforce Skills, Product Quality and Economic Performance' in A. Booth, D. Snower (eds) *Acquiring Skills: Market Failures, Their Symptoms and Policy Responses*, pp. 177–197.

Matheson, David (1999) 'Lifelong Learning and Economics in Switzerland' in Nafsika Alexiadou and Colin Brock (eds) *Education as a Commodity*, John Catt Educational, 135–148.

Maynard, Alan (1985) 'Performance Incentives in General Practice' in George Teeling Smith (ed.) *Health, Education and General Practice*, Office for Health Economics.

Max Planck Institute (1983) *Between Elite and Mass Education/Education in the Federal Republic of Germany*, Albany, State University of New York Press.

Merriman, Linda (1998) 'Degrees of Difference', unpublished PhD thesis, University College Northampton.

Mill, John Stuart (1994) *Principles of Political Economy*, edited with an introduction by Jonathan Riley, Oxford, Oxford University Press. First published 1848.

Mill, John Stuart (1974) *On Liberty*, London, Dent. First published 1859.

Mill, John Stuart (1867) 'Inaugural Lecture at the University of St. Andrews' in F. A. Cavanagh (ed.) (1931) *James and John Stuart Mill on Education*, Cambridge, Cambridge University Press.

Miller, David (1993) 'In Defence of Nationality', *Journal of Applied Philosophy*, 10, 1, 3–16.

Montesquieu (1973) *The Persian Letters*, London, Penguin.

Morley, J. (1993) *Edmund Burke*, introduced by Brendan Clifford, Belfast, Athol Books.

Mounce, H. O. (1996) *The Two Pragmatisms*, London, Routledge, 1996.

National Commission on Education (1993) *Learning to Succeed*, London, Heinemann.

Nietzsche, Friedrich (1888) (1954*) The Twilight of the Idols, in The Portable Nietzsche*, edited and translated by Walter Kaufmann, London, Penguin.

Nozick, Robert (1974) *Anarchy, State and Utopia*, Oxford, Blackwell.

Oakeshott, Michael (1962) *Rationalism in Politics*, London, Methuen.

O'Hear, Anthony (1981) *Education, Society and Human Nature*, London, Routledge.

O'Neill, John (1998) *The Market: Ethics, Knowledge and Politics*, London, Routledge.

Orchard, Lionel and Hugh Stretton (1994) *Public Goods, Public Choice and Public Enterprise*, London, Macmillan.

Ormerod, Paul (1994) *The Death of Economics*, London, Penguin.

Osterheld, Horst (1996) 'Konrad Adenauer' in Hans Klein (ed.) *The German Chancellors* Berlin (edition q).

Paul, R. (1990) *Critical Thinking: What Every Person Needs to Survive in a Rapidly Changing World*, Rohnert Park, CA, Centre for Critical Thinking and Moral Critique.

Peters, R. S. (1966) *Ethics and Education*, London, Allen and Unwin.

Plato (1950) *The Republic*, J. Llewelyn Davies and D. J. Vaughan (eds) London, Macmillan.

Plato (1961) *The Sophist* in *Parmenides and Other Dialogues*, John Warrington (ed.) London, Dent.

Polanyi, Michael (1958) *Personal Knowledge: Towards a Post-Critical Philosophy*, London, Routledge.

Prais, S. J. (1991) 'Vocational Qualifications in Britain and Europe: Theory and Practice', *National Institute Economic Review*, 136, May, 86–89.

Prais, S. J., Valerie Jarvis and Karin Wagner (1989) 'Productivity and Vocational Skills in Services in Britain and Germany: Hotels', *National Institute Economic Review*, November, 52–74.

Pring, Richard (1995) *Closing the Gap: Liberal Education and Vocational Preparation*, London, Hodder and Stoughton.

Rainbird, Helen and Pat Ainley (eds) (1999) *Apprenticeship*, London, Kogan Page.

Ricardo, David (1951) *On the Principles of Political Economy and Taxation*, Cambridge, Cambridge University Press. First published 1817.

Robinson, Joan (1962) *Economic Philosophy*, London, Penguin.

Robinson, P. (1996) 'Rhetoric and Reality: The Evolution of the New Vocational Qualifications.' Centre for Economic Performance, London School of Economics.

Rojas, Mauricio (1999) *Millennium Doom: Fallacies about the End of Work*, London, Social Market Foundation.

Ross, David (1995) *Aristotle*, sixth edition, London, Routledge.

Rousseau, J.-J. (1762) (1966) *Emile ou l'Education*, Paris, Editions Flammarion. English edition translated by Barbara Foxley, London, Dent, 1911.

Ryle, Gilbert (1949) *The Concept of Mind*, London, Hutchinson.

Sanderson, Michael (1994) *The Missing Stratum: Technical Education in England 1900–1990*, London, Athlone Press.

Shackleton, J. R. (1976) 'Adam Smith and Education', *Higher Education Review*, Spring, 80–90.

Schön, Donald (1991) *The Reflective Practitioner: How Professionals Think in Action*, Aldershot, Avebury.

Schurfeld, Angela and Markus Fredebeul-Krein (1999) 'Ein Mittelälterliches Sieb gegen neuzeitliche Bönhasen', *Franfurter Allgemeine Zeitung*, 28 August, 15.

Searle, John R. (1995) *The Construction of Social Reality*, London, Penguin.

Sheaff, Rod (1996) *The Need for Health Care*, London, Routledge.

Simpson, Evan (1989) *Good Lives and Moral Education*, New York, Peter Lang.

Smith, Adam (1776) (1981) *The Wealth of Nations*, Indianapolis, IN, Liberty Fund.
Smith, Adam (1759) (1984) *The Theory of Moral Sentiments*, Indianapolis, IN, Liberty Fund.
Smith, Frank (1985) *Reading*, Cambridge, Cambridge University Press.
Smith, Richard (1987) 'Skills: The Middle Way', *Journal of Philosophy of Education*, 27, 2, pp. 197–202.
Strawson, P. F. (1974) 'Freedom and Resentment' in *Freedom and Resentment and Other Essays*, London, Methuen.
Streeck, W. (1989) 'Skills and the Limits of Neo-Liberalism', British Sociological Association, *Work, Employment and Society*, 3, 1, March, 92–101.
Streeck, W. (1992) *Social Institutions and Economic Performance*, London, Sage.
Streeck, W. (1998) *Mitbestimmung und neue Unternehmenskultur*, Hans Böckler Stiftung.
Strike, Kenneth (1998) 'Freedom of Conscience and Illiberal Socialisation: The Congruence Argument', *Journal of Philosophy of Education*, 32, 3, 345–360.
Szporluk, R. 1988) *Communism and Nationalism: Karl Marx versus Friedrich List*, Oxford, Oxford University Press.
Taylor, Frederick (1911) *The Principles of Scientific Management*, New York, Norton.
Taylor, W. (1963) *The Secondary Modern School*, London, Faber and Faber.
Thomson, Judith Jarvis (1971) 'A Defence of Abortion', *Philosophy and Public Affairs*, 1, 1.
Thompson, Paul, Terry Wallace, Jorg Flecker and Roland Ahlstrand (1995) 'It Ain't What You Do, It's the Way that You Do It: Production Organisation and Skill Utilisation in Commercial Vehicles', *Work, Employment and Society*, 9, 4, 719–742.
Tolstoy, Leo (1954) *Anna Karenina*, London, Penguin.
Tooley, James (1995) *Disestablishing the School*, Aldershot, Avebury.
Tooley, James (1998) 'The Neo-liberal Critique of State Intervention in Education: A Reply to Winch', *Journal of Philosophy of Education*, 32, 2, pp. 267–282.
Verdon, Michel (1996) *Keynes and the Classics*, London, Routledge.
Vico, Giambattista (1968) *The New Science*, translated by Thomas Goddard Bergin and Max Harold Fisch, Ithaca NY, Cornell University Press.
Walden, George (1997) *We Should Know Better*, London, Fourth Estate.
Weber, Max (1904–05) (1958) *The Protestant Ethic and the Spirit of Capitalism*, New York, Scribner.
Wells, C. G. (1981) 'Some Antecedents of Early Educational Attainment', *British Journal of Sociology of Education*, 2, 2.
White, J. P. (1982) *The Aims of Education Restated*, London, Routledge.
White, J. P. (1990) *Education and the Good Life*. London, Kogan Page.
White, J. P. (1997) *Education and the End of Work*, London, Kogan Page.
White, J. P. (1997) 'Philosophy and the Aims of Higher Education', *Studies in Higher Education*, 22, 1.
White, J. P. (1999) 'Thinking About Assessment', *Journal of Philosophy of Education*, 32, 2, 201–211.
White, J. and P. Gordon (1979) *Philosophers as Educational Reformers*, London, Routledge.
Wickens, Peter (1995) *The Ascendant Organisation*, New York, St Martin's Press.
Williams, Gwydion M. (2000) *Wealth Without Nations*, London, Athol Books.
Williams, Kevin (1994) 'Vocationalism and Liberal Education: Exploring the Tensions', *Journal of Philosophy of Education*, 28, 1, 89–100.
Winch, Christopher (1990) *Language, Ability and Educational Achievement*, London, Routledge.
Winch, Christopher (1996) *Quality and Education*, Oxford, Blackwell.
Winch, Christopher (1995) 'Vocational Education: A Liberal Interpretation', *Studies in Philosophy and Education*, 14, 4, 401–415.

Winch, Christopher (1998a) *The Philosophy of Human Learning*, London, Routledge.

Winch, Christopher (1998b) 'Markets, Educational Opportunities and Education: Reply to Tooley', *Journal of Philosophy of Education*, 32, 3, pp. 429–436.

Winch, Christopher and John Gingell (1994) 'Dialect Interference and Difficulties with Writing: An Investigation in St. Lucian Primary Schools', *Language and Education*, 8, 3, 157–182.

Winch, Christopher and John Gingell (1999) *Key Concepts in the Philosophy of Education*, London, Routledge.

Winch, Peter (1972) *Ethics and Action*, London, Routledge.

Wiseman, Stephen (ed.) (1973) *Intelligence and Ability*, London, Penguin.

Wittgenstein, Ludwig (1953) *Philosophical Investigations*, Oxford, Blackwell.

Die Zeit (1998) 'Modell mit Zukunft', 22, 20 May, p. 1.

Index